UTOPIAS

Frontispiece. Fourier's Ideal Society (J. J. Grandville, 1844).

UTOPIAS

edited by
Peter Alexander
Roger Gill

OPEN COURT PUBLISHING COMPANY
LA SALLE, ILLINOIS 61301

✳

OPEN COURT and the above logo are registered with
the U.S. Patent and Trademark Office

Published by arrangement with Gerald Duckworth & Co., Ltd., London

OC 855   10 9 8 7 6 5 4 3 2 1

ISBN 0-87548-364-X

Utopias.

Includes index.
1. Utopias—Congresses.   I. Alexander, Peter,
1917-   . II. Gill, Roger.
HX806.U7935   1984b   335'.02   84-18971
ISBN 0-87548-364-X

Printed and bound in Great Britain

Contents

Preface

Each year a Colston Symposium is held in the University of Bristol under the auspices of the Colston Research Society. The Society's financial contribution makes it possible to bring together eminent scholars from all over the world to promote their discussions and to publish the results as an annual Colston Paper. Its funds are contributed by the citizens of Bristol and one of its chief aims is to foster relations between the City and the University. The range of subjects covered in Colston Symposia is extremely wide. This volume is Colston Papers No. 35.

We wish to thank the Council and members of the Society for their support of the symposium in 1983 which produced this book, and in particular the President, Mr A.A. Anson, who took a keen interest in the planning and running of the event. We also wish to thank the British Academy for a generous grant.

The editing of the volume was made much easier by our authors who agreed to many cuts in their papers and in several cases redrafted large sections in order to reduce the length of the book, and by our publishers who accepted a substantial increase in the number of words over the original target figure.

Finally, we owe a debt of gratitude to Doreen Harding and Yvonne Kaye for their help in organising the symposium and preparing the final typescripts.

P.A. & R.G.

Contributors

Peter Alexander, Emeritus Professor of Philosophy, University of Bristol.

W.H.G. Armytage, Emeritus Professor of Education, University of Sheffield, and now Professor, Kent State University.

C. West Churchman, Chairman, Center for Research in Management Science, University of California, Berkeley.

J.C. Davis, Reader in History, Victoria University of Wellington, New Zealand.

Robert Fishman, Professor of History, Rutgers University.

Roger Gill, Lecturer in Architecture, University of Bristol.

Barbara Goodwin, Lecturer in the Department of Government, Brunel University.

Keith Graham, Lecturer in Philosophy, University of Bristol.

Peter Hall, Professor of Geography, University of Reading.

J.F.C. Harrison, Professor of History, University of Sussex.

Mark Holloway, author of *Heavens on Earth: utopian communities in America 1680-1880.*

Ruth Levitas, Lecturer in Sociology, University of Bristol.

Steven Lukes, Fellow of Balliol College, Oxford.

Alasdair Morrison, Lecturer in Politics, University of Bristol.

Donald E. Pitzer, Professor of History and Director of the Center for Communal Studies, Indiana State University, Evansville.

Milan Šimečka, formerly Professor of Philosophy and Literature in Bratislava. Deprived of his position for political reasons, he has been a labourer for ten years. He was unable to attend the Symposium.

Bernard Suits, Professor of Philosophy, University of Waterloo.

Plates

Frontispiece. Fourier's Ideal Society

Introduction

This book was designed with 1984 in mind. Its main aim is to explore questions concerning the present value of and need for utopian thinking in planning and organisation for the future. Is there a case for utopian thinking in spite of the undesirable consequences predicted by recent dystopias? Are such consequences inevitable or do they merely indicate weaknesses in particular versions of utopia? Are utopias realisable in practice, and is theoretical utopian construction valuable even if they are not? What conclusions should we draw from the failure or success of actual attempts to put utopian ideas or whole utopian organisations into practice in large or small communities? Are New Harmony, Oneida, Jonestown, Soviet Russia, Cuba and Nazi Germany, for example, all rightly regarded as the result of attempts to realise utopias?

There are two main approaches to utopian thought: the theoretical and the practical. These approaches may be distinguished in both the construction and the analysis and criticism of utopias. Of the chapters that follow, those of Part I are largely theoretical, those of Part III have a practical bearing, as does Pitzer's Colston Lecture, while those of Part II may be seen as transitional. But we would stress that no such classification can be more than rough-and-ready.

Utopian constructions may take the form either of a picture of an unrealisably ideal social order criticising an existing order, teaching us lessons about organisation and promoting understanding of the concepts involved, or, alternatively, of a blueprint intended to guide the actual reorganisation of a society. The critical discussion of utopias may involve an exploration either of the nature of utopias and the intentions of their creators, or of their value for practice and their possible means of implementation.

Part I

None of our authors has attempted to construct a utopia, with the possible exception of Suits, whose paper therefore constitutes a fitting peroration; we are mainly in the business of analysis and criticism.

The chief concern of the authors of the papers in Part I is the understanding, rather than the implementation, of utopian ideas. They are therefore interested in conceptions, definitions and intentions.

In the discussion of utopias the question whether we should try to define such terms as 'ideal society', 'utopia' and 'perfection' has been controversial. This is probably not something that has concerned, or need concern, the constructors such as Plato, More, Wells and B.F. Skinner, but it has concerned the commentators. Their opinions range widely. At one extreme we have, for instance, the Manuels who regard attempts to define 'utopia' as constricting and even intellectually dangerous, obscuring 'plural meanings' that the term has acquired through history. At the other extreme we have Davis who sees the attempt to define 'utopia' as a necessity for clear discussion, delimiting the field and guiding what we include in or exclude from our consideration. It is worthy of note that these radically opposed views both come from historians.

No one can suppose that there are no difficulties attached to the idea of definition: by its very nature a definition will omit features that some would regard as central in some applications of the word in question. However, accepting a definition is merely the beginning, not the end, of discussion – it does not commit us to ignoring those features that the definition does not mention. Indeed, we do so at our peril. It is clearly mistaken to suppose that a definition of 'utopia' can give us a final understanding of utopias; that requires a great deal of further investigation of uses of the term, whether actual or proposed, and analysis of what it is taken to designate. A good definition can, however, serve as a preliminary delimitation within which we can proceed to amass detailed differences and similarities between the various things the term denotes.

This is the approach adopted by Davis in his chapter, as in his earlier book. Regarding 'ideal society' as a generic term, he delineates under it five specific terms applied to kinds of ideal societies that are different enough to deserve separate discussion. This is not to imply that social organisations falling under different headings have nothing of interest in common, only that their differences form a useful point of departure for discussing them. It has been objected, as it always will be when a definition is proposed in any context, that his category 'utopia' excludes some things that ought to be included. For example, it is alleged that some anarchist societies should be included in utopias but do not fit Davis's definition. That can probably be countered. Many anarchists have stressed that an anarchist society is not one without *order* but one without *rulers*, as the derivation of the word implies. They do not reject all organisation, only organisation imposed by legislation from above; Davis's definition does not imply legislation as the means to utopian ends and so does not run against anarchist ideals in this respect. There are clearly matters here for further examination.

Davis's classification is adopted by Alexander, at least for the purpose of getting discussion off the ground. Alexander explores certain other features, not excluded by Davis's definition, of well-known theoretical utopias in an attempt to understand the nature of the utopian project and the intellectual stimuli lying behind it. Some exception has been taken to his use of the distinction between the conceivable and the achievable; it has been said that utopias, to be interesting, must at least be theoretically achievable. More discussion of that is needed, but Alexander's point does not rest on theoretical or logical, but only practical, unachievability, which may be a function of the time at which utopia is devised. The theoretical construction of a utopia, he urges, may be valuable whether or not it is, or is thought to be, practically achievable at the time. He also connects theoretical utopias with fairy-tales, and this is implicitly criticised in other papers in this volume. Holloway, for example, asks for the establishment of a 'definable frontier between Utopia and fantasy'. One's view on this no doubt depends upon one's view of the purpose of utopian construction.

By contrast, social, emotional and appetitional factors stimulating the construction of utopias are examined by Levitas. She is not hostile to the idea of definition but, favouring a wider definition of 'utopia', she leans slightly away from Davis and towards the Manuels. Consequently she includes under that heading some organisations that Davis excludes, such as William Morris's Nowhere. Her central theme concerns need. She adopts a view of needs, likely to be favoured by sociologists, according to which needs are not natural but are 'socially constructed'. This, of course, invites the question 'constructed out of what?', and it has been urged that there is an important distinction to be made between needs as socially constructed and as socially influenced. Further analysis of social construction would seem to be urgently required. Its relevance is that Levitas uses it to conclude that there is no possibility of a universal utopia and that, far from arising from natural needs, 'utopianism has as one precondition a disparity between socially constructed experienced needs and socially prescribed and actually available means of satisfaction'. The first of these conclusions could probably be arrived at from a much weaker premiss. All this probably conflicts with the view that practical achievability is not an overridingly important feature of theoretical utopias and with Davis's view of the relations between needs and satisfactions in utopian thought.

More particular concepts related to utopianism are examined by Churchman and Graham. Churchman considers the idea of perfection historically and philosophically and sees as unsatisfactory what he calls the 'add-on' view of it found in Descartes and, in a more modern version, in E.A. Singer Jr. It depends, he holds, on a rather simple-minded psychology of desire. Nevertheless he sympathises with Singer's claims that perfection in a society rests upon omnipotence and omniscience, to allow the making of infallible predictions, and upon 'ideal co-operation' such that 'when A begins to attain his goal, he increases B's chances of obtaining his'. This leads Churchman to pessimism about the realisation of a perfect society. Moreover, its success would contain the seeds of its downfall: affluence breeds indifference and so militates against co-operation. Human beings 'do not know enough to design utopias' and, he suggests, never will. However, he finally sounds a note of approval for theoretical utopian construction: it may 'reveal areas of ignorance that need to be addressed by the coming generations' and that is essential if we are to survive. The whole basis of this, and of other familiar ideas of utopia, has been challenged on the grounds that it is a mistake to think of utopias in terms of *perfection*; but acceptance of that makes it difficult to distinguish utopias from many other different kinds of proposal which seek merely to improve the lot of mankind.

Graham asks questions about consensus in decision-making, in particular, whether it is utopian and whether, if it is, it should be simply ignored. There are moral objections to majority rule because it involves thwarting the *bona fide* moral convictions of minorities. So, the argument goes, 'collective decisions ought to be based upon unanimity', and this requires that a whole community '*think* in concert'. There are obvious objections to the idea that unanimity could be achieved, but Graham implicitly suggests that the situation has not been adequately formulated and argues that the utopian has ways of meeting the objection through ideas of rational persuasion, the non-specificity of the demand for unanimity and the possible effect of the general approval of unanimity on the form of social organisation reached. The views he considers (Nozick, Strawson and Wolff) all rest on various forms of individualism which, he urges, presume too narrow an ontology; corporate entities may make moral decisions and act in ways open to moral appraisal without being reducible to individuals. So it may be rational to consider not only one's own interests in making decisions but also those of the collective. If the correct ontology is recognised, unanimity will seem not only the right thing to strive for but also possibly achievable. Conflicts of interests would be less severe if we saw it as 'essential that we are parts of units larger than individual human beings'. Perhaps the knottiest problems posed by this view concern the acceptability of these larger units as moral agents: this is one direction in which it seems important to push enquiry.

Harrison, in comparing and contrasting millenarianism with utopianism, shows a greater gulf between the theories of the two groups than between their practices and throws light on religious elements in utopianism. His suggestions may well be profitably considered in conjunction with Pitzer's account.

Graham's paper points forward to questions about the impact of utopian thought, discussed in Part II, as well as to the more practical political bearings of the papers in Part III.

Part II

Opening this part, Goodwin deals with economic and social innovations related to utopianism and particularly with inequality, private property, work and the position of women. On the economic side, many specific proposals of utopians, especially from the nineteenth century, have been at least partially implemented in Western societies, e.g. progressive taxation, minimum wages and welfare services. But their effects are muted by the overall capitalist framework within which they have arisen, and one result has been that people search for maximum satisfaction with minimum contribution. The prophets' motives have been obscured by the profit-motive. Goodwin contrasts utopians who wish to abolish capitalism and those who favour an 'improved capitalism' which aims to civilise the profit-motive. She cites many other partial and piecemeal influences of utopian thought but stresses the difficulty of identifying such influences. On the social side, direct influence is perhaps even more difficult to identify, but many utopian ideas have become common currency, even though their practical implementation has been slow; she mentions, as examples, ideas about women's rights, marriage and eugenics. However, some ideas in these areas may have origins other than utopian ones. The slowness of implementation may largely be due to the dependence of social inequality on economic inequality, which appears firmly entrenched in the Western world and, indeed, beyond it. There seem to be some pressing questions about the extent to which conservative views about social matters depend upon conservative views about economic matters and whether, as some evidence suggests, they are relatively independent.

Goodwin's final likening of utopians to poets who inspire practical people to realise desirable states of affairs and her deploring of the current shortage of poet-utopians perhaps relates to the assimilation of utopias and fairy-tales.

The many signs of the implementation of utopian ideas also constitute Armytage's theme, especially those related to technology and education. He refers mainly to ideas put forward during and since the nineteenth century, when the enormous possibilities of technological development began to be obvious. One may perhaps be forgiven for asking, apropos his many fascinating examples, 'What is the importance of motives in all this?' Most applications of technological innovations are probably stimulated by motives of power and profit rather than moral or humanitarian considerations, and it may be that this infects the results in undesirable ways. One suspects that there is a certain haphazardness about the improvements in the human lot that they may have brought about, and it would be worth examining the extent of such applications which have had harmful effects. What is to prevent harmful innovations from being introduced if they promise a profit to the innovator or power to the sponsor in spite of losses to most of those affected? It is noticeable that Armytage, unlike Holloway, has little to say (for example) about the millions spent on the nuclear arms race. It may be that, as is argued in both preceding and later papers, thinking in terms of whole utopias would have a beneficial effect on piecemeal innovations by giving direction to them and rendering them principled rather than random in relation to human well-being. This too presents problems, some of which are exposed in Pitzer's Colston Lecture.

A special variety of utopia is the ideal city, celebrated in the history of architecture, which by promoting a natural harmony between man, society and the environment transforms society in all its aspects. The physical setting of the ideal society is seen not as one factor among many, as in most utopias, but as that from which all social change follows. This attitude contrasts with that of most architects, who have respected the limits of the existing social order. Like other utopias, the ideal city typically has no history but is pictured as a going concern for our consideration. It is seen as an achievable end with, usually, a severely practical reliance on the wealthy patron as means. Fishman examines three examples and argues that the consequences in practice have usually been the exact opposite of those intended. Plans for ideal cities are important in the education of architects, most of whom, lacking the vision of a new social order, have incorporated elements from them piecemeal into existing cities, producing disorder rather than order. Fishman believes that in the end this is beneficial. Diversity, in contrast to the totally organised ideal, is a source of urban vitality. However, although the end of the ideal city may seem to be at hand, the advent of the 'third industrial revolution' may create a need for a new breed of ideal city.

The ideal city once again raises questions of individual freedom and the concentration of power. However, one may wonder whether the horrors of modern cities may not be due, in part, to the piecemeal application of utopian ideas, and whether these alone are likely to stimulate new generations of utopias. Features which in a utopian context would be valuable may be dangerous in isolation from that context; the next best thing to a particular ideal society may not be the closest possible approximation to it.

Such problems no doubt exercise Gill, and later Hall. Gill takes the plans produced for Central London during the last war and shows that the strategic ideas they use are to be found in written and practical utopias of earlier centuries. He argues that this is a necessity of effective planning and development because an overall vision of a better society is an important controlling influence on the details of the contemporary working plan. Lacking this, the development of a modern city may be haphazard and even tend to make things worse because motives underlying it may depend upon sectional and conflicting interests rather than an interest in general, overall improvement. Karl Popper's 'piecemeal social engineering' can be effective in desirable ways only if it is undertaken by people with the highest motives and, probably, some vision of a bearable society.

In his Colston Lecture Pitzer considers attempts to realise whole utopian systems in small communities. He concentrates on a wealth of religious communities in America, because they have been, on the whole, more enduring, efficient and productive than secular communities, and seeks to make clear some lessons to be learnt from them. These may be relevant both to similar future projects and to piecemeal reform. Some of them sound a grim warning, others a note of hope.

The lessons fall under three headings: collectivism, community and commitment. Some communities have shown strikingly the efficacy of collective economic ventures, even to the extent that their commercial success has proved embarrassing to their members, and the mere fact of collectivism may sometimes be seen as increasing moral sensitivity. This may also be one of the lessons of community, which are more elusive but nevertheless real. Many communities have achieved a sincere concern for the welfare of others and the ability to co-operate in personal as well as commercial relations; we may be reminded of Graham's suggestion of the possibility of unanimity. The lessons of commitment are probably more diverse and, sometimes, more worrying; the dangers are clear in the activities of the Rev. Jim Jones and the eugenic policies of the Oneida Community. As Pitzer says, 'Commitment holds the key to their constructive solidarity and their destructive authoritarianism.' The main hazard lies in commitment to a leader's authority rather than a co-operatively devised set of ideals or the individual conscience.

It is noteworthy that moral sensitivity has not, even among utopians, always increased with collectivism and community: success in the manufacture of animal traps and the fund-raising activities of some leaders are open to moral questioning; a sincere concern for others may entail restrictions in freedom and privacy. A question that calls out for careful scrutiny is one of scale: Are the successes of these communities likely to be possible, and their weaknesses likely to be avoided on the larger scale of the nation-state? We are probably not yet in a position to give an answer.

Part III

Even Morrison, who declares himself to be predisposed against utopianism, when he sets out to make his best case for it, sees both the point of considering such questions and the desirability of some controlling view of an end. His fear is that a utopia on a large scale would eliminate *voluntary* participation and would be likely to fail because of the difficulty of specifying its structure and operation well enough to allow testing in advance. Nevertheless, he sees value in small experiments for encouraging and testing new ideas, especially in an era of rapid technological change. Such experiments have usually been controlled by a vision of an ideal and have taught valuable lessons about the faults of some alleged ideals and about the dangers inherent in too rigid an allegiance to one person's ideal. As he says, 'if we must be open-minded about what the future can be like, we cannot afford to be empty-headed about it'.

Lukes discusses the relation of Marxism to utopianism and argues that although Marxism sees itself as scientific, revolutionary and anti-utopian and has explicitly criticised utopianism, there are embedded in the theory both a utopian and an anti-utopian viewpoint which are distinctive. He argues that Marxism's anti-utopianism has had detrimental effects on the theory and practice of Marxism. Marx and Engels, even while criticising Saint-Simon, Fourier and Owen, expressed considerable respect for their total vision and incorporated it into their own vision of human emancipation. Their criticism was mainly that the utopians were unscientific in their manner of predicting future states of affairs. The knowledge they lacked, and which Marxism was to provide, was knowledge of social and economic forces already at work, of a 'self-transforming present, not of an ideal future'.

Lukes asks how we can have that kind of knowledge without a knowledge of the shape of future society, and how we can justifiably assist the transformation without knowing that the new society will *be* emancipatory. He seeks to identify the reasons behind the failure of Marx and Engels to appreciate this objection. A serious consequence, he claims, is that they failed to reflect seriously and systematically upon *their* utopia, that is, full communism or human emancipation. This in turn led them to neglect discussion of moral and political notions that would be necessary in judging whether the new society was better than the old, and of more practical problems concerning the distribution of resources, economic, social and industrial organisation, and so on. Lukes begins and ends by referring to

Šimečka's paper in this volume, suggesting that the evils he finds in one example of 'actually existing socialism' may be traced to these weaknesses in Marxist theory.

It may be thought rather arbitrary to include Lukes's paper in Part III rather than in Parts I or II. However, although Lukes is primarily pointing to a lack of clarity in Marx's theory, it can be argued that this weakness underlies the unsatisfactoriness of an alleged application of that theory. Moreover the theory is perhaps correctly regarded as a blueprint for social reconstruction rather than as a purely theoretical exercise. Another feature marking the transition from Part I to Part III is a move from the more general to the more particular. For these reasons it seemed desirable to juxtapose Lukes's chapter to Šimečka's.

Šimečka also makes the point about criteria for judging the worth of societies. He begins by writing with the bitterness of one who has had all his utopian illusions shattered by living in a caricature of a socialist state and witnessing the betrayal of Marx's ideals. His first reaction is to despair of utopian thinking and to stress elements in utopias leading to their corruption. His strictures are just those that Popper stresses in urging the totalitarian tendencies of utopias. But then, after Šimečka has led us inexorably up the path toward a total rejection of utopias, he asks us to imagine a world without utopias. A broader view of humanity now leads him to reason his way out of his first bitter reaction. Without a desire for order, beauty and harmony in society, without a concern for human brotherhood, we should lack criteria even for criticising our present condition, for defining a better or for condemning a failed utopia. Ants are efficiently organised but have no appreciation of Greek tragedies. The world needs new utopias, not their abandonment: 'a world without utopias would be a world without social hope, a world of resignation to the status quo.' Without a minimal utopia based on a respect for humanity, as such, there would be no human dignity.

Many of the features that Šimečka regards as important, such as peace, freedom, the satisfaction of basic needs and the rejection of the profit-motive are those which Holloway considers likely to be furthered by utopian thinking or as having been partially achieved because of it. Like Armytage and Goodwin he thinks that various piecemeal changes within our lifetime have been promoted by past utopian thinking. Going beyond this he sees many of the harmful changes as the result of the neglect of central features in utopian thought.

At first sight, Hall seems to take a view contrary to Fishman's, since he considers that attempts to plan for the future *necessarily* involve speculation about ideals. However, their views may not be very far apart. Fishman stresses that constructors of ideal cities typically hold that desirable social changes follow from features of the ideal city, but he sees advantages in the incorporation by architects of some of these features in non-ideal existing cities even without reference to the ideal. However, his conclusion may suggest that new utopias are needed to enable us to cope with technological innovation even if we are not ideal-city planners. Hall is more concerned than our other authors that planners should embrace the art of the possible, without which utopia becomes divorced from utility; perhaps this is to be expected from one whose primary interest lies in the actual reconstruction and reorganisation of our cities.

Finally, Suits confounds us all in the continuation of his fable of the Grasshopper and the Ant by claiming to show that there are logical reasons why any thought for the future, including the rejection of utopianism, necessitates our being utopians. If this is so, it is not surprising that Graham should be disposed to argue for the possibility of consensus, that Šimečka should ultimately return to utopianism and that Marx and Engels should turn out to be utopians despite themselves. Do we conclude, then, by merely stating a truism and accepting a necessity beyond our control that gives no guidance for future procedure? No – since even if Suits is right, necessity does not justify fatalism. The argument continues about whether we should pursue an explicitly stated utopian policy and, whatever our answer, about how to avoid any unwelcome consequences of a view with which we are necessarily saddled.

PART I

Conceptions, Definitions
and Intentions

1

The History of Utopia:
the Chronology of Nowhere

J.C. Davis

The history of utopia has, until very recently, been indifferently written. Its interest has resided in the curious details of apparently futile dreams and their nostalgic associations for us, or in the coincidences of prophecies fulfilled across more or less elongated tracts of time. But the evolution of a structure, the revolution of a paradigm, the metamorphosis of a genre have barely been discernible.

If the essence of history is change through time, and if the history of ideas is consequently about the flux of conceptual configurations and/or their linguistic contexts through time (23a; 27a, b, c,)* the historiography of utopian thought has scarcely begun. One might discern its beginnings in the 1960s and 1970s in the writing of, for example, Judith Shklar and Elisabeth Hansot with their concern to distinguish the shift from classical, transcendent utopias to modern utopias concerned with 'actualisation in time' (26a, b; 9). But it was as recently as 1979, with the publication of Frank and Fritzie Manuel's *Utopian Thought in the Western World*, that the conceptualisation of the history of utopia and, inseparably, of the varieties of utopia reached a point of sophistication from which patterns of dissimilarity and change could be distinguished. One should not therefore underestimate the achievement of the Manuels in their monumental work. This is a necessary caveat because in this paper I shall question their historiographical *schema* of constellations and in particular their depiction of the varieties of utopia. I want to end by raising again the issue of the possibility and the nature of the history of utopia.

Until the mid-1960s such views as there were on the historiography of utopia had to be derived from three types of rather unhelpful source. The first consisted of catalogues or bibliographies wrestling with

* Numbers in brackets refer to the bibliographies at the end of each chapter.

inadequate definitions (5; 8; 21). The second amounted to a chronologically arranged commentary on little more than a list of any, all or selected visions of imaginary societies (20;10; 1a, b). This is an approach which has been characterised by the Manuels as 'the daisy chain' and dismissed by them as 'fragmented and particularistic' (16). Sometimes the daisy chains were put together with an ideological intent (11; 12; 2; 19) or by those wishing to pursue a special interest in social idealism (17; 7). The third consisted of those who wrote extended studies of, exhortation to, or admonition against utopian activity based on an assumed rather than demonstrated necessity for, utility of, or danger from utopian thought (4; 25; 24; 30). The reawakened interest in utopianism of the 1960s saw a continuation of these kinds of writings alongside a new search for a historiographical footing for the study of the phenomenon through time. The special edition of *Daedalus* devoted to utopias in 1965, and subsequently republished with additions, typified this mix (15).

The reordering of utopia's past was not without its difficulties and, given a degree of definitional uncertainty, these readily focussed around chronology. While Judith Shklar could proclaim the end of utopia in the shattering of classicism and classical political theory in the late eighteenth century (26a, b, c), Adam Ulam saw the emergence of utopia in the succeeding period coincident with socialism, rationalism and the nineteenth century (29). Some attempt at reconciliation of this kind of chronological conflict was made by Elisabeth Hansot in her attempt to distinguish two modes of utopian thought, both theoretically and diachronically distinctive (9). She saw the shift occurring in the seventeenth and eighteenth centuries from the static, contemplative classical utopia to the modern utopia, incorporating change and concerned with viability. Plato, More and Andreae typified the former; Bellamy, Wells and Howells the latter. Classical utopias were ultimately aimed at individual reformation; modern utopias at social reconstruction. There are problems involved in the readings necessary to sustain this. For example, Thomas More's insistence that individuals inside and outside Utopia remained the same, equally reasonable (18, pp. 237-9), seems to cut across these categories, and one is expected to accept a position in the unresolvable debate about More's social intention in publishing the *Utopia*. From a more general perspective, it might be thought too crude an operation to reduce what has variously been seen as a diverse cultural expression sustained through four centuries or an impulse to imaginative social idealisation traceable back to the fourth millennium B.C. if not before, to such simple dichotomies. There are clearly problems of definition, description and chronology (i.e. of a certain kind of history) involved here.

From the latter – problems of description and chronology – the

Manuels have richly provided for our escape. But they have ignored the former – problems of definition – deliberately, self-consciously and almost entirely. It is worth examining the consequences of definitional obscurity for their work and indeed for the whole enterprise of writing a history of utopian thought, for like Nietzsche they believe that history and definition are antithetical (16, p.5). In 814 large, closely-printed pages supported by 51 pages of notes *Utopian Thought in the Western World* presents us with a great wealth of 'utopian' writings, carefully described, periodised, categorised and chronologically arranged in deliberately untidy groupings called constellations. The main body of the literature discussed runs from the Renaissance to the present day, although a preliminary tenth of the book surveys the ancient and medieval background to the sixteenth-century birth of the Western Utopia. It is a prodigious display of modern scholarship; a book which by sheer weight of learning, sustained enthusiasm and overall critical insight, puts the historiography of ideal society thought on a new plane. In it we are presented with seven major constellations of utopian thought and several minor ones – though it should be confessed at once that there is a degree of numerological uncertainty arising out of the untidiness of the categories. '... the perimeters of the concept of utopia,' we are told, 'have to be left hazy' (p.5). The Manuels' endeavour is 'to identify historical constellations of utopias with reasonably well marked time-space perimeters and common elements that are striking enough to permit framing generalisations, while still respecting the concreteness of the individual experience. The origin of the utopian propensity is, in an absolute sense, not knowable; its application and incorporation in given utopian configurations or constellations are. They become the main subject of our inquiry' (p.13). Not all utopias can be squeezed into these constellations, but new and innovative utopias are held to be embraced by them (p.15). The utopian story proper begins with a threefold configuration or set of constellations: More's witty fiction, the *città felice* of Patrizzi, Alberti and Filarete, and the radical vision of a new heaven on earth for the common man of Thomas Müntzer. In the fourth constellation, images of these dreams are conflated with science in the pansophic enterprises of Bruno, Bacon, Campanella, Andreae and Comenius. Loosely associated with this are two lesser configurations, the radical outpourings of the English Civil War and its aftermath and the critique of Bourbon absolutism implicit in works of Vairasse and Fénelon. There then follows a rather heterogeneous collection of people brought together in the constellation of Enlightenment eupsychias, embracing Diderot, Rousseau, Turgot, Condorcet and Kant amongst others. Slightly to one side appear the sexual visionaries, de Sade and Restif de la Bretonne. A sixth constellation incorporates the visions of social justice engendered by the French

Revolution and the utopian socialism of Saint-Simon, Fourier and Owen. There is then a digression to consider Marx and Engels in a utopian context, Comte and the anarchism of Godwin, Proudhon, Kropotkin and Sorel. The last and seventh major constellation is that of the late Victorian, progressivist, evolutionary utopias of Bellamy, Hertzka, Morris, Bulwer-Lytton and Wells. The book culminates in a sustained examination of the impact of Freud, Darwin and Marx on visions of this sort. Here then is an ambitious work, transcending the biography with commentary, the backward-looking rescue job, the daisy chain and the polemic. Utopia and its transformations are related to successive intellectual, social and biographical contexts. We have a work of history of sophistication and resource. Does it work?

Let us begin with the rationale of chronologically arranged historical groupings or clusters of these writings. The Manuels' constellations of utopias are perceived by them to be linked by common elements arising out of a chronologically delimited historical context. Thus we can distinguish, for example, Renaissance from Enlightenment utopias. There is nothing particularly new about these kinds of distinction. The Manuels' originality lies in the detail and sophistication with which they elaborate the map of their constellations. Nevertheless, if we recognise the fundamentally traditional basis of these groupings or constellations we can see that the historian's capacity to explain them depends upon the ability to make either or both of two sorts of connections. By the first, utopian constellations as intellectualist phenomena might be associated with a perceived social requirement for a new vision, with social transitions or the prospect of them. So it is that certain constellations may be associated with periods of political revolution and their aftermath. 'At such times all things seem possible, and the utopian appears no madder than other men' (pp. 14, 332). Under scrutiny, however, these assertions seem of questionable value. It may be possible to find chronological relationships between some utopias and the English Civil War or the French Revolution, but where are those for the American or Russian Revolutions or for the Frondes or the Spanish Civil War? The phenomena we are dealing with are too gross to enable us to establish specific relationships in these terms, and what of all those utopias associated with periods of peace or relative stability (More, Bacon, Burton, Morris)? Unless we adduce something as general and as vacuous as 'the rising spirit of capitalism', it appears difficult to categorise all utopias as associated with certain types of social happenings.

Social idealism of the utopian type is always a rejection of the contemporary world and its processes. Yet the rejection is never entire. There is something in the metaphor of the photographic negative, the utopian's inversion, but it too is not completely satisfactory. At the level of political theory the problem of utopia is that however bizarre it might seem in terms of the present world – however unrealistic – its order is legitimated in the end by some principle taken from this unideal world. Its ideal quality – to put it another way – is derived from a world which is found most unideal. So Swift, abandoning all realism, imagines an ideal world not of men but of horses. Even so, the qualities which make the society of the Houyhnhnms so admirable – honesty, rationality and decency – are taken precisely from the society which Swift found wanting. Indeed, the force of these principles can arguably only be maintained if we continue to hold the ideal and the unideal in juxtaposition. The relationship between the utopian manifestation and the real world is consequently bound to be ambivalent and idiosyncratic. Hence it becomes hard to see how whole groups, or constellations, of utopias could be related to common features of a social landscape and, significantly, the Manuels do not attempt this. In any case, our perception of the social reality of the past – as of the present – is itself an intellectual construct. What we may be being asked to do then is to reduce an intellectual phenomenon (utopian thought) to an epiphenomenon of something which is itself an intellectual construct (our perception of past reality). Giving no place a circumscribed location, it can be seen, is no easy matter.

From this indeterminate point we can move on to the second sort of historically explanatory connection which might be envisaged for utopias. This is the association of intellectualist phenomena (utopias) with other intellectualist phenomena, and hence, where there are common intellectual associations, to constellations. Naturally, this too the Manuels practise. 'Religious schisms and intellectual revolutions like the emergence of the new science in the seventeenth century ... have all sparked novel utopian ideas and led to the formulation of startling new utopian constellations' (p.14). Thus we may relate utopian writing to the intellectual currents of the Renaissance or the Enlightenment or the Scientific Revolution. But at what level are connections being made between these rather slippery semantic constructs and specific utopias? And what type of influence is it which we are discussing? Is it the details, the fashionable finish, that is conditioned by the intellectual climate or is it the essence of the utopian structure that is influenced so that each intellectual movement of European history recasts the shape of utopia? Yet, of course, we are not dealing with all intellectual movements in European history. To *demonstrate* the precise and presumed connections between milieu and artifice we would need a comparative history of counterinstances, just as the comparative history of social revolutions requires one to examine those situations in which revolutions did not occur (28). Thus, for example, it might be held that the Enlightenment excited certain types of utopian imagination. Why did scholasticism have no comparable effect – or did it? The Manuels do not, perhaps understandably, examine this sort of question, but the consequence is that we are left too often with presumed connections, and presumptions do not persuade. A further presumption is involved in deciding what level or quality of intellectual movement influences utopian constructs. There are 120 pages on the influence of the Enlightenment but not one on the influence of what has come to be called the Scots Enlightenment. Is this because it does not meet the standards – which haven't been revealed to us – of a fully-qualified intellectual movement? Or because the mental constructs of utilitarianism and classical economics are not considered to be utopian enough, however vaguely that term is defined? (Should Bentham's 'Panopticon' be completely disregarded? For a classical economist turned utopian see W.H. Beveridge (3).) It is important to recognise, if there are rules to the game, that the vaguer or more elastic one makes one's operative definitions, the more carefully one has to justify exclusions. This should not be confused with querulousness about individuals or individual works which have somehow been omitted. Given the scale of the Manuels' aspiration and the nature of human fallibility such omissions are inevitable. But we are talking here of the omission of schools of thought or intellectual movements so significant in the development of western consciousness that their exclusion can only be regarded as deliberate. For another example, take the case of classical republicanism, the significance of which for western culture has been so dramatically restated by J.G.A. Pocock (23b); Macchiavelli, Gianotti and Guicciardini certainly dreamed of an ideal republican society but their dreams are not dealt with in this work. Why not? What tests have they failed to meet? This case is all the more baffling since all three can be regarded as constitution makers, and for the Manuels 'all constitution making is in a way utopian' (p. 366). Harrington's *Oceana*, assaulted by the Manuels – 'As arid a work as has sprung from the mind of utopian man' – is not recognised as the offspring of a great intellectual tradition and perhaps a dead end for it (23c; 6b).

There are problems then with the Manuels' constellations. Their nature remains unclear and, in consequence, their linkage to other phenomena, difficult at best, remains indeterminate, a matter of assertion or presumption rather than demonstration. As a further consequence, their number and size, arising partly from common elements vaguely defined, partly from indeterminate linkages with other intellectual movements or social phenomena, remain purely arbitrary. One can rearrange the constellations, querying omissions and redistributing individual works almost at will. (For example, should Campanella be in chapter 5 or chapter 10?) The history of utopia becomes a game of snakes and ladders with each player free to accept or redefine the characteristics of the snakes or the ladders or both.

Why, given the appearance of grasp, control, and *schema* that pervades the work, does *Utopian Thought in the Western World* end up by dissolving the history of utopia in a fine mist of blurred categories, tenuous relationships and imprecisely conceived movements? I want to suggest that there are two reasons why the Manuels' constellations cannot provide an adequate framework for a history of utopian thought. One is their failure to define and distinguish utopia and, intimately connected with that, their failure to grasp that utopian thought poses and attempts to settle an essentially political question. The other is their failure to confront the conceptual problem of a history of utopia.

Given, on the one hand, an absence of definition and, on the other, a lack of contextual precision (p.24), how can any history but a purely speculative one be written? The Manuels' defence of their evasion of sharp categories to determine what falls into the investigation of utopian thought in the past is both cursory and half-hearted (pp. 5-7, 252). At various points, arcadianism, millennialism, anarchism and moral reform programmes are equated with utopia (for examples, see part 1, chapter 1, pp. 103, 109, 124-7, 130, 133, 134, 232-5, 381-5, 528, 535). At others, the Manuels imply distinctions between 'proper' utopias and others, or between utopias and other forms of ideal society, without ever telling the reader what those distinctions are (for examples, see pp. 1, 33, 48, 109, 111, 112, 123, 251). The two authors acknowledge the apparent absence of utopian thought in Spain, 'though', they say, 'free-floating utopian affect may have somehow attached itself to the figure of Don Quixote' (pp. 14-15). Whatever this may mean, it seems to imply that utopia is in the air we breathe. Searching for precise connections, the ligaments of a history, seems futile. Like the air around us, utopia has no history and yet is in the history of everything. The failure to establish criteria by which to distinguish what is going on in the dialogue of the works of individual authors, like Cervantes, is also a failure to discriminate the body of material over which the historians must work and which gives potential shape to their history.

Whether we are dealing with the origins, the utility and necessity or the history of utopia we will not get as far as we might unless we are prepared to distinguish utopia as one type of ideal society and to differentiate it from the others. If society were ideal there could be no origin, no utility, and no necessity for dreaming of a better or ideal society. Such aspirations would be subsumed in description. The ideal-society thinker begins by recognising the unideality of the society in which he lives. Ideality implies the solving of a social dilemma. In this sense, all ideality is rooted in social reality. But, like ideality, reality is perceived from many different vantage points and the set of social problems to be solved is ordered according to different priorities. Hence, there begin to emerge different types of ideal society. In my book, *Utopia and the Ideal Society*, I have tried to distinguish five broad types of ideal society. We might, using the diverse material to be found in the Manuels' constellations, rehearse these types according to their utility and necessity.

Those who give priority above all to material and sensual satisfaction may take the short cut to the Land of Cockaygne by wishing away all physical and sensual limitations. They see a world of instant gratification, of wishing trees, fountains of youth, rivers of wine, self-roasting birds, sexually promiscuous and ever-available partners (16, pp. 78-81). The Ranters, if they existed at all, represented the desire for this self-fulfilment in the stress of the English Civil War. But to call their individual indulgence and satiation utopian is to rob utopia of all meaning as a social construct (cf. pp. 355-8).

In a second type of ideal society, arcadia, an aesthetic or moral sense is added to the concept of natural abundance. Nature is bountiful but in a restrained way. Appetites are satisfied but in a temperate way. Fénelon's vision, for example, is that of 'a natural idyllic existence without great struggle' (p. 385); arcadia rather than utopia.

Those who would push restraint further, envisaging a society capable of enduring hardship and want, create a third type of ideal society, one with a prescriptive moral order, perfectly realised by all its members. This I have called the perfect moral commonwealth. Kant's appeal to the good will and experience of all men in the perfecting of society betokens final adherence to this ideal-society type (p. 528). If we were all good, all would be well. As a mode of ideal society, this is, in essence, institutionally conservative and conformist. In the Manuels' reading, More's *Utopia* comes close to being only a preparation for this type of society, giving men 'a large measure of doing what they would, as long as they caused no pain to themselves or others; a quiet stable existence free from anxiety, marked by honest allowable pleasures' (pp. 133, 134). This is to blur and conflate the utopian vision of More with a minimal state á la Robert Nozick (22). But dress, housing, work, leisure, residence, travel, talk, eating, sitting, marriage and death are regulated by the state in *Utopia* (6a, pp.53-4). They are so regulated and sanctions provided for enforcement because men cannot be relied upon or even inspired to act well.

The fourth type of ideal society, the millennium, assumes that nature and man will be transformed by a force arising and acting independently of the wills of individual men and women. The origins of this hope lie not so much in the fear of chaos but in the fear of systematic and triumphant evil – the historical triumph of anti-Christ, however defined. The answer is in the depiction of a force greater than anti-Christ and therefore greater than man, anti-Christ's victim. Moral powerlessness will be overcome by a *deus ex machina*. Given that, the details of the new order tend to remain blurred. The emphasis is on the process of transition and its timing. Pressed as to the details of the new society envisaged, in so far as both man and nature will be transformed by the process, the millennial prophecy tends to dissolve into perfect moral commonwealth or arcadia (5a, pp. 35-6). 'We fleshly earthly men become gods through Christ's becoming human and thus we are pupils of God with Him, taught by Him Himself and made divine by Him. Nay far more. We become altogether transformed so that the earthly life changes over into heaven' (Thomas Müntzer, quoted in 16, p. 192). Not only do the Manuels fail to note the typicality of this but their conflation of the millennial with utopia (ch. 6) leads to consequent misreadings such as those on the Fifth Monarchists or on the development of Gerrard Winstanley.

In utopia we see no invocation of a *deus ex machina*, nor any wishing away of the deficiencies of man or nature. Systems have to be devised whereby men will be able to offset their own continuing wickedness and cope with the deficiencies of nature. Such systems are inevitably bureaucratic, institutional, legal and educational, artificial and organisational. Arcadia and Cockaygne idealise nature. The perfect moral commonwealth idealises man. The millennium envisages an external power capable of transforming man and nature. The utopian idealises not man nor nature but organisation. Threats to organisational perfection come from *fortuna*, the play of contingency; from moral inefficiency, the wavering of intention in the face of the uncertainty of moral results; and from corruption, the perversion of institutional and organisational processes. The perfection of organisation implies by definition attention to those details which will prevent and surmount those threats. The contingent must be eliminated, moral intention must be made efficient, and the choice which corruption implies must be taken away.

It is important that the political significance of these distinctions be grasped. If politics is about the distribution of opportunities, rewards and satisfactions, the setting of norms of human behaviour and policing the abnormal, then ideal societies are, in a sense, all about the end of politics. But the terminus is arrived at in different ways and those differences are instructive. In Cockaygne satisfactions are multiplied to the point of universal satiation. There is no problem of distribution and, since all appetites are satisfied, no problem of restraint. In arcadia men police themselves in temperance and find their moderate wants blissfully satisfied. As Cockaygne is a land of satiation, so arcadia is a land of rest. In neither case is redistributive work required. The perfect moral commonwealth is a land of perpetual moral striving, of ethical heroics, where men endure privation stoically and altruistically. Though scarcity persist, distribution is no problem where self-abnegation is the common response. The millennium envisages the cataclysmic transformation of the situation by some transcendent or immanent power beyond the will of men and therefore beyond the realm of politics. Utopia, by contrast, accepts the distributional problems posed by the deficiency of resources and the moral disabilities of men. Unlike the others, therefore, it accepts the bases of the problem from which politics arises. Out of the minds and wills of human beings must come organisational forms and practices which will guarantee the just distribution of finite resources and contain the anti-social proclivities of men and women. Utopia is thus political in a fuller sense than the other ideal society types. But, like the Hobbesian citizen creating Leviathan, the depiction of utopia is a once-for-all political act; a set of decisions against which there is no appeal. In the perfect and immortal commonwealth there is no room for improvement or even for change. Utopia begins with dissatisfaction with the present state of politics as, at its best, social engineering. Why aren't things put to rights; problems solved, without creating further problems? To visualise a world put to rights, while still accepting the limitations of nature and humanity, utopia has to confront political problems and political deficiencies. This is what distinguishes it from those forms of social idealisation which wish the problem away, and their failure to recognise it mars the Manuels' work. Once the utopian has solved the political problem by organisational means there is no longer need for politics in utopia. So, in Utopia, political discussion outside the senate is prohibited as a capital offence (6a, p. 53). When politics stops, so does change. Perfection is not relative. The dynamic utopia is a myth. Its conception would involve the depiction of a continuous and endless sequence of legal, institutional and administrative devices adapted to successive changes in society and capable of guaranteeing their own transformation while maintaining harmony and stability in societies where resources are presumed to be limited and everyone, including the administrators, is assumed to be wicked. I am not aware of a serious attempt to set down such a vision.

By contrast with the Manuels' engagingly relaxed attitude to categories, I am suggesting that we should be much more careful, and perhaps more pedestrian, in distinguishing the varieties of ideal society and utopia amongst them. But are my taxonomies too restrictive and do they have any historiographical value? It would be possible to retain utopia as a synonym for ideal society but then we would have to invent a new term for that category of social idealisation dependent upon detailed organisational, legislative, administrative and educational imagination. Since Thomas More did exactly that over four and a half centuries ago and since, I believe, we have to treat his work as a defining *locus classicus* for the genre, there seems little point. The categories have, I have tried to argue elsewhere, both historiographical and theoretical value. To demonstrate that requires more detailed analysis than there is room for here. I would like instead to illustrate that value by turning to three problems in the historiography of utopia posed by the Manuels' eclecticism – anarchism and the case of Proudhon; the Enlightenment; and utopia and science – and finally to ask what, if anything, it might mean to talk of the history of utopia from the perspective of my typologies.

Chapter 31 of the Manuels' book, dealing with 'Anarchy and the Heroic Proletariat', is a marvellously sensitive piece of writing about a difficult area. Niggling through the reader's experience of it, however, is a sense of unease about what is going on. '... the order of anarchy as a utopian condition for mankind dates from the end of the eighteenth century' (16, p. 735). But, 'There is no significant utopian novel or full-bodied description of a future utopian society whose author would identify himself as an anarchist.' Even worse, 'a utopian blueprint of anarchy would be self-contradictory'. But again, compounding our problem, anarchy, we are told, remains 'a definable species in utopia' (p. 737). How can this be when there is no definition? The Manuels are clearly hesitating before a critical problem. Can anarchism – the absence of a constraining social order – ever be an ideal society? For Kropotkin there can be no coercion, only an appeal to goodwill (p. 741). In William Godwin's *Political Justice* the conversion of all members of society had to precede the implementation – if that is the right word – of anarchy (p. 736). George Sorel's is 'a utopia of heroic conduct' (p. 747). It will be clear by now that, in terms of my typologies, the Manuels are discussing a perfect moral commonwealth solution and confusing it with utopia. Does this matter? I think it does for two immediate reasons.

The first is that an anarchism of heroic conduct can be associated with a long tradition insistent that society could be made perfect by the moral performance of all its members. In many respects that tradition retained a conformist, conservative aspect. If kings were wise and sought their subjects' welfare, judges were just, merchants honest, lords good and kind, peasants laborious and obedient, and so on, all would be well. But even in its most conservative form such a vision could be perceived – as it was, for example, by Thomas Lupton writing in the late sixteenth century (13; cf. 14) – to dissolve social, institutional and governmental structures. For what was there for judges to be just about when all men were law abiding? The anarchist version of this ideal-society type goes straight to this position. It is an important transition, but one which we shall miss entirely if we conflate perfect moral commonwealth with utopia.

Secondly, it is important to recognise the profound antagonism between an ideal which places its faith in the moral capacities of free human beings and one which insists that human beings – for their own good, of course – must be subject to legal, bureaucratic and administrative controls and be punished for breaching them. Unless one distinguishes them, one cannot grasp the radical anti-utopianism of the anarchists. What else does Sorel's hatred of the bureaucratisation of Marxism betoken? Or take Proudhon's classic attack on the utopians: 'What is Association? It is a dogma ... Thus the Saint-Simonian school, going beyond what it received from its founder, produced a system; Fourier, a system; Owen, a system; Cabet, a system; Pierre Leroux, a system; Louis Blanc, a system; like Babeuf, Morelly, Thomas Morus, Campanella, Plato, and others, their predecessors, each one starting with a single principle, gave birth to systems. And all these systems, excluding each other, are equally progressive. Let humanity perish rather than the system, this is the motto of the utopians, like that of fanatics of all ages' (16, pp. 742-3, 754). The failure to identify the anti-utopianism of Proudhon and Sorel springs, in the last resort, out of the failure to define utopia and so to distinguish it from other forms of ideal society.

Similar problems emerge with the Manuels' treatment of the Enlightenment. Determining the constellation under scrutiny is a cavalier business. The 'utopian digressions' of Montesquieu, Voltaire and Diderot are out (p. 413). Why this should be so, when Leibniz, who (like Rousseau, p. 438, or Marx, p. 713) never composed a 'proper utopia' (p. 392), is in on the strength of his digressions or what might be culled from phrases of his, is difficult to say. It is a manifestation of the Manuels' untidiness. We may find it liberating. We may smile indulgently – if we are prepared to take the risk of being caught in a patronising attitude. Far more serious is the failure to grasp what is going on in terms of ideal-society types in the Enlightenment by seeing it all in terms of a broad utopianism. For the disposition of most of the writers enlisted by the Manuels in their constellation is, again, anti-utopian. It may indeed be argued that the Enlightenment rejected utopia with all its repressive and constraining devices in favour of three possible alternatives. The first was a secular perfect moral commonwealth, and here the difficulty was to find a secular basis for social morality. Rousseau's attempt to find the ideal secular self (p. 441) should perhaps be viewed in this context as should the neglected utilitarians' attempt to find a scientific basis for individual moral calculation. The second was that pervasive, ambiguous and best known Enlightenment ideal, the intellectual arcadia. Finally, there was the attempt to rehabilitate the classical republic in a commercial world, to lay the ghost of its vulnerability to corruption. Here the Scots Enlightenment played its part, while across the Channel, figures like

Turgot and Condorcet offered to rescue the republic from *fortuna*, by flattening her wheel and unveiling the prospect of progress. But progress and utopia are not compatible. The dynamic utopia is a myth. My claim against the Manuels then is that the Enlightenment cannot, even partially, be interpreted in terms of utopia, and that anti-utopianism, arcadianism and the search for a secular morality are more typical of it. Constellations and typologies, in this context, are only of value if, through their use, the continuities and transitions of European thought become clearer.

The relationship of utopia and science forms a third area that we might briefly examine to illustrate problems arising out of the Manuels' definitional imprecision. Their view is one of a natural, complementary relationship between science and utopia, and they feel that the future of utopian thought 'is bound up with the destiny of science and scientists in modern society' (p. 782). We can see, however, that science has had differing relationships with various ideal society types, and these differences may have been of some significance in the evolution of western culture. Millennialism and a kind of scientific aspiration had strong affinities in the seventeenth century (31). They have more sinister affinities today. Science has been seen as a means of overcoming natural deficiencies, producing a cornucopia or arcadia of play and rest. The scientific community has been seen as a perfect moral commonwealth, a self-ruling republic of qualified citizens notable for their *virtu*. But the relationship between utopia, as I have defined it, and science has been far more ambiguous and central than the Manuels are able to allow (6c). The instrumentality of science offered to confer plasticity of the environment upon the utopian designer, as also it offered to reduce contingency to law and so give predictability to the design. In return, utopia offered social stability and a resource base for scientific activity. But the stability of utopia was jeopardised by the restless and relentless innovations of science. At the same time, the utopian impetus towards order and control could threaten the freedom of scientific enquiry. The relationship between the two has remained ambivalent and forms one of the central dilemmas of modern western culture, but it cannot be perceived, assessed or its history traced if it is confused by the association of utopia with the broad category of ideal society.

This brings me to my last question and an ironic twist. Can there be a history of utopia as I have typified it? Can an intellectual construct, like utopia, have, in a general sense, no history? Is utopia out of time in the historiographical, as well as conceptual, sense? Obviously individual utopias have a history which is bound up with the biography of their author or the bibliographical contingencies of their experience as artefacts, or their perlocutionary effects as linguistic contexts, but does utopia, as a species of social commentary or as a construct of the political imagination, have a history? If it has, then we may look at its manifestations in terms of mutability, tracing the internal changes and relating them to changes in social context, the technology and social import of the relationship between conceiver and receiver and so on. We may look for periods of absence of the phenomenon or periods of its abundance, arrange them into chronological sequences or constellations, and try to explain their variations. Or we may look at the structural patterns within utopias and explain their diversity synchronically or diachronically.

Now, *theories* may have a history which can transcend individual biography or – as I understand it – the perlocutionary effect of individual semantic constructs. Thus we can talk of the history of Marxism or of classical economics or of classical republicanism, although we find ourselves quarrelling endlessly about definitions. Theories can have a history because of what they aspire to do intellectually, that is to set up a framework of hypothesis attempting to show the validity, or legitimacy, of one way of looking at the phenomena, or of acting upon them, rather than any other. The legitimacy of the framework can be tested against the acknowledged authorities, be they empirical fact, Holy Writ, the rules of the game, the opinion of the Master and so on. Many of these relationships can alter through time. The theory may be amended to accommodate new facts, interpretations, dilemmas, or pronouncements. Or it may be reformulated in order to recover what is held to be the purity of past meaning. These changes constitute its history. But if we talk of politics, apparently an area of endless flux and change, it is clearly possible to think of positions which deny a need for adaptability and therefore the need for a prospective history. They are a negative instance, a no-politics. For example, we may cite the notion that politics is a waste of time, a fruitless activity, a sphere of indifference. We are aware of the attitude. Books have been written to defend politics against it. Let us assume, not altogether unreasonably I suspect, that this attitude has had a more or less continuous existence through time. What would a history of it be like? One could perhaps write a history of the changing nature of those who have adopted the attitude and the use to which they have put it. But is the concept itself sufficiently flexible to permit the kind of change through time that would permit a history of it to be written? I know of no such history and fear for its impossibility. It may be that utopia falls into the same category.

If we define utopia vaguely as any kind of ideal society, the appearance of a history, confused and unstable as it might be, can be conferred upon it. But its vagueness as a category will limit its capacity to illuminate those intellectual movements or histories of theory with which it comes into conjunction. If we identify utopia more precisely, however, the problem takes on a different dimension. As a mode, or type, of ideal society, utopia assumes the imperfection of man and nature and the validity of institutional and organisational means of producing stable and ordered societies. This configuration of assumptions has not changed through time. Nor has its confrontation with other ideal society modalities and their assumptions of a perfect humanity or a perfect nature or of a transforming power beyond the will of men. As a mode confronting other modes of ideal society utopia barely has a history.

In relation to history, utopia is like a train journeying each day from one point to the other. Different passengers get on and off. They differentiate the journeys, for the vehicle and its route remain the same. So science, transforming the secrets of nature into its laws; class, reducing vertical bonds to horizontal ones; feminism, asserting a wider citizenship against domestic subjection; the human soul, emerging from its battle with original sin into the conditioning of the unconscious; these, amongst others, may be seen to get on and off at varying points, illuminating their own history in the process but in relation to utopia only again demonstrating its potentialities and limitations. As a vehicle of the mind, utopia remains with us. In distinguishing it from other varieties of ideal society we can see more clearly the nature of those potentialities and limitations and hence, perhaps, gauge its necessity and utility in our changing historical circumstances more accurately.

References

1. Armytage, W.H.G. (a) *Heavens Below: utopian experiments in England 1560-1960*, Routledge, London 1961. (b) *Yesterday's Tomorrows: a historical survey of future societies*, Routledge, London 1968.
2. Berneri, Marie Louise, *Journey Through Utopia*, Routledge, London 1950.
3. Beveridge, W.H., 'My Utopia' in *Planning under Socialism*, London 1936.
4. Bloomfield, P., *Imaginary Worlds or the Evolution of Utopia*, Hamish Hamilton, London 1932.
5. Blum, Irving D., 'English Utopias from 1551 to 1699: a bibliography', *Bulletin of Bibliography* 21:6 (1955) pp. 143-4.
6. Davis, J.C. (a) *Utopia and the Ideal Society: a study of English utopian writing 1516-1700*, Cambridge University Press, 1981. (b) 'Pocock's Harrington: Grace, Nature and Art in the Classical Republicanism of James Harrington', *The Historical Journal*, 24:3 (1981) pp. 683-97. (c) 'Science and utopia: the history of a dilemma', *Yearbook in the Sociology of the Sciences*, vol. 8 (1983?).
7. Fuz, J.K., *Welfare Economics in English Utopias: Francis Bacon to Adam Smith*, Nijhoff, The Hague 1952.
8. Gibson, R.W., & Patrick, J. Max, 'A bibliography of utopiana', in R.W.

Gibson (ed.), *St. Thomas More: a preliminary bibliography*, Yale University Press, New Haven & London 1961.

9. Hansot, Elisabeth, *Perfection and Progress: two modes of utopian thought*, M.I.T. Press, Cambridge, Mass. 1974.

10. Hertzler, J.O., *The History of Utopian Thought*, Allen & Unwin, London 1923.

11. Kaufman, M., *Utopias; or, Schemes of Social Improvement from Sir Thomas More to Karl Marx*, Sydenham, London 1879.

12. Laidler, H.W., *Social-Economic Movements: an historical and comparative survey of socialism, communism, co-operation and utopianism: and other systems of reform and reconstruction*, Routledge, London 1949.

13. Lupton, T., *The Second Part and Knitting up the Boke Intituled, Too Good to be True*, London 1581.

14. Luther, M., 'Secular Authority, To What Extent it Should be Obeyed', in John Dillenberger (ed.), *Martin Luther, Selections from his Writings*, New York 1961.

15. Manuel, Frank E. (ed.), *Utopias and Utopian Thought*, Houghton Mifflin, Boston and Cambridge, Mass. 1966.

16. Manuel, Frank E. & Fritzie P., *Utopian Thought in the Western World*, Blackwell, Oxford 1979.

17. Masso, Gildo, *Education in Utopias*, Teachers College, Columbia University, New York 1927.

18. More, Sir Thomas, *Utopia* (1516) edited by Edward Surtz, S.J. and J.H. Hexter, Yale University Press, 1965.

19. Morton, A.L., *The English Utopia*, Lawrence & Wishart, London 1952.

20. Mumford, Lewis, *The Story of Utopias*, New York 1962: 1922, 1950.

21. Negley, Glenn, *Utopian Literature: a bibliography*, Lawrence, Kansas 1977.

22. Nozick, Robert, *Anarchy, State and Utopia*, Blackwell, Oxford 1974.

23. Pocock, J.G.A. (a) *Politics, Language and Time: essays on political thought and history*, Methuen, London 1972. (b) *The Machiavellian Moment: Florentine Republican thought and the Atlantic Republican tradition*, Princeton University Press, 1975. (c) (ed.) *The Political Works of James Harrington*, Cambridge University Press, 1977.

24. Polak, Fred L., *The Image of the Future*, 2 vols, Sythoff, Leyden, 1961.

25. Ruyer, Raymond, *L'Utopie et les utopies*, Presses Universitaires de France, Paris 1950.

26. Shklar, Judith (a) 'The political theory of utopia: from melancholy to nostalgia', in Manuel (ed.) 1966. (b) 'Rousseau's two models: Sparta and the Age of Gold', *Political Science Review* 81:1 (1966) pp. 25-51. (c) *After Utopia*, Princeton University Press, 1969.

27. Skinner, Quentin (a) 'Meaning and understanding in the history of ideas', *History and Theory* 8 (1969) pp. 3-53. (b) 'Conventions and the understanding of speech acts', *Philosophical Quarterly* 20 (1970) pp. 118-38. (c) 'On performing and explaining linguistic actions', *Philosophical Quarterly* 21 (1971) pp. 1-21.

28. Skocpol, Theda, *States and Social Revolutions: a comparative analysis of France, Russia and China*, Cambridge University Press, 1979.

29. Ulam, Adam, 'Socialism and Utopia', in Manuel (ed.) 1966.

30. Wagar, W.W., *The City of Man: prophecies of a world civilisation in*

twentieth-century thought, Houghton Mifflin, Boston 1963.
31. Webster, Charles, *The Great Instauration: science, medicine and reform 1626-1669*, Duckworth, London 1975.

2

Need, Nature and Nowhere

Ruth Levitas

In examining the social origins of utopianism, our first question must be, 'What constitutes a utopia?' Many, if not most, societies have some kind of myth of an earthly paradise, and, in spite of variations, these reveal a number of similarities. Their content revolves around common human concerns of survival, ageing, pain and death, with an emphasis on abundance and physical ease. Many mythological paradises not only have clement weather and abundant food and water, but also contain a tree of life, a source of eternal youth, a substance with miraculous powers of healing (10; 16). Such themes occur in the biblical account of Eden, and in the Celtic tales of the Isles of the Blessed, and recur in modern fiction, for example *The Chronicles of Thomas Covenant the Unbeliever* (7).

Whether such myths are considered utopian or not depends on the definition used. Some would argue that they are utopian precisely because there is no prospect (or intention) of realising them (e.g. 8). Mannheim's view (14) would be that they are ideological rather than utopian, since they tend to compensate for and therefore support rather than transform the status quo. Williams (23b) also argues that the transformative impulse is an important element in utopianism. Riesman would probably exclude them on grounds of irrationality, defining utopia as 'a rational belief which is in the long-run interests of the holder; it is a belief, not in existing reality, but in a potential reality; it must not violate what we know of nature, including human nature, though it may extrapolate our present technology and must transcend our present social organisation' (19, p. 70).

I have argued elsewhere (13a, b) that such definitions unnecessarily limit the category 'utopia', and that it is preferable to define utopia inclusively and non-evaluatively as that state of society ultimately aspired to by an individual or group, irrespective of whether or how it could be realised. This facilitates exploration of differences in the content, form, location and social role of utopias between societies and over time. In particular, the role of utopia as a future state acting as a political catalyst then becomes visible as a cultural form predicated on particular conditions – belief in progress and in human (though not necessarily democratic) control of social change – rather than its normal and definitive characteristic. Now, however, most people are fatalistic about their own ability to influence the process of social change, and, more importantly, about the possibility of anyone else doing so. Any 'advance', technological or social, is seen as likely to have deleterious side-effects. Such despair is illustrated in *The Lathe of Heaven* (11a), in which every attempt to make positive changes results in unintended, unimagined, disasters. Each governmental appeal to the inevitability of, for example, mass unemployment, every denial of responsibility, reinforces this fatalism. The nineteenth-century status of utopia as future goal and catalyst of present action has been eroded. People have not stopped writing utopias in the broad sense, but they are no longer seen as likely to be reached from the present, and are less closely linked to the political process.

Such changes in the location and social role of utopia are also associated with changes in content. Where there is no intention of perceived possibility of implementation, imagination is not limited by perceived plausibility. Thus substances treating all possible ills can be included because they are desirable; one does not need to suppose that people have believed this possible, although they may have done. I very much doubt whether medieval peasants or anyone else ever believed in the literal possibility of ready-cooked larks flying into the mouth, or pigs running around crying, 'Eat me, eat me.' Such utopias may indeed violate what we know of nature and human nature. Where utopia is to be constructed, and especially where it is to evolve out of the present, the constraints of plausibility are much more immediate. The severance of the connection between utopia and political action has released contemporary utopias from the constraints which apply to overtly political programmes. In this respect, they have as much in common with early accounts of the earthly paradise as with nineteenth-century utopias; and this is one reason why they are frequently classified as fantasy.

Observers using a restrictive definition of utopias may interpret this as a decline in the utopian impulse. The inclusive definition suggests that it is more properly to be seen as a shift in the mode of its expression, and, moreover, one which, in freeing utopia from the exigencies of the present, encourages the exploration of true human needs and the best (though not necessarily possible) society for meeting these. In practice, however, the dissociation of political struggle and utopian imagining which has occurred in the West (and which has been thoroughly detrimental to the political process) has not had this result, although it has to some extent allowed utopias to address less immediate issues (see, for example, 11b; 17).

There are two reasons for this disjunction between expectation and actuality, arising from the nature of the inclusive definition itself. Suggesting that it is *only* the mode of expression of the utopian impulse which varies implies an essentialist view, a view that such imagining is 'natural'. But one cannot assume this to be the case, and it is misleading to imply that utopianism will be expressed in some form in all circumstances. In spite of the recurrent theme of an earthly paradise in mythology, it is recurrent, not universal. There is every reason to suppose that some societies are more conducive to such speculation than others, and that it is not *only* the form of speculation which varies. Thus a culture as fatalistic as our own produces utopias of a particular kind, utopias which are 'fantastic', both in the intrinsic sense of violating our knowledge of nature and human nature, and in the extrinsic sense of being so defined for ideological reasons. Individuals, too, may seek escape through fantasies of winning vast amounts of money from Pools or Premium Bonds (5). But it may also be the case that fewer utopias are produced than in more hopeful times, and that the same forces which liberate content may discourage the entire genre. Not only form and content, but the actual possibility of creating alternatives, are socially constructed. To suggest that the utopian impulse is 'natural' is both wrongly to dichotomise nature and culture, and to distract attention from this process of social construction; in so far as the inclusive definition tends to do this, it is problematic.

Secondly, and more importantly, the notion of an intrinsic impulse towards utopias is closely linked to the idea that there exist basic human needs, independent of specific social formations, which lead people to attempt to transcend the actual conditions and means of satisfaction which they experience. The idea of 'true' human needs is, I think, central to the utopian endeavour, and highly problematic in that it necessarily dichotomises nature and culture at the level of need itself. One cannot disagree with Bauman (4, p. 14) that 'utopian ideals ... are shaped ... under the double pressure of the feeling of deprivation and the ... squeeze of ...stubborn realities', and clearly the stubborn realities are more pressing for utopias that are perceived as realisable. But it is important to note that the feeling of deprivation is itself not a 'natural' response to any given conditions, but is socially constructed in the context of realities, stubborn or otherwise.

There would be nothing remotely contentious in arguing that feelings of deprivation are socially relative. However, utopians (and politicians) commonly try to distinguish between 'real' needs, which would of course be met in the good society (or ought to be met now), and false needs, which would disappear (or illegitimate ones which should be denied). Problems of defining poverty involve the same distinctions, between 'needs' and 'wants', or 'basic' and other needs.

If such needs could be distinguished, it would indeed make sense to argue that the severing of utopian thought from practical politics and social engineering would encourage the exploration of these needs and the means for their satisfaction. However, I am not arguing merely that the experience of deprivation is socially relative, or that the *perception* of basic needs is so; but that it is not possible to define a set of basic human needs which utopia can then be designed to meet. The problem of distinguishing basic needs from others, or needs from wants, has been best expounded by Leiss (12); I shall outline his argument, and go on to develop its implications for utopian thought.

Leiss does not deny that there are certain objective needs which can be identified, such as the need for 'a minimum nutrient intake, proper conditions for retaining or dissipating bodily heat, and socialisation experiences to maintain group cohesion in social animals such as man' (p. 72). But not only are these needs common to many species, and thus hardly definitive of basic *human* needs; they are also expressed at a level of abstraction which obscures the problem. Expressed in this way, they might be seen as 'natural', the objective conditions required for the survival of the organism. Yet the argument about 'basic' needs is never conducted on this level: the problems arise when these are translated into needs for particular kinds of food, in specified quantities, with specified qualities, and likewise for clothing, fuel, shelter, and facilities for meeting needs for social contact; and, of course, in the relationship between these. Human beings never experience their own or each others' needs at the first level of abstraction. They are always confronted in socially mediated forms which specify needs for certain concrete objects or processes. And because the socially prescribed ways of meeting material needs also have symbolic meanings, one cannot distinguish some needs, at this less abstract level, as more 'natural' or basic. Thus:

> there is no aspect of our physiological requirements (the famous basic needs for food, shelter and so forth) that has not always been firmly embedded in a rich tapestry of symbolic mediations. Likewise what are called the higher needs – love, esteem, the pursuit of knowledge and spiritual perfection – also arise within a holistic interpretation of needs and are not separated from the material aspects of existence (12, p. 75).

In other words, the distinction between nature and culture is inappropriate, since we cannot experience nature other than in a culturally mediated way, and the interpretation of different sorts of needs in a single system also prevents us from constructing hierarchical orders of needing.

Further, Leiss argues, such complex systems of needs develop in interaction with the means for their satisfaction. This is not contradicted by the fact that utopians frequently include means for need-satisfaction which do not exist, such as the cure-alls of mythological paradises, and Cockaygne's ready-cooked larks. The first example merely 'extrapolate[s] ... present technology' (19), since diseases were and are cured by the application or ingestion of specific (and sometimes rare) substances; and both may in any case be understood symbolically rather than literally. Leiss is not arguing that no need can be experienced unless the means for its satisfaction (theoretically) exists. The stress he places on the interaction between needs and satisfactions arises from his concern with the impact of commodity production for exchange, on the construction of needs. He argues (p.77) that 'the general tendency of the present day market economy ... is ... to orient needs entirely towards commodities'. The proliferation of commodities for the satisfaction of needs creates a refinement or fragmentation of those needs themselves. For example, leaving aside entirely the symbolic aspects of the goods concerned, one no longer 'needs' soap, but a proliferation of cleansing agents for particular specialised tasks. This specialisation creates a problem, but it is not, as critics of consumerism might think, a problem of the creation of false needs to provide a market for commodities which have only exchange value and no use value. Indeed, in view of the symbolic meanings attaching to material objects, it is difficult to make an absolute distinction between these forms of value. Rather, a state of confusion results from the difficulty of 'determining the suitability of produced objects for the requirements of needs' (p. 95). An immense amount of knowledge, time and energy is necessary to identify the precisely correct product to meet a specific need. One might observe in support of this claim that the entire justification for the publication *Which?* is that people do experience difficulty and confusion in product selection (which they attempt to solve by buying another product); the problem is similar even with items less expensive and durable than those *Which?* considers, as can be ascertained by observing children choosing sweets or crisps.

It is significant that Leiss is not arguing that these needs are artificially created and false. They are of course artificial rather than natural in the sense of being socially constructed, but since all needs are socially constructed, this cannot be a criterion of falsity. The problem that is located here is the process by which a particular mode of social organisation creates needs whose satisfaction is always problematic, and involves an increasing burden of time and energy, so that the individual is under increasing pressure in seeking satisfaction of his needs, and is increasingly anxious about the possibility of doing so.

Most utopian writers concern themselves with the meeting of needs. The good society is that in which 'true' needs are met, but which does not allow the intrusion of 'false' needs to create dissatisfaction. Conversely, dystopias derive their negative force from representing the way in which individuals are produced to meet the needs of the social system, or particular groups within it, as manipulation and suppression of 'true' needs, which are not met. To some extent at least, the anxiety about the way in which fictional societies, utopian or dystopian, create members who do not experience needs the society cannot meet is misplaced. It arises from an assumption that there *are* basic human needs that are 'natural', and a failure to recognise that these are all socially mediated. Both the notion of manipulation, and that of the 'education of desire' (a concern imputed to Morris which has recently become fashionable: see 21; 1; 23a) imply a core of human needing/wanting which transcends the social context, and which, if not distorted or repressed, can be used as a source of transformative power.

The reason for this is that we seem to be faced with a serious dilemma. Either we assert the existence of basic human needs, or we appear to have no criteria for evaluating societies beyond the degree of fit they achieve between the needs they construct and the means they prescribe and supply for their satisfaction. The latter position intuitively feels unsatisfactory, so we opt for the former. Yet the dilemma is miscast. The appeal to needs is ideological, in so far as the attribution of naturalness is used to avoid, disguise or deny the need for value-based choice between forms of social organisation, as opposed to an objective measure of their virtue.

The contemporary school of thought which most explicitly makes this appeal to 'naturalness' is sociobiology. Sociobiologists posit a model of human nature which is genetically programmed even at the level of behaviour. They also argue that this genetic programming, produced by evolution, produces particular behavioural characteristics, different for men and women, which imply that certain sorts of social arrangements are more fitted to this nature, and therefore better. (See 24a, b; 2a, b; 6). Barash, for example, manages to produce biological 'explanations' (although he denies that they are justifications) not only for a double standard of sexual morality, but also for rape and child-battering (especially by adoptive or step-parents); yet he still implies that social organisation should take account of human nature, and that if we choose social arrangements which oppose what is natural, we must take the consequences.

Many opponents of sociobiology simply reject the notion of 'human nature' for much the same reasons as Leiss rejects the distinction between basic (or natural) needs and wants (which are socially constructed): 'nature' is never present except in socially mediated forms. This does not mean that there is no such thing. As Marvin Harris has said (9):

In principle there can be no disagreement that *Homo sapiens* has a nature. One does not have to be a sociologist to hold such a view. As every science-fiction fan knows, a culture-bearing species whose physiology was based on silicon rather than carbon and that had three sexes instead of two, weighed a thousand pounds per specimen, and preferred to eat sand rather than meat would acquire certain habits unlikely to be encountered in any *Homo sapiens* society ... Hence the disagreement about the human biogram is entirely a matter of substance rather than principle – that is, precise identification of the content of the biogram.

Yet although this statement appears to locate an area where there is no disagreement, it does so by reverting to the level of abstraction at which even Leiss recognises identifiable survival needs, and thus removing us from the actual ground of the dispute, namely, how far the 'culture-bearing' nature of the species to which Harris refers affects individual behaviour and social organisation – or how much, as well as what, is given by the biogram. This renders Riesman's assertion that utopia 'must not violate what we know of nature, including human nature' far more problematic than it appears at first glance, since what we know is in dispute, and in dispute precisely because of its legitimising and delegitimising potential with respect to actual or proposed social arrangements. Those social scientists who have attempted to engage with biology without lapsing into biologism have found this difficult, precisely because our nature is such as to make intrinsically difficult the distinction between nature and culture and thus the identification of processes of social mediation (see 3; 20a, b). This problem is both raised and illustrated by Timpanaro (22), who argues that any properly materialist explanation of social and cultural processes (including the production and content of utopian imagery) must take into account not just social production, with which materialism has generally been concerned, but the biological givens which are an inescapable part of the human condition. Those to which he refers are illness, ageing and death, which he claims to be universally and necessarily unpleasant experiences, in spite of his clear recognition that these, like other biological phenomena, are only ever experienced in socially mediated forms.

It is notable that the concerns which Timpanaro identifies here correspond closely to the recurrence of utopian themes relating to life, youth and health, to be attained by the acquisition of appropriate elixirs. The survival needs identified by Leiss link with the stress on abundance. However, this location of 'indisputable' biological givens (which in Timpanaro's case oddly exclude sex and reproduction, to which sociobiologists give such overwhelming centrality) does not provide a key to 'true' human needs or nature, precisely because they are so general. All societies attach meanings to bodily states; but the meanings attributed to ageing and death vary, as does the identification and interpretation of illness, particularly mental illness.

What utopias do is to make statements about needs, in the sense of translating abstract physical and survival needs into concrete terms, and positing other human needs (conviviality, creativity, self actualisation); and they make statements about the best way of meeting these needs. In so doing, however, they do not (and should not) proceed from those biological givens to 'needs' to 'satisfactions'. To do so would be to treat as secondary emotional and symbolic needs, to adopt a hierarchy in precisely the way Leiss has argued to be inappropriate because of the intermingling of material and symbolic spheres of human culture; and it would make nonsense of the frequency with which individuals and groups choose to forgo safety, comfort or physical survival in the interests of altruism or self-respect. But in legitimising these statements, utopias are concerned with making statements about human nature. It is notable that it is primarily in feminist critiques of biologistic arguments that the notion of human nature currently impinges on the social sciences, although this takes the form of counter-assertions about what that nature is as much as stressing its necessarily socially constructed quality; and correspondingly, a disproportionate amount of contemporary utopian writing is by women.

The origins of the utopian 'impulse' then, are not to be found in some natural propensity to invent, or want, better social arrangements. Nor are they to be found in a disparity between basic needs given by human nature, and the means available to satisfy these. Rather, utopianism has as one precondition a disparity between socially constructed experienced need and socially prescribed and actually available means of satisfaction. This is usually disguised, even for utopians themselves, since needs are primarily legitimised by their designation as 'natural', i.e. by invoking an (illegitimate) nature/culture distinction and denying their socially constructed aspect. This has a number of implications. First, there can be no universal utopia, not simply because all cultures perceive needs differently, but because all societies construct them differently, so that they do actually vary. Secondly, utopias must make (contentious) claims about human nature. The alternative to this is to make explicit the values involved in particular constructions of individuals and societies, which renders them questionable and thus ambiguously utopian. Thirdly, in theory at least, if a perfect fit could be achieved between needs and satisfactions, the utopian impulse could be extinguished. In practice, this is a trivial possibility, since any complex system of needs is likely to contain contradictory elements, both for and between individuals, and also because there are much more immediate dangers to the flourishing of utopian thought.

If utopianism is not a response to a gap between natural needs and available satisfactions, nor is it a natural response to a disparity between two socially constructed systems. It has frequently been observed that peasants do not generally rebel against being oppressed, only against being oppressed more than is customary. Similarly, the industrial working classes do not rebel against exploitation *per se* – indeed, in many cases they do not recognise it – but only against not receiving a wage perceived through social definition as fair. Ideological struggle here centres not around eliminating exploitation, but around the competition by different interest groups to make their definition of 'fair' predominate. Rebellion and utopianism are not the same thing, but they share the precondition of a perceived gap between needs and satisfactions. Rebellion, however, and all forms of political action oriented towards change, necessitate the perception that an alternative state of affairs is possible and can be brought about by human intervention. If utopianism is defined broadly, to refer only to the imaginative construction of alternative states, then it involves only the perception of desirable alternatives, which need be seen neither as possible in themselves nor as attainable. While this illuminates the fact that a declining belief in progress and a fatalistic cultural climate have detached utopia from a primary role of political catalyst and consigned it to the realm of fantasy, it obscures the fact that the possibility of creating utopias at all cannot be taken for granted. One cannot assume that utopian thought has been or is being extinguished because its form has changed; but nor can one assume that such changes in form have no relevance to its survival. And there seem to me to be problems about expressing more than cautious optimism, in view of the ways in which both needs and satisfactions are expressed in contemporary Western society.

While the inclusion of 'fantasy', whether in literary form, or in the millennial form of, for example, Rastafarianism, in the category of utopia helps us to see that there is still a (confined) place for imagining other worlds, the transition to this form is important. We have already noted, following Leiss, that the tendency of modern industrial society is to orient needs increasingly towards commodities, and that the resultant proliferation of needs and commodities results in confusion. A further confusion, however, is created which Leiss does not comment on. There is also an elaborate process whereby the legitimacy of certain needs (and the right to relevant commodities) is debated. This is true of everyone engaged in wage-bargaining, but more particularly in relation to low pay and state benefits – and about a quarter of the population of Great Britain live at or below the officially-defined poverty line. Argument about benefit levels, and about social services, the NHS, education, is a way of constructing 'what people have a right to expect', which applies more widely than to those immediately affected. Thus people must also handle messages which say that at least some categories of people do not need or should not want certain commodities or services; and the identification of a need/product fit is not facilitated by denial of the reality of the need.

The greater the proliferation of needs, the more difficult is the problem of choosing between them. This means that contemporary utopias have as a central task that they must not only tell people how they can get what they want, but that they should tell people what they should want. These two tasks may be seen as separate enterprises, and the emphasis does seem to be on the latter. Indeed Williams identifies this shift as taking place in the nineteenth century, towards utopias that are heuristic (concerned with values, which inform choice) rather than systematic (concerned with blueprints for social organisation). It is not only utopias which do this. The appeal of sociobiology, particularly in its popular forms which lack any conceivable intellectual respectability (2b; 6), is that in spite of not overtly prescribing any particular social organisation, they 'explain' and legitimise some needs in terms of nature, and simultaneously, though silently, delegitimise others: they tell people what they 'naturally' want. The concern with the 'education of desire' is similar, although less ideological so far as it is less disguised: people must learn to 'find out their wants ... to want more ... to want differently' (21, p. 806). *The Dispossessed* (11b) is a utopia in which not all needs are met; the benefits and costs of the prescribed values are stated, but nevertheless some needs are accorded greater legitimacy than others.

The effect of this is that utopian thought at the moment probably has more relevance to arguments about human nature, through uses of 'naturalness' as a legitimising quality, and challenges to this, particularly in feminist utopias, than it has to the sphere of practical politics. In itself this need not lead to a decline in utopianising, but in practice it is likely to result in a limitation of audience and participants, and a focus on the construction of selves rather than of societies. This is a marked alteration in the utopian enterprise: but is it a decline, and does it matter?

My own, frankly evaluative, answer would be yes, for three reasons. Morris (15) said 'it is essential that the ideal of the new society should be always kept before the eyes of the ... working classes, lest the continuity of the demands of the people should be broken, or lest they should be misdirected'. Williams (23b) has argued that 'the element of transformation rather than the more general element of otherness' is central to the utopian mode; and that there is a particular danger that the heuristic utopia can 'settle into isolated and in the end sentimental "desire", a mode of living with alienation'. For those of us who are concerned that political decisions should be informed by 'a vision of the world transformed' (see 18), the retreat into fantasy is clearly a loss, although it is a loss whose cause and compensation must be sought in the decline of hope and of political will, not in the failure of desire and imagination.

Secondly, even without such a vision, political decisions will be informed by notions of legitimate and natural need, and the argument should be as extensive as possible. Without utopia, the fatalism of sociobiological thinking may prevail. Here, though, it must be noted that utopianism is a double-edged weapon; while it can be used to explore needs, it must also make choices about which needs are legitimate, and assign them priorities.

Thirdly, if Leiss is correct about the relationship between the social construction of needs and means of satisfaction, the exclusion of the transformative element from utopianism is likely to lead to a decline in such imagining. Experienced needs are *identified* by reference to at least theoretically possible means of their satisfaction. If we have no idea how the world might be transformed, how we might get what we want, we may cease to be able to imagine alternatives, because we will not be able to identify what we want. Either desire must result in hope and political will be restored, or the loss of hope will end in the loss of desire; next come senility and death.

References

1. Anderson, P., *Arguments within English Marxism*, New Left Books, London 1980.
2. Barash, P., (a) *Sociobiology and Behaviour* (1977), Heinemann, London 1978. (b) *Sociobiology: the whispering within* (1980), Fontana, London 1981.
3. Barker, M., 'Human biology and the possibility of Socialism' in J. Mepham & D.H. Ruben (eds) *Issues in Marxist Philosophy*, Harvester Press, Hassocks 1981.
4. Bauman, Z., *Socialism: the active utopia*, Allen and Unwin, London 1976.
5. Cohen, S. & Taylor, L., *Escape Attempts* (1976), Penguin, Harmondsworth 1978.
6. Dawkins, R., *The Selfish Gene* (1976), Paladin, London 1978.
7. Donaldson, S., *The Chronicles of Thomas Covenant the Unbeliever*, Fontana, London 1978-80.
8. Engels, F., *Socialism: utopian and scientific* (1892) in Marx & Engels, *Selected Works*, Progress Publishers, Moscow 1975.
9. Harris, M., 'Sociobiology and biological reductionism', in A. Montagu (ed.) *Sociobiology Examined*, Oxford University Press, 1980.
10. Jobes, G., *Dictionary of Mythology, Folklore and Symbols*, Scarecrow Press, New York 1961.
11. Le Guin, U., (a) *The Lathe of Heaven* (1972), Panther, London 1974. (b) *The Dispossessed* (1974), Panther, London 1975.
12. Leiss, W., *The Limits to Satisfaction*, Marion Boyars, London 1978.
13. Levitas, R., (a) 'Sociology and utopia', *Sociology*, Jan. 1979.

(b) 'Dystopian times', *Theory Culture and Society*, 1982, vol.1, no.1.

14. Mannheim, K., *Ideology and Utopia*, Routledge, London 1936.

15. Morris, W. and Belfort Bax, E. *Socialism – its Growth and Outcome*, Sonnenschein, London 1896, p. 278.

16. Patch, H.R., *The Other World in Medieval Literature*, Harvard University Press, 1950.

17. Piercy, M., *Woman on the Edge of Time* (1976), The Women's Press, London 1979.

18. *Political Quarterly* 52, 4, Oct-Dec 1981.

19. Riesman, D., 'Some observations on community plans and utopia' (1954), in *Individualism Reconsidered*, The Free Press, New York 1964.

20. Rose, S. (ed.), (a) *Against Biological Determinism*, Allison & Busby, London 1982. (b) *Towards a Liberatory Biology*, Allison & Busby, London 1982.

21. Thompson, E.P., *William Morris*, Merlin Press, London 1976.

22. Timpanaro, S., *On Materialism* (1970), New Left Books, London 1975.

23. Williams, R., (a) *Politics and Letters*, New Left Books, London 1979. (b) *Problems in Materialism and Culture*, New Left Books, London 1980.

24. Wilson, E.D., (a) *Sociobiology*, Harvard University Press, 1975. (b) *On Human Nature*, Harvard University Press, 1978.

3

Grimm's Utopia: Motives and Justifications

Peter Alexander

I

The word 'utopian' is frequently used pejoratively with the intention of denigrating some proposal because it could not possibly be carried out. The implication for deliberate utopian thinking is usually clear: we waste our time if we indulge in the construction of utopias because they are incapable of practical realisation. A criticism which is related to this, though not in an immediately obvious way, is that utopian thinking leads to totalitarianism. I think that the theoretical construction of utopias is, and should be, a far more complex affair than such criticisms suggest. In particular, to say that utopians propose *impossible* social organisations, *tout court*, is highly misleading and calls for a consideration of the complexities of the word 'impossible'. This is a matter that both utopians and their critics have sometimes neglected with considerable resulting confusion. I shall be largely concerned with motives underlying the *theoretical* construction of utopias.

II

The literature contains various definitions of 'utopia'; I mention one or two merely to give a rough preliminary indication of the way in which I use the term.

I leave aside Karl Mannheim's definition (14, pp. 173-7) as unserviceable, at least for my purpose. His distinction between utopias and ideologies has the bewildering consequence, because it rests heavily on realisability, that it is impossible to tell until the end of history that a plan is an ideology rather than a utopia. As I shall argue, the constructors of utopias have been, and should be, much less concerned with practical realisability than he suggests.

My own approach to this depends especially on the classification and definitions of J.C. Davis (7, ch. 1). In the main I rely on his classification of ideal societies and dwell upon those he classifies as utopias. He distinguishes five varieties of ideal society: the Land of Cockaygne, Arcadia, the Perfect Moral Commonwealth, Millennium and Utopia. Here it suffices to say that, according to him, constructors of ideal societies set out to solve problems posed by unlimited human wants in the context of limited possibilities of their satisfaction. Constructors of utopias, as distinct from some of the other ideal societies, accept the probable permanence of human deficiencies, moral, emotional and intellectual, and of limited resources, and aim to show how a well-ordered and well-functioning society might be designed in the face of them by organisation through social institutions.

I also rely on the views of George Kateb (13). He defines 'utopias' in a rather wider way than Davis, but I am concerned rather with what he calls the 'causes' of utopian thinking which would perhaps be better called the motives behind it. As a political philosopher Kateb appears to be mainly interested in motives or stimuli related to intellectual considerations, which is my allotted theme. His list of motives includes intellectual playfulness and the attempt to rearrange social phenomena into a more rational or beautiful pattern; the desire for moral clarity and an understanding of the relations between the ideal and the acceptable; the wish to subject existing society to a total indictment and to propose a radical alternative; the wish to achieve reform and the belief that overstatement will help to do so; and the desire to impart, and encourage action based upon, the whole truth about social harmony, taken as known.

These motives appear to me to be closely related, although I think Kateb sees the predominance of one or other of them as historically delineating various forms of utopia. I see no reason why there should not be traces of two or more of them lying behind all utopias, and I am inclined to think that this is true of the utopias with which I am familiar.

I should perhaps say that I do not accept the claim that a clear distinction can be made between 'classical' and 'modern' utopias, at least on the bases of the features in which I am here interested (12).

III

I approach utopianism as a philosopher in the belief that most utopians have had as a central aim, though not their only aim, the solving of certain philosophical problems. I believe that thinking about utopias, whether favourable or critical, inescapably involves one in the analysis of certain moral and political concepts and that this often leads to the recommending of certain normative judgments.

This brings me back to an earlier remark about the need to examine the word 'possible' and cognate words. Politics has been described by, among others, R.A. Butler, as 'the art of the possible', but without further elaboration that does not distinguish politics from various other activities. Specifically, philosophy, in at least one of its aspects, might also be described as 'the art of the possible'. A distinction I would make, as at least rough and ready but needing elaboration, is between 'possible' meaning 'achievable' and 'possible' meaning 'conceivable', and then I would say that politics is the art of the possible in the first sense and philosophy in the second sense.

A state of affairs may be conceivable, involving no logical contradictions, without being practically achievable, now or ever. It is conceivable that a computer could solve a problem that no human being could ever solve unaided, but not conceivable that it could solve the problem of squaring the circle. Both solutions would be unachievable by human beings; the first would be achievable by the computer and conceivable by a human being that it was so but the second would be inconceivable both for us and, if I may so speak, for the computer.

It has often been said that one of the things philosophers do is to invent conceivable but not necessarily achievable states of affairs in order to gain an understanding of everyday concepts used in the description of those states of affairs. Like an engineer testing the strength of a beam, we strain a concept to its limits by considering extreme situations in an effort to discover when we reach the breaking point, the point at which the concept is no longer applicable to the situation. For example, in trying to understand human freedom and to decide whether there is any such thing we may ask such questions as 'Would anyone say we had freedom of choice if we worked exactly like the most sophisticated computer we can conceive?' or 'Would anyone say we had freedom of choice if nothing whatever restricted in the slightest anything we did, thought, said, desired or felt?' The invention of such extreme situations is of the nature of a thought-experiment intended to clarify the concepts involved.

I illustrate my contention about the philosophical aim of utopias by reference to Plato's *Republic* (17), but there are many others which I might choose. Understanding the feature of Plato's project on which I wish to focus involves attending to the way in which he embarks on the construction of his ideal society. The dialogue begins as an explicit attempt to give an account of justice. After various attempts to elicit a satisfactory statement of what justice is by questioning participants with differing views, Socrates finds that 'justice' has been defined either in a trivial, unilluminating way or in a way that involves the rejection of justice as something valuable and desirable in itself. There must, Socrates thinks, be some confusion, since people do profess to value justice and regard it as important. He then uses an analogy. The subject of justice is an obscure one and it needs keen sight to see what justice is. Short-sighted people may have difficulty reading a notice written in small letters; they would do better if they found the same words written in large letters. Justice is to be found in communities as well as in individuals; we have been considering what we take to be just people but perhaps if we looked at just communities we should more easily discern what justice is. Finding justice 'writ large' in the community may help us to discern and understand it 'writ small' in the person.

This all relates to the platonic conceptions of the tripartite division of both the human soul and the organised community and of harmony between the parts. It will waste a great deal of time, Socrates seems to be saying, to consider existing communities because none is without its faults, there will be disagreement about where the faults lie and about whether a particular community is just or not; better to construct an imaginary community which we might all agree is a just one, examine it for the qualities that prompt this agreement and then look for these in the individual. The agreements on the way will help us to clarify the idea of justice. This Socrates sets out to do.

Thus, I believe, a central aim of Plato's construction of an ideal society was to provide an analysis of the concept of justice. Closely related to this is the desire to persuade people to accept certain values; the correct analysis of justice will show it to be valuable in itself. I am not here concerned with questions about whether Plato's methods and conclusions are satisfactory; I merely wish to urge that he had certain aims. For my present purpose these other questions are relatively unimportant. What is important is that the pursuit of these aims requires that the ideal state be conceivable but not that it be achievable.

Socrates says as much:

> when we set out to discover the essential nature of justice and injustice and what a perfectly just and perfectly unjust man would be like, supposing them to exist, our purpose was to use them as ideal patterns ... We did not set out to show that these ideals could in fact exist.

and, he asks

> Is our theory any the worse, if we cannot prove it possible that a state so organised should be actually founded? (17, 472)

Moreover, the point is made again very near the end of the whole work (592).

The closing sentence of More's *Utopia* (15, pp. 246-7) is 'But I readily admit that there are many features in the Utopian commonwealth which it is easier for me to wish for in our countries than to have any hope of seeing realised.' Northrop Frye comments 'The implication seems clear that the ideal state to More, as to Plato, is not a future ideal but a hypothetical one, an informing power and not a goal of action' (10, p. 121). The publisher of the first edition of *New Atlantis* wrote 'Certainly, the model is more vast, and high, than can possibly be imitated in all things' (3, p. 256). In general, Frye says, 'Utopian thought is imaginative, with its roots in literature, and the literary imagination is less concerned with achieving ends than with visualising possibilities' (p. 116). I might add that the philosophical imagination is concerned with the exploration of the implications of those possibilities.

I am inclined to think that this motive underlies most well-known utopias, whether ancient or modern. Their authors have been concerned with conceivability rather than achievability and with the clarification of familiar moral and political concepts. Few of them have discussed methods of getting from our present society to the ideal one. If this is a central motive of utopian construction then it is no criticism of that activity that the ideal society can never be reached because of human frailty or recalcitrant nature. Whether our *practical* aim is to revolutionise society or merely to reform it, the theoretical construction of utopias will be valuable if it helps us to clarify our ideas of sovereignty, freedom, equality, justice, law and related concepts.

Fully to establish my hypothesis that this philosophical concern is central to most well-known utopias would require a detailed scholarly examination of each of them. I can do no more here than present a few pieces of evidence which may incline some towards it, but primarily I wish to suppose it to be true and explore some of its implications. Moreover, I have a position to which to retreat if the hypothesis cannot be accepted as a correct historical account of utopias; our best hope of justifying the construction of utopias lies in regarding this as an important feature of them, whether their authors intended it or not.

It is striking that most well-known utopias are cast in fictional form and describe social organisations in some distant time or place whose accessibility is difficult. Even their names are suggestive; we have *Utopia, Erewhon, New Atlantis, The City of the Sun, Looking Backward, Antiquity Reviv'd* and many others. Few instructions, if any, are given about how to get there from here, in either sense of that expression; we seem to be intended to *contemplate* the alleged ideal and decide whether it is ideal, or better in some or all respects than the existing social order.

The interest in philosophy is almost ubiquitous and often explicit. Plato's rulers are philosopher-kings, Campanella's supreme ruler is Metaphysic, whose assistants are Power, Wisdom and Love, Andreae's leading characters are personifications of virtues. More's main narrator is a sailor but also, and more importantly, a philosopher (15, pp. 49-50), and More distinguishes between, on the one hand, philosophy and practical politics (p. 57) and, on the other hand, academic philosophers and a more civilised variety, who speak only with an awareness of contexts (p. 99). Bacon's Fellow of Salomon's House (3, pp. 277ff.) had as his ideal Bacon's own philosophy of a knowledge of the world through a knowledge of causes, and his philosophers were in some sense the most powerful in his society, being above the state (7, p. 120). Utopian cities frequently exemplify the ideas of physical perfection, symmetry and harmony, in buildings, fixtures and fittings, and overall plan in the form of circles or spheres, thus embodying ancient cosmological and philosophical ideas.

I think that the significance of the use of philosophers as rulers, by Plato and others, is not that it is thought that philosophers should *be* kings in practice but that the construction of an ideal society requires philosophical skills, that is, the ability to understand through analysis the concepts we use in the context of moral, social and political thought. What do we mean by 'perfection', 'freedom', 'justice', and so on? Some grasp of the answers to such questions is essential for those who are to conceive the creation and preservation of ideal societies.

Even H.G. Wells, who is not nowadays usually thought of as a philosopher, makes a relevant point in his *A Modern Utopia* (20, p. 315):

> Our business here is to be Utopian, to make vivid and credible if we can, first this facet and then that of an imaginary whole and happy world. Our deliberate intention is to be not, indeed, impossible, but most distinctly impracticable by every scale that reaches only between to-day and to-morrow.

If we take 'to-morrow' to refer to the time at which Utopia will be in existence we may see this as indicating that his concern is with a conceivable ('imaginary') state rather than with an achievable ('practicable') one and that he does not know how we could get from one to the other.

In some utopias there is another feature that suggests philosophical interests and methods. Philosophers engage in thought-experiments in which understanding is sought through the consideration and comparison of alternative possibilities. In the *Republic* Socrates considers in a somewhat abstract way various possible social organisations with a view to deciding in which of them, if any, we find what we would be prepared to call justice. Doni (8) finally accepts a possible world which is the sixth out of an envisaged seven, located in various parts of the universe. Hence the plural form of his title *I Mondi* (11, p. 60).

IV

Closely related to the philosophical motives for constructing ideals is the fictional setting of most utopias. Moreover, among fictions, utopian writing is perhaps more closely related to fairy-tales than to other forms. Philosophers, too, may be thought of as writing fairy-tales when in their pursuit of conceptual clarity they invent conceivable but highly improbable situations. They deal in extremes which are *ex hypothesi* unlikely to arise; they talk of perfectly good and wise men, of ideal observers, of perfectly rational men, of omniscient beings, of perfectly random behaviour, of souls of princes being transferred to bodies of cobblers, and many more marvels. They ask, as if they could ever know, what precisely it is like to be a bat. Commentators on utopias often hint at a fairy-tale element in them; Mannheim stresses their incongruence with the existing reality, Davis calls them 'curious essays in the rejection of social reality' (7, p. 12ff.) and Kateb talks of 'intellectual playfulness' and of the author's 'playing at being God' (13).

In the utopias themselves there are explicit features also found in fairy-tales. There are cities of a structurally fabulous kind, magic significance given to numbers, prophetic dreams, miraculous transportations, strange animals and people, personifications of abstractions as well as unlikely social structures and events. More's Utopia exists *beyond* a fairy-tale land, beyond 'waste deserts scorched with continual heat' which are 'inhabited by wild beasts and snakes' and 'men no less savage and harmful than are the beasts'. Here we come upon a green and pleasant land with gentle beasts and civilised men. What interests the narrator is not Raphael's stories of monsters and mythical figures, since 'Scyllas and greedy Celaenos and folk-devouring Laestrygones and similar frightful monsters are common enough, but well and wisely trained citizens are not everywhere to be found' (p. 53). That is, they are even rarer than fairy-tale creatures. From time to time, More stresses the absurdity of Utopia; he says 'many things come to my mind which seemed very absurdly established in the customs and laws of the people described' (p. 245). The very names of his characters and peoples, such as Hythlodaeus and Polyleritae, derive from words meaning 'nonsense' and we have also 'no-country', 'no-people' and 'Utopia' ('no-place') itself.

Campanella describes the City of the Sun in terms that might fit into a fairy-tale as well as into an ancient treatise of perfection based on circles, spheres, symmetry and precise mathematical proportions (6, pp. 218ff.). An analogy with the seven planets figures largely. There is beauty and rich decoration everywhere and the city is well-nigh impregnable. The ruler is Metaphysic, his assistants are Power,

Wisdom and Love. The city possesses the only real phoenix. The punishment for minor misdeeds is banishment from the common table which reminds one of one of the child's worst fears: bed without supper.

Andreae's ship is called the *Phantasy* and it sails over the Academic Sea to reach Christianopolis (2). The city is a geometrically regular structure dominated by towers in each of which lives an official whose tower is larger or smaller according to his rank.

Eberlein's *Wolfaria* (9) went in for the kinds of punishment one finds in the most frightening of fairy stories, such as drowning for marrying secretly and drunkenness (4), and Doni's city, like so many Renaissance town plans, is star-shaped with a temple at its centre having a hundred doors and a hundred streets leading from it to the hundred gates of the city. The account of his city is given, in a vision, by Jove and Momus (11, p. 171).

Bellamy's *Looking Backward* (5) is perhaps the account of utopia that seems least like a fairy-tale on the surface, but nevertheless he said of it:

> In undertaking to write *Looking Backward* I had, at the outset, no idea of attempting a serious contribution to the movement of social reform. The idea was of a mere literary fantasy, a fairy tale of social felicity. There was no thought of contriving a house which practical men might live in, but merely of hanging in mid-air, far out of reach of the sordid and material world of the present, a cloud-palace for an ideal humanity (16, p. 303).

Moreover, access to it is via a dream.

Wells's Utopia is another planet, which may remind us of Putnam's 'Twin-Earth' (19) except that it is identical with our own at only one point in its history. His narrator is magically transported to it and finds its people speaking a familiar language.

V

It is a short step nowadays from Plato to Popper. I do not propose to enter into scholarly dispute with Popper over the interpretation of the details of Plato's arguments, although I believe there is room for such dispute. I want, rather, to return to my consideration of Plato's general aims and, in the light of what I have already said, to dispute some of Popper's general conclusions about utopian thinking.

Popper places great emphasis on Plato's view that kings should be philosophers and accuses him of causing 'a lasting confusion in political philosophy' by asking the wrong question, namely, 'Who should rule?' (18a). To that question, he says (p. 120) 'it is hard to avoid some such reply as "the best" or "the wisest" or "the born ruler" or "he who masters the art of ruling" (or, perhaps, "the General Will" or "the Master Race" or "the Industrial Workers" or "the People")'. Popper claims that these answers are useless because they may lead us to suppose that a fundamental problem of political philosophy has been solved, whereas in fact they merely blind us to the really fundamental problem. Political rulers are not always sufficiently good or wise to justify our relying upon the goodness and wisdom of governments. We must face the problem of bad governments and should 'prepare for the worst leaders, and hope for the best' (p. 121). This leads to a new approach forcing us to replace the question 'Who should rule?' by the question 'How can we so organise political institutions that bad or incompetent rulers can be prevented from doing too much damage?'. Popper calls the view that political power is *essentially* sovereign, i.e. is, in fact, or ought to be, unchecked 'the theory of (unchecked) sovereignty', and regards the question that leads to it as a dangerous one for political philosophers to ask or, at least, to regard as fundamental because it prevents their developing a theory of checks and balances.

In the first place, I believe that the fault lies not in the question but in the answers proposed by Popper. I do not find it difficult to avoid these answers, and his phrase 'some such reply as' allows the proposing of other answers which imply the need for checks and balances. In the second place, I think that it is gratuitous to suppose that Plato was unaware of the fallibility in practice of rulers and the need for checks and balances. The story of Gyges' ring (359-60) has application not to the truly just man but to the man with a reputation for justice (612), that is, not to the perfect philosopher but to those who have, without deserving it, that reputation and by whom we might be ruled in practice. Questions about sovereignty may be fundamental and may imply, rather than preclude, Popper's preferred question. The question 'Who should rule?', understood as I believe Plato understood it, leads to the question 'What is the best, and the worst, we can expect in a ruler?' and 'How can the worst be coped with?' as soon as we consider the realisability of the ideal society.

The route to an understanding of this lies through my contention about Plato's central aim in the *Republic*. We may construct, on paper, an ideal society in the belief that the best we can conceive is a society governed by entirely wise and good, i.e. incorruptible, rulers. We may learn a great deal about what we do, or ought to, value from this construction even if we think that there is no practical possibility of our ever finding such rulers and so of realising that ideal. We may also hold that in such an ideal society there would be no need for checks on rulers but that *only* in such a society should sovereignty be unchecked. I see no evidence in the *Republic* that Plato did not hold this.

None of this implies that we need suppose that sovereignty should ever in practice be unchecked because the construction of utopias, in so far as it is a philosophical project, does not imply the belief or hope that the ideal society could be achieved in practice. The conception of an ideal society may be none the worse for its practical unrealisability if it improves our understanding of political and moral concepts. One important motive for its conception will have been satisfied.

The conviction that we have described an ideal society does not confer upon us the responsibility of working to achieve that society as a whole, although it may confer the responsibility of at least not obstructing progress towards some features of it if they are practical possibilities. The construction of utopias need neither conflict with nor blind us to the importance of Popper's 'piecemeal social engineering' and it does not commit us to his 'Utopian social engineering' (pp. 157-8). Utopias may be as useful for guiding reform as for stimulating revolution.

I have been relying on a distinction between political philosophy and political theory, a task of the first being to understand and evaluate conceivable or actual political organisations and ends, a task of the second being to consider how valued ends might be achieved by acceptable means. This latter task would involve consideration of actual or probable psychological, social, economic and environmental factors. When a political philosopher constructs an ideal society there are likely to be many problems lying in the way of its practical realisation, and I see these as the concern of the political theorist. In particular, if an ideal society involves the conception of perfectly good and wise rulers, one task of the political theorist who considers the realisation of as close an approximation to it as may be possible is, as it were, to 'apply corrections' to the ideal to accommodate probable ineradicable weaknesses of human beings likely to become rulers. My analogy is with the scientific procedure of stating laws for ideal cases, such as the ideal gases, and then specifying corrections that allow them to be applied to actual cases. My suggestion is that Plato's reason for not considering the corrections necessary in working towards the realisation of his ideal society was not, as Popper suggests, that he accepted 'the general theory of sovereignty' (pp. 125-6) but that he regarded this consideration as lying beyond his present project of clarifying moral and political concepts.

The importance of his philosopher-kings, I think, is not that he thought that such perfectly wise and good rulers were available or likely to be available, but rather that the best society he could conceive would be governed by such rulers and that such rulers would only be produced, if at all, by a particular sort of philosophical training. Perhaps he was exploring the consequences of a hypothesis: if such truly good and wise people could be produced by this training what would follow for social organisation?

These comments are not intended to cover merely the *Republic*. What I have couched in the form of a defence of one of Plato's aims is intended to be the basis of a justification for the construction of utopias in general, given what I take to be an aim of most utopians. It should be obvious, too, how my interpretation may be applied to the criticism that utopias lead to totalitarianism and violence (18b). My contention that the practical unrealisability of utopias does not destroy and may even enhance their value is directly relevant to this criticism.

It seems to me of considerable importance that those interested in political and social organisation tend to speak as if they value the same things; it is difficult to find among them people who will say that they do not value justice, peace, freedom, happiness, equality, and so on, and yet there may be very little agreement beyond this between various groups. There is sometimes a disagreement about how such values should be realised in practice, but more often, and even more basic than this disagreement, I think, there is a disagreement about what these honorific words *mean*. Mr Bresznev, Mrs Thatcher and Tony Benn all claim to value democracy, but they appear to value different things under that rubric. That is why the construction of utopias seen as having as a central aim the clarification of such concepts and as recommending, through the provision of acceptable analyses of them, certain values appears to me to be a worthwhile activity.

I would not have it thought that I am claiming that the philosophical task is merely to explore the meanings of words. Adequate conceptual clarification leads one to see complex interrelations between whole clusters of concepts; this in turn may lead one to see relations between moral and political principles involving them and suggest particular judgments or recommendations for action. It may thus have an indirect bearing on practice and may even lead the philosopher down from the ivory tower in which he reputedly lives to support or oppose particular courses of action. He might be said to be studying rationality in various areas, and being rational in the end involves rejecting certain sorts of judgment and action and favouring other sorts.

I think it is important to regard utopians as foster-siblings of the Brothers Grimm, working in their tradition although their messages are directed at adults. The Brothers Grimm played upon the fears and longings of children and no doubt intended to teach them certain things about morality as well as to entertain. Utopians play upon the fears and longings of adults and intend by rational argument to lead them to a better understanding of political and moral matters and, with the help of entertainment, to incline them towards valuing certain things. There are probably no knock-down arguments about values and even if there were we could not hope to find perfectly rational people to act on them. It may be salutary for both anti-utopians and utopians to bear this in mind as well as the elucidatory and the fairy-tale elements in utopias; anti-utopians may become clearer about the nature and value of such projects, and utopians may be prevented from getting too big for their arguments.

References

1. Armytage, W.H.G., *Yesterday's Tomorrows*, Routledge, London 1968.
2. Andreae, Johann Valentin, *Christianopolis* (1619), ed. F.E. Held, New York 1917. See also 7, pp. 73ff.
3. Bacon, Francis, *New Atlantis* (1627) ed. Thomas Case, Oxford University Press, 1969.
4. Bell, Susan Groag, 'John Eberlin von Gunzburg's *Wolfaria* ...' in *Church History* 36, 2, 1967, pp. 122ff.
5. Bellamy, Edward, *Looking Backward* (1888), New American Library, New York 1960.
6. Campanella, Tomasso, *The City of the Sun* (1623) trans. Thomas W. Halliday in Henry Morley (ed.), *Ideal Commonwealths*, Routledge, London 1887.
7. Davis, J.C., *Utopia and the Ideal Society*, Cambridge University Press, 1981.
8. Doni, Anton Francesco, *I Mondi* (1553). See also 7 and 11.
9. Gunzberg, Johann Eberlein von, *Wolfaria* (1521). See 4.
10. Frye, Northrop, 'Varieties of literary utopias', in *The Stubborn Structure*, Methuen, London 1970.
11. Grendler, Paul F., *Critics of the Italian World, 1530-1560*, University of Wisconsin Press, Madison 1969.
12. Hansot, Elizabeth, *Perfection and Progress*, M.I.T. Press, Cambridge, Mass. 1974.
13. Kateb, George, 'Utopias and utopianism', in *The Encyclopedia of Philosophy*, ed. Paul Edwards, The Macmillan Co. & The Free Press, New York 1967.
14. Mannheim, Karl, *Ideology and Utopia*, translated by Louis Wirth & Edward Shils, Kegan Paul, Trench, Trubner, London 1936.
15. More, Thomas, *The Complete Works of St Thomas More*, vol. 4, *Utopia* (1516) ed. Edward Surtz and J.H. Hexter, Yale University Press, 1965.
16. Parrington, Vernon Louis, *Main Currents in American Thought*, vol. 3, Harcourt Brace, New York 1930.
17. Plato, *The Republic*, translated by F.C. Cornford, Oxford University Press, 1955. References are given to the traditional paragraph numbers.
18. Popper, K.R. (a) *The Open Society and its Enemies* (1945), vol. 1, Routledge, London 1963. (b) 'Utopia and violence', *Hibbert Journal* 1948, reprinted in Popper, *Conjectures and Refutations*, Routledge, London 1963.
19. Putnam, Hilary, 'The meaning of "meaning" ', in *Philosophical Papers*, vol. 2, Cambridge University Press, 1975, pp. 215ff.
20. Wells, H.G., *A Modern Utopia*. Quotations are from an undated edition published by Odhams Press, London; the volume also contains *Tono Bungay*.

4

The Design of a Perfect Society

C. West Churchman

The main topic of this chapter is the concept of perfection. I want to apply this concept to the design of societies. Hence I will define 'utopia' as a perfect society. Of course, utopia does not have to be defined in such a manner. It could mean the best that we as humans can do; but I am choosing to use the definition as given above. This means that the chapter consists essentially of two parts: the first is a discussion of perfection in general, the second a discussion of a perfect society.

It is worthwhile trying to place the discussion of perfection in its historical setting. To do so accurately, one would have to trace the idea, at least in Western philosophy, to Plato, for whom the idea was central (the idea of the good). One would then go on to ask whether Aristotle's *Nicomachean Ethics* defines perfection. Then one would go to the Stoic version of a perfectly rational world and possibly from there to St Augustine's confusion regarding God's perfection and evil. Then, on the historical voyage, in the eleventh century one would pause to talk to St Anselm about his famous proof of God's existence from the idea of his perfection (the so-called ontological proof).

But my historical setting is made much easier by Descartes because he wanted to start all of his ideas from scratch. Hence I will make the historical beginning a quotation from Descartes's third Meditation:

> Hence there remains alone the idea of God, concerning which we must consider whether it is not something that is capable of proceeding from me myself. By the name God I understand a substance that is infinite (eternal, immutable), independent, all-knowing, all-powerful, and by which I myself and everything else, if anything else does exist, have been created. Now all these characteristics are such that the more diligently I attend to them, the less do they appear capable of proceeding from me alone; hence, from what has already been said, we must conclude that God necessarily exists.

This quotation is quite astonishing in at least two ways. In the first place, it is not St Anselm's ontological proof, which was based on Anselm's notion of logic. Instead, Descartes provides a psychological proof. He is interested in the 'me, myself', that is, he is interested in the psyche and in particular his own psyche. He believes he recognises what his own psyche has created. This, indeed, is the essence of Cartesian psychology, meaning that each mind can determine which of its contents has come from that mind alone. As he goes over the list, Descartes tells us that he becomes more and more convinced that the characteristics of the perfection of God could not have proceeded from his own psyche and, therefore, were caused by a being outside his psyche and, indeed, must have been caused by a perfect being, namely God.

The point has some historical interest because when Kant, in the first *Critique*, criticises the proofs for the existence of God, he gives us Anselm's version and not Descartes's.

The other interesting feature of this quotation from the third Meditation is that Descartes lists the properties of a perfect being. They are:

1. eternal
2. immutable
3. independent (not caused by anything other than himself)
4. omniscient
5. omnipotent
6. the creator of all.

I call the method of defining perfection that Descartes used the 'add-on' method. One thinks of all of the properties that a perfect being could have, defines the maximum along each of the properties and joins all of these together to define perfection. Not all philosophers have used this method. Spinoza, for example, seems to have argued that God has an infinity of attributes of which we humans can only understand a small number.

One of the things that is interesting about Descartes's list is that it omits benevolence. A Satanist might very well argue that Descartes's list defines the perfectly evil being, the devil. But it is easy enough to add perfect benevolence to the list.

The Cartesian question still stands: how in the world did the human mind come to the idea of perfection? There are a number of candidates:

First, there are our parents, who in childhood rearing instilled in us the notion of better and worse, e.g., in eating habits and cleanliness. They in turn borrowed these opinions from their parents. If we assume that we all have a mental function that carries the mind from better to best, then we can understand how our parents taught us perfection. This explanation of how we acquire the idea of perfection seems to be somewhat shaky, depending as it does on a long line of parental teachings.

Or one might take Jung's notion of the collective unconscious and say that the categories of perfection come from the archetypes, although I suspect that this response is something like saying that colds are produced by cold-influencing germs.

We should not forget that Descartes might be right, namely, that the idea of perfection came from a perfect being.

If we go back to Descartes's list, there are some additional mysteries. 'Eternal', 'immutable', and 'independent' could probably be defined in the language of classical physics. 'Omniscient', on the other hand, is not so easy. I think I can guess what Descartes might mean because Spinoza and Leibniz did try to define 'omniscience'. An omniscient being simultaneously knows all the correct axioms and definitions as well as all the theorems. In modern-day technology, one would say that an omniscient being is a perfectly programmed computer with a zero processing time.

But this rationalistic definition may not be what we are really after, especially for utopias. Nor would a perfectly empirical mind be a satisfactory condition because a mind that knew all the facts of nature would not necessarily be useful in a society, especially if we did not know how to gain access to it.

Edgar A. Singer, Jr. tried his hand at an approximate definition of omniscience as well as omnipotence. He imagined a society in which each person (a) knows his own wants, (b) knows the instruments for satisfying his wants, (c) has perfect instruments available, and (d) has access to those instruments and knows how to use them. Such a person could be said to be pragmatically omniscient and omnipotent.

Singer was aware that in such a perfect society one would also need co-operation; that is to say, the wants of the members of a society would have to be so aligned that no one would want something that would reduce other people's capabilities. I think the three items of perfection which Singer selected, namely, omniscience, omnipotence and co-operation, really reflect his nineteenth-century mind. He actually straddled two centuries. In the nineteenth century, the dream of Western Europe and America was a world in which technology had been brought as near as possible to the ideal of perfect want satisfaction and in which the citizens were given the kind of education that would enable them to use this technology perfectly. There was in fact a model of ideal approximation in the nineteenth century, namely, the approximation of perfect measurement, which can be measured in terms of the probable error of a measuring process.

The twentieth-century side of Singer was a flaw in the nine-teenth-century idealism; namely that if an approximately ideal society should come into being, where we would have little work to do and all the means of satisfying our wants, we would all be utterly bored after a while. In other words, the decay of civilisation would occur in so affluent a society.

Secondly, Singer's twentieth-century side invented the notion that, as human beings, we are constantly dissatisfied no matter how close we come to the technological ideal. He called this 'ideal dissatisfaction' and claimed that in a society which is advancing towards perfection, eternal dissatisfaction would characterise the mood of the individuals in the society. Of course, he was getting this idea from science. No true scientist ever rests content with his state of knowledge. To him the storehouse of knowledge is always mostly empty compared to what is not known. The restless scientist looks to the future with great hope that some of the deepest mysteries he has encountered will be explained but also with the expectation that, once these mysteries are explained, even deeper mysteries will appear.

Singer's is one utopia based on the 'add-on' definition of perfection. There are lots of questions to ask about this version of perfection.

First of all, it is unfortunately based on a very simple-minded eighteenth- and nineteenth-century psychology of desire. There probably has never been a more simple-minded psychologist than Jeremy Bentham, who states in *Introduction to the Principles of Morals and Legislation* that we are all driven towards pleasure and away from pain. A slightly more sophisticated theory says that we all have an ego which, during our whole lives, seeks to attain what it wants. As Singer remarks, given but one wish, what wish would you select? The obvious answer is that you would wish that all your wishes come true.

But in point of fact I don't wish anything of the kind. I am continually delighted that some of my wishes do not come true, especially the wish to overeat or to overdrink. Furthermore, I have studied enough about the human psyche to realise that the conscious ego is only a small part of it. I think Jung is right that the major ethical principle in the design of one's life is the process of individuation, which is not based on the satisfaction of ego desires. In fact, there is nothing new about Jung's idea because it appears quite explicitly in much Hindu philosophy, e.g., in the *Bhagavad-Gita*.

But one does not have to go into depth in psychology to see the weakness of a utopia based on ego satisfaction. I can certainly say, as I have said above, that I do not want my wishes to be satisfied because I do not approve of them.

One more point in fairness to Singer. He seems to have adopted the notion that ego satisfaction is not the main drive. Since he had no theory of the unconscious to work with, his fourth ideal turns out to be a difficult one for him to express.

Now I want to turn to another point: whether the 'add-on' philosophy of perfection is tenable.

I am not a scholar of modern philosophy, but I can find no references to philosophers who worried about the 'add-on' theory of perfection, with the possible exception of Leibniz in *Discours de Métaphysique*. Leibniz put the task of the ontological proof to be one of demonstrating God's existence, if God is possible. This seems to reflect Leibniz's concern that adding on a new quality of perfection may create a contradiction. For example, is it possible that a being could be omnipotent and benevolent at the same time? There are certainly plausible arguments that show it is not possible.

Rather than using logic as my argument, I will choose history. History does seem to say that as a nation becomes more powerful, i.e. in our current language, 'more developed', it seems to have a great deal more difficulty in carrying out co-operative policies.

This brings me back to Singer's notion of ideal co-operation. He thought of co-operation in terms of teleology. Specifically, A co-operates with B to the extent that when A begins to attain his goal, he increases B's chances of attaining his. But I very much question whether this concept of teleology captures what Kant was trying to say in *Foundations of the Metaphysic of Morals*. Kant also imagined a utopia, which he called a kingdom of ends. In it, the basic underlying structure rested upon a universally shared moral law: 'Never treat humanity either in yourself or another as means only but as an end withal.' He imagined that every member of his kingdom of ends was self-motivated by this law so that no individual or group legislates for the rest, but everyone legislates in exactly the same way with respect to the others. I think Singer's definition of teleological co-operation hardly captures what Kant was trying to talk about.

There are other versions of the Kantian notion of co-operation, for example, in Romans, St Paul talks of 'every one members one of another'. Much more recently, Jung wrote about the process of individuation in which he seems to describe individual development of each person in terms of his or her relationship to others.

If we consider these richer and deeper meanings of co-operation, might it not be the case that as persons or nations become more powerful they become less co-operative? I am afraid that there is almost overwhelming evidence from history that up to now this has been the case, as large powerful nations have displayed such horrifying inequities. At the present time, we estimate that something like 25 to 50 per cent of the children of the world go to bed hungry even though there is enough food in the world to feed everyone adequately. In other words, affluence in a nation creates indifference.

If all this is the case, it may very well be true that progress in the direction of omnipotence may cause retrogression in the direction of co-operation. To put it another way, we do not know how to increase affluence and co-operation at the same time. This may be the deepest mystery that we face; far deeper than black holes in space or any other conundrum the physical sciences have raised.

My conclusion is that human beings do not know enough to design utopias. The design of perfection and certainly the design of perfect societies must rest on knowledge, but at present it is a knowledge that we have not attained even approximately. The study of utopias and conferences on utopias are thoroughly worthwhile, however, because they reveal the areas of ignorance that need to be addressed by the coming generations, if there are to be any: I certainly hope there will be.

5

Consensus in Social Decision-Making: Why is it Utopian?

Keith Graham

Consider the following Utopian suggestion. In any form of collective decision-making, decisions which issue from the will of a minority *or* a majority are a moral affront. The individual has a moral duty to follow the dictates of his or her own conscience. If we assume, therefore, that any member of a collective actually has a preference that some particular state of affairs should exist and (what is no doubt a larger assumption) that he holds this preference as a matter of *bona fide* moral conviction, then the institution of some contrary state of affairs will thwart his will: it actually prevents him from conforming to the requirements of morality. True, if it is the majority's will which prevails then fewer unfortunates will end up in this position than otherwise, but some will nevertheless. Accordingly, *collective decisions ought to be based upon unanimity.* The right to impose ought not to be the prerogative of *any* social group, whatever its numerical relation to the remainder. The only way for the autonomy of the moral subject to be preserved is for the whole community to act in concert. And since such acts are to be the expression in the outside world of moral conviction arrived at in the inner sanctum of conscience, it must also be a requirement that the whole community *think* in concert.

By virtue of this last feature, if no other, it will perhaps readily be conceded that the suggestion here is a utopian one. We can then raise a series of questions about it. *Why* is the suggestion utopian? What facts about ourselves and our aspirations license describing it in those terms? What assumptions does it rest on, and what is wrong with them? What *follows* from the fact that the suggestion is utopian? Ought we then to ignore it or does it still have some legitimate role to play in serious, practical thinking about the acceptability of different forms of social decision-making?

In pursuing these questions in this connexion I hope to be able to

shed some more general light on the role of utopian considerations in
moral and political thought. A suggestion of this kind, about modes of
decision-making, seems to me a promising place to start. Argument
about the way decisions are to be made, and who is to make them,
necessarily bulks large in social theorising in any case, but especially
so in connexion with utopian thought. It is, after all, a strongly felt
objection to some depictions of utopia that decision-making (at least
for the general run of the populace) is left out of the reckoning
altogether. We feel that it is worthless for people to be in a succession
of good and desirable states if someone else behind the scenes is
pulling all the levers: there is something inappropriate and demeaning
in mature human beings living in such a way. Furthermore, we are
familiar with the objection that utopian schemes are in the end
necessarily totalitarian: not everyone will share the proposer's view of
what the perfect society looks like, there will be recalcitrants ready to
spoil the scheme of things, and consequently the opportunity to do so
must be removed.

Now the suggestion of unanimous social decision-making at least
avoids *that* charge. Coercion, whether issuing from a totalitarian
structure or from some putatively more legitimate arrangement, has
been excluded from the scene altogether. But in avoiding that charge
it may incur two further, connected ones. First, that it avoids lapsing
into totalitarianism only because it is even more utopian than the
ordinary run of suggestions: people are not merely to be perfectly good,
or perfectly happy, or perfectly rational, they are actually never to
disagree – surely a taller order than usual? Secondly, it may be
objected that strictly speaking the suggestion is not even a utopian one.
It is, significantly, merely a formal one, it is silent about the content or
the structure of a community run according to the unanimity principle.
And the suspicion would be that there is simply no plausible way of
taking steps to make good that deficiency. In classical utopias at least a
genuine picture is offered to us, with people exhibiting certain definite
characteristics, living in a particular kind of way and pursuing
particular courses of activity. Indeed, the specificity of such details in
some utopias is notorious. But in the suggestion as described no clue is
given as to how we might envisage the community looking or how it
might develop, and this may be no accident.

These preliminary reflections provide a useful starting point for
pursuing some of the questions mentioned above. They furnish some
of the considerations which will figure in the most obvious way of
accounting for the rejection of the unanimity proposal as utopian, if it is
allowed even to qualify for that status. People are diverse – infinitely
so, perhaps, but in any case indefinitely so. They have widely differing
preferences and aspirations, their life-styles may be utterly different
one from another; in short, people simply do have utterly diverse views

on the kind of world they wish to inhabit. Nozick (5) offers a list of thirty-odd such diverse people and asks rhetorically whether there is really *one* kind of life which is best for each of them (p. 310). It perhaps makes the point with sufficient strength to note that three of the names on his list are Wittgenstein, Elizabeth Taylor and Ayn Rand. It is, surely, utterly incredible that they could be got to agree, with no note of dissent, on matters of social policy, and it would surely be utterly irresponsible to make proposals based on the contrary assumption without any indication of how to cope with such a central stumbling-block. It is this thought which leads Nozick to the conclusion that there cannot be one utopia, that utopia will consist of utopias – many divergent communities in which people lead very different kinds of lives.

That is one way of grounding the charge against the unanimity proposal – to advert to some undeniable facts about human beings. It is also possible to urge the point in a different way: to argue not merely that such diversity exists and is ineradicable but also that, even if it were possible to eradicate it, this would not be desirable. Thus Strawson (6) calls attention to the diversity of the conflicting ideal images of worthwhile human life and suggests that 'this statement itself may be seen not merely as a description of what is the case, but as a positive evaluation of evaluative diversity. Any diminution in this variety would impoverish the human scene' (p. 29). For him, there is no absurdity in desiring that two conflicting attitudes towards life – say, those of Bertrand Russell and D.H. Lawrence – should co-exist: 'steadiest adherence to one image may co-exist with the strongest desire that other and incompatible images should have their adherents too' (p. 28).

Clearly there are points of contact between Nozick and Strawson. For Nozick, '... utopia is meta-utopia: ... the environment in which people are free to do their own thing ...' (5, p. 312). It is perhaps only a translation of Californian 1970s idiom into Oxford 1960s which gives Strawson's view that the desirable combination of attitudes is (i) a first-order view which favours particular ideals and (ii) a meta-view that such ideals, even where they conflict, should be allowed to flourish, and his belief that this combination of attitudes will be most at home 'in a liberal society, in a society in which there are variant moral environments, but in which no ideal endeavours to engross, and determine the character of, the common morality' (6, p. 44). There are also, it seems to me, limited points of contact between these views and the utopian one to which they stand in contrast. For their complete success they require in a limited area what it requires in general: they require that the entire populace should reach agreement on the illegitimacy of interference in others' experiments in living and their attempts to realise their ideals. As such they must cope with the empirical consideration that strong commitment to an ideal has very often brought with it precisely a fervent desire that the ideal be shared by everyone and, where power has been available, actual imposition on unwilling populations. They must further cope with the theoretical challenge that at least wholehearted *moral* commitment to an ideal logically requires the belief that the ideal is valuable not just for its aspirant but universally. In these ways the stability of the combination of attitudes which they presuppose would itself come under threat.

It may still be felt, however, that this does not reduce by very much the gap between the utopian position we began from and these responses to it. The question is therefore whether the utopian has any more considerations to offer which might increase the plausibility of the suggestion, without flying in the face of obvious facts about human beings or implying a commitment to some unacceptable normative position. Consider, then, some possible rejoinders to the points made earlier. It may be argued that it is an unfair representation of the original suggestion to suppose that it never allows for any disagreement between people. What is not permitted is the resolution of disagreement in a particular way, namely by the imposition of arrangements favoured by one party to the disagreement. It is perfectly compatible with this that there should *be* disagreement, provided only that some other means is envisaged for its removal. And the means favoured by the utopian will be rational persuasion. The only force which will be allowed as legitimate is the force of rational argument, for to subject opponents to this is in no way to deny their status as autonomous agents. On the contrary, it is to behave in the way which most obviously respects that status. (This is to reveal a little more of the assumptions on which the utopian position rests, a question I shall devote more attention to subsequently.) The utopian will then argue that, of course, we have to envisage people settling their disputes in a very different fashion from the one they often follow now: but they do sometimes follow the favoured procedure, and it would require a well-substantiated theory of human behaviour, not mere prejudice about human nature, to show that this pattern could not be established in a more thorough-going way.

Next, the utopian will argue that the lack of specificity complained of earlier in connexion with the proposal is a positive advantage. It avoids precisely the objectionable feature of presuming to know what is good for other people, and instead concentrates on developing a form of decision-making in which people themselves are free to decide what is good for them with the highest possible degree of non-harassment by others. To that extent it ought especially to find favour with anyone who shares the attitudes evinced by Nozick and Strawson, for to that extent it is a second-order, or one might even say liberal, utopia. As an argument *ad homines* this seems to me to have at least some force; but the difficulty it leaves us with is the fear that the constraint it places on the making of social decisions is such as to ensure that not enough social decisions will be made to provide the type of environment favoured by its critics (I will take up this point later).

Thirdly, the utopian will argue that the effect which the evident diversity of people has on the proposal can easily be misunderstood. After all, it will be said, where Russell and Lawrence, or for that matter Wittgenstein and Elizabeth Taylor, do not share the same view about what constitutes a worthwhile life, there is at least a higher degree of plausibility in imagining that they can eventually be got to agree to keep out of each other's hair and go their separate ways than there would be in imagining a total capitulation of one party to the other's views. And this may provide the model for larger and even more diverse populations achieving a *modus vivendi* based on unanimity. Moreover, the reply continues, we should be careful how much we concede to the argument from human diversity, whether it is stated in factual or in normative form. We should expect diversity in an atomised society where ideas of unanimity are given virtually no serious consideration: in a climate where consensus was more actively searched for, things might be very different. Nor should we necessarily deplore a decrease in diversity: we ought rather to give close scrutiny to the view which holds that diversity as such is to be encouraged, and ask whether its appeal may not rest implicitly on the assumption that the ideals which provide diversity are in fact independently commendable or at least not objectionable. What is the merit in letting a hundred flowers bloom, rather than ninety, if ten of them are bindweed?

This, I think, is as far as we can go (indeed, in some respects it is further than we can go) in reducing the distance between the original utopian suggestion and the opposing positions so as to minimise the stigma of utopianism. But we can go further in reducing the distance between them for other purposes. The views, I suggest, have more in common than we have yet noticed, and when this is realised it affords a better understanding of the utopian nature of the original suggestion. This further common ground lies at a deeper theoretical level than supposedly obvious facts about human nature. In exposing it, therefore, I move to another of the general questions raised at the outset about the original suggestion, namely 'what assumptions is it based on and what is wrong with them?'

The utopian suggestion under consideration is no mere fanciful construction, specially invented for knock-about purposes in the present context. It is precisely the challenging view put forward by Wolff (7) that unanimous direct democracy furnishes the only form of social decision-making which is morally compatible with the requirements of autonomous moral agency. Unfortunately, if we enquire what assumptions his position is based on, he tells us disobligingly if candidly that he has 'simply taken for granted an entire ethical theory' (7, p. viii). A certain amount of extrapolation and reconstruction is possible, however. The background assumptions are, in a number of senses to be distinguished, individualist, and they overlap with those of the other positions described. For Strawson it is individual ideals which ought to be fostered (the role he allots to social morality will be considered in a moment). For Nozick, notoriously, in the very first sentence of his preface, 'Individuals have rights, and there are things no person or group may do to them (without violating their rights)' (5, p.ix). How are we to expand on this? Clearly, a certain kind of *moral* individualism is being presupposed. (The terms employed to distinguish different types of individualism here differ in their sense from those employed by Lukes (3), to whose discussion I am greatly indebted.) The individual is the primary object of moral regard, the entity deserving of protected status in any disputes with other, e.g. collective, entities. Whether that entity is seen chiefly as a bearer of rights, a formulator of ideals and experimenter in living, or an autonomous decision-maker, and whether its protected status is seen as inviolate or just extremely important, that is the common thread which can be discerned. Very closely connected with this is a kind of *psychological* individualism. This is not necessarily stated, but implicit in the view is the picture of the individual as, in a strong sense, originator of moral decisions, life plans, ideals, etc. The theories begin, as Descartes did, with the individual and build out from that, rather than beginning from a social context as a frame within which the individual's activities, aspirations and judgments must be viewed. They tend to underplay the extent to which an individual's identity is bound up with the nature of the group(s) of which he or she is part, the extent to which individuals must take options and decisions from stock rather than arriving at them out of their own resources. They tend to give minimal weight to an observation like Mannheim's: 'We belong to a group not only because we are born into it, not merely because we profess to belong to it, nor finally because we give it our loyalty and our allegiance, but primarily because we see the world and certain things in the world the way it does (i.e. in terms of the meanings of the group in question).' (4, p. 19)

Now if Mannheim's observation were accurate this would be a fairly serious matter for these theories. Unless it is to be a gratuitous or dogmatic assertion, the claim that individuals ought or ought not to be treated in certain ways needs support, and I take it that it is the role of theories about what individuals are like, what sort of creatures they are, to provide that support. That is why I suggested that the psychological individualism involved here is closely connected with the moral individualism. And if the former proves to be inadequate then the latter is cast adrift.

But is the former inadequate? Certainly Mannheim's observation in its unqualified form can be questioned. The point can readily be conceded that the values, concepts and institutions of a group play a central role in the formation of an individual, without its being agreed that the individual just *is* the net result of internalising these things. As Lukes has argued, respect for persons requires us to treat them in their concrete specificity, and this means on the one hand taking account of them as social selves, but on the other hand recognising them as 'actually or potentially autonomous centres of choice ... able to choose between, and on occasion transcend, socially-given activities and involvements ...' (3, p. 149).

Indeed, it might be said that this necessary corrective to both excesses of psychological individualism and a Mannheimian reaction against it is already present in Strawson's argument. He does, after all, call attention to the importance of the training we receive in the formation of our moral beliefs and suggests that we should temper to some extent the picture of ourselves as self-consciously choosing moral principles in complete freedom (6, pp. 39, 36). This in its turn he connects with the fact that certain human interests are so fundamental that they must be recognised to some degree in any community, and it is the obligation to observe the protection of such interests that gives rise to social morality. Demands may be made of an individual in matters such as the infliction of injury and the deceiving of others, where some standards are necessary if there is to be any society at all, and these demands may legitimately be backed by social sanction if that is the only means of enforcing them (6, pp. 37, 32). In these ways, therefore, Strawson may be said to be less clearly committed to the kind of psychological individualism which I described, a fact which is reflected in an equally modified commitment to moral individualism. By the same token it might be pointed out that Nozick spends one-third of his time charting the rise of the minimal state in a way which violates no individuals' rights. In view of all this, does it not look as though my attempt to assimilate these positions to the utopian one is beginning to falter?

Some preliminary points in reply. First, the issue of psychological individualism is one which is difficult to settle satisfactorily (or perhaps it would be more accurate to say that it cannot be settled satisfactorily without a more adequate specification of the doctrine than the one I have given). Once the two extreme positions have been abandoned, differences of opinion may appear to be no more than a matter of emphasis, one side saying, 'The individual may be formed by the group but still has the capacity for personal choice, rejection of the group's values, etc.', the other saying, 'The individual may make personal choices but the limit to such choices is set by the material and conceptual possibilities present in the social context.' Further progress can be made only via consideration of the meaning which is to be attached to notions such as 'group' and 'social context'. As I shall suggest in a moment, that would bring us to the heart of the matter.

As far as moral individualism is concerned, the difference remains between the utopian position and these others by virtue of their initial specification; but it is not clear that they *ought* to arrive at different positions given their background assumptions or that the non-utopian positions are as consistent as the utopian. Strawson notes that the demands with social sanctions attached which he thinks are legitimate will not form part of a system of morality unless they are at least to some extent acknowledged as claims by those subject to them. This is fair enough, and surely it is hard to imagine a human community, none of whose members recognise the validity of some regulation of conduct with regard to human injury, deception and so on. The problem, however, lies precisely in the *detail* of such regulation and the fact that individuals of good will can and do have conflicting views on it. Unless they hold to an absolute prohibition on injury, deception, etc. (itself an unwise and perhaps inconsistent position), then, in an actual concrete case, they are liable to disagree over, say, the acceptability of those in power deliberately disseminating false information about the results of armed conflict which their forces are involved in, and over the acceptability of taking part in the conflict itself. It should be stressed that this problem arises between *bona fide* moral agents. None of the positions under review carries a commitment to allowing psychopaths, or for that matter ordinary rogues, to have their way. But anyone who espouses one of these positions has to confront the possibility, to adopt a phrase of Devlin's, of 'a number of people doing things he himself would disapprove of, but doing them earnestly and openly and after thought and discussion in an endeavour to find the way of life best suited to them as individuals' (1, p. 107). Strawson applauds the pursuit of individual ideals subject to the constraint of minimal social morality; so does the individual who does things of which he disapproves. But they also disagree on what constraints that social morality should impose, and that is what makes the content and the enforcement of social morality problematic for one who places this kind of value on the pursuit of individual ideals. Though I shall not argue the point, I believe that similar difficulties arise for Nozick's position.

The difficulty can be put in the form of a dilemma: the dilemma of the liberal wet and the dictator. Suppose that you have accepted the importance of individuals' shaping their own lives, forming their own ideals, making their own moral decisions. This you express in the dangerously seductive belief that individuals ought to do what they think they ought to do. Some years ago I knew a philosopher who held this as his primary ethical belief. On the occasion of a South African cricket tour of England, against which a protest movement had been formed, he therefore ended up with (and explicitly embraced) the following beliefs: (i) that the South Africans should come and play; (ii) that the protestors should prevent them from playing; (iii) that the police should prevent the protestors from preventing them from playing. Now I doubt that this triad can be shown to be formally inconsistent, but it does cry out for an answer to the question, 'What state of affairs do you think ought to obtain in the world?' It is the inability to give a straight answer to this question which allows us to characterise this position as wet.

Now it may be objected that an answer can be given – by whatever the philosopher thought *he* ought to do in the circumstances. But this is where we run into the other horn of the dilemma. Imagine, this time, a dictator who announces to his subjects that he too has been won over to the importance of autonomy for individuals' lives. Henceforth he will urge them to reach their own decisions about what they ought to do. Of course, he adds, since he *is* the dictator he will not allow them to translate such decisions into action except where they coincide with what *he* thinks they ought to do, and he will secure this by coercion and the threat of coercion. We should rightly conclude that such 'respect for autonomy' is a sham. The question then is: where a non-dictatorial individual intervenes in the plans which another individual in good faith adopts as morally acceptable, because the first individual, also in good faith, believes that they are not, is this any more compatible with serious respect for individual autonomy?

The utopian, in the shape of Wolff, argues that it is not and prefers the first horn of the dilemma, giving it the title philosophical anarchism rather than my own ruder label. In this he seems to me to have the consistency of his convictions in a way the other positions do not. What should perhaps be given greater stress than it receives from Wolff is the motivation which his position provides for argument and debate before individuals make their decisions, in the hope that a consensus can be reached.

Yet this is no comfortable resting-place. I have argued elsewhere that where consensus is not achieved it is clear that some individual's autonomous will *must* be thwarted (2, p. 133). Even doing nothing on the grounds of lack of unanimity will ensure this. I also argued on that previous occasion that Wolff's views, in these circumstances, commit him to the acceptance of majority decisions. I do not know whether that argument was successful, but I do know that it conceded too much to Wolff's views. It was largely *ad hominem*, based on the precept: Disagree with as few of your opponent's assumptions as you need to, because then you are more likely actually to secure his agreement. On this occasion it is necessary to call attention to one implicit assumption of Wolff's which I had left unchallenged, the one which I believe is most importantly held in common by the positions under examination.

Each implicitly accepts a kind of *ontological* individualism, the view that in the end the only real moral agents are individuals. When due allowance has been made for social influences on the individual and for the moral demands which society can make on the individual, it remains true that the locus of moral decision is the individual conscience and the fit object of moral appraisal is the individual's action. In this way, this form of individualism undercuts the previous two and survives differing degrees of commitment to them. It is reflected in Strawson's case in the fact that socially sanctioned demands on one are possible because of what one may do *to other individuals*, closely echoed in Nozick's rejection of the idea of a *social* good: 'But there is no *social entity* with a good that undergoes some sacrifice for its own good. There are only individual people, different individual people, with their own individual lives. Using one of these people for the benefit of others, uses him and benefits the others. Nothing more' (5, pp. 32-3). That Wolff subscribes to this kind of ontological individualism is evident from his entire argument.

This doctrine seems to me importantly false. I believe that, in addition to individuals, there are corporate entities which make moral decisions and act in ways open to moral appraisal but which are not, in the required way, reducible to individuals. Take, as an example, a university senate. It can decide that people are to be fired or close a department (perhaps subject to ratification by equally corporate entities). Now its deciding and acting in these ways does not, of course, involve anything over and above a number of individuals themselves deciding and acting; but they have significance for that process only insofar as they can be identified by reference to the corporate entity in question. It is as a member of senate, not as John Smith, that anyone does anything which contributes to the entity's decision. That is why I hold that this corporate entity is not, in the required way, reducible to individuals. Another example would be an electorate. This entity, not individuals, returns a government to power; but it is their actions *as voters*, i.e. members of the electorate, which constitute that act on the part of the electorate. A less institution-dependent example would be that of a populace which gives expression to a climate of opinion, where this is again constituted by the individual acts of its members.

This has implications for the old chestnut 'Why should I be moral?' and related questions about the acceptance of social decisions. Traditionally, it has been feared that any answer must be tautological ('Because you ought to do what you ought to do') or must connect the demands of morality with an individual's self-interest in an external, problematic way, giving *carte blanche* to cheats, hypocrites and free-riders ('Because it will pay you to do what you ought to – most of the time.') But now it looks as though such questions may have been wrongly framed. It is not just that there are other entities than individuals and other interests than individual interests: when I am taking a decision which has significance merely as one component in a collective decision, it is not clear that it is appropriate or rational for me to take it merely by reference to my individual interests or to look for some fortuitous, contingent link between them and those of the collective entity. (It is not clear that this is inappropriate either. More of that in a moment.) Relatedly, it is not clear what the appropriate and rational limits are to resistance to the implementation of a corporate decision. In purely individual matters, I take it, a central consideration is the causal fact that *I* bring my actions about – I am in that sense responsible for them – and that this brings with it the presumption of *moral* responsibility and therefore the insistence on freedom to follow the dictates of my conscience. Since I take the rap, I should make the choice. But the causal locus is elsewhere in the case of corporate action – it is not in any one place but more or less widely dispersed – and if moral responsibility and the right to autonomy come in on the back of causal responsibility, then they may not here be allocated in the same way.

Now it would not be mere intellectual error, it would be politically dangerous to make matters here seem simpler than they are. Individuals may be constituents in corporate entities which they do not want to be part of or which they would prefer to be non-existent. The internal structure or dynamics of a corporate entity may be such as to nullify the apparent contribution of an individual to the collective decision. An individual may be a constituent in several distinct corporate entities which stand in complicated relations to one another, e.g. a member of a society and a particular class in a class-divided society. There is therefore no simple recipe for how the individual is to behave insofar as he or she is acting as part of some larger entity. Nothing less than an entire social theory will give the answer to this in any particular case. But that is what is required, and it is utopian to discuss social decision-making in terms which ignore the fact.

The peculiarity of the original utopian suggestion is that it compounds its inadequate ontology by aspiring to a condition – consensus – which that ontology is precisely least likely to serve. Where people see themselves as the atoms to which anything else is reducible then their preferences, plans and projects are correspondingly likely to be literally self-ish. In contrast, where they consciously recognise that their identity is not exhausted in their own selves and that part of their selves has significance *only* as a constituent in a larger entity, they will recognise the inadequacy of posing questions simply in the form 'What is in my interests?', and they will not feel under a constraint from some external source when they ask 'What is in the interests of the group?' Not that the self-image which the utopian suggestion fosters is the only, the ultimate or even necessarily the most important determinant of how people approach their responsibilities as participants in social decisions; but it makes its contribution, and that contribution is, from the point of view of the desired end, pushing in the wrong direction.

If the utopian suggestion harbours these deeper theoretical weaknesses, as well as flying in the face of hallowed common sense, does it have any role to play in serious discussion? It would be boring to say no. It would be only marginally less boring to say that it has a role as an unattainable ideal to which real arrangements can approximate. Rather, if it has a role to play it is precisely because it raises wider issues. Like many utopian suggestions, it is in a way not utopian enough. As it stands, it is simply a suggestion about decision-making made against a background of atomistic, individualist assumptions and with no serious regard for the source and nature of conflicts in contemporary reality. As such it stands condemned because it wants the halfpence without the kicks, while not being prepared to do anything about the origin of the kicks. But as part of a more wide-ranging proposal, based on firmer theoretical grounds, it would deserve to be taken more seriously. The converse of ontological individualism, a strong sense of community, is largely lacking from our thinking because community is largely lacking from our social lives. The problem is not so much that people like Elizabeth Taylor are very different from people like Wittgenstein: it is rather that conflict of interests is endemic in the most basic aspects of our social relations. That itself would have to change for consensus to have any chance. And it is reasonable that it should, in recognition of the essential communality of human life – that is, of the fact that for the satisfaction of both material and psychic needs it is essential that we are parts of larger units than individual human beings.

References

1. Devlin, P., *The Enforcement of Morals*, Oxford University Press 1965.
2. Graham, K., 'Democracy and the autonomous moral agent', in *Contemporary Political Philosophy*, ed. K. Graham, Cambridge University Press 1982.
3. Lukes, S., *Individualism*, Basil Blackwell, Oxford 1973.
4. Mannheim, K., *Ideology and Utopia* (1936) Routledge, London 1976.
5. Nozick, R., *Anarchy, State, and Utopia*, Basil Blackwell, Oxford 1974.
6. Strawson, P.F., 'Social morality and individual ideal', *Philosophy* 36, 1961, reprinted in *Freedom and Resentment*, Methuen, London 1974.
7. Wolff, R.P., *In Defense of Anarchism*, Harper & Row, New York 1970.

6

Millennium and Utopia

J.F.C. Harrison

The starting point of this chapter is the hypothesis that utopia may be a secular equivalent of the millennium (5) or, alternatively, that the millennium may be a religious form of utopia. A presentation of the issues involved should be a contribution to both the origins and utility of utopian thought; for it will show the religious strand in utopian thinking and also suggest its functional significance for the participants. In other words, we shall be helped to understand how and why people arrived (and still arrive) at utopian beliefs. Millennialism, like utopianism, has existed in many different types of society, in various countries, and over a long period of time. The material here is drawn mainly from Britain and America in the period *c.* 1780-1850, though it could easily be supplemented by both earlier references and links with today (3).

Millennialists believed that the world was to be transformed by the second coming of Christ and the establishment of the kingdom of God on earth. This state would last for a thousand years, after which would come the last judgment. During the period of the millennium the saints (that is, the Christian martyrs and all faithful Christians who have suffered) would reign with Christ. There were differences of view, however, between those Christians who believed that Christ's second coming would precede the millennium (premillennialists) and those who thought that it would follow the millennium (postmillennialists). From these differences stemmed others. The premillennialists were predisposed towards the establishment of the millennium by divine, cataclysmic action, whereas the post-millennialists were prone to think that the kingdom of God would come gradually as the result of Christian, human instrumentalities. For either of these views there was ample scriptural support, so that the choice between a revolutionary or reformist interpretation had to be made on other than theological grounds. Among premillennialists there was a further division between those who believed that the

second advent had already occurred and that the millennium had
begun, and those who still looked for these events in the future. Again,
among both pre- and postmillennialists anticipation of the millennium
could provoke either pessimism or optimism, depending on whether the
imminent end of the world was dreaded or welcomed.

From these differences in interpretation and emphasis a variety of
types of millennial concern was possible, ranging from sophisticated
study of the biblical books of prophecy to divine revelations concerning
the immediate arrival of Christ on earth. Throughout the eighteenth
and first half of the nineteenth centuries the first of these forms never
lacked able exponents. Contemporary events like the Lisbon
earthquake of 1755 were interpreted as evidence of the fulfilment of
biblical prophecies. Above all, the French Revolution excited a spate of
interpretations on both sides of the Atlantic designed to show that the
world was entering upon the last days. Millennialism was widely
espoused by leading scholars and divines. In America the names of
Timothy Dwight (President of Yale), John H. Livingston (President
of Rutgers) and Joseph Priestley come to mind: in Britain, George
Stanley Faber, Edward King and Edward Irving. A spate of pamphlets
and sermons by Church of England clergy and orthodox American
ministers poured forth from the 1790s; and there was constant
reference back to the prophetical studies of Sir Isaac Newton, Joseph
Mede, and William Whiston.

In addition to these intellectually sophisticated millennialists there
were also many popular, largely self-educated, adventist millenarians.
These are the people condemned by the opulent classes as fanatics and
imposters, and by historians as cranks and the lunatic fringe. The
distinction between what may be called respectable, orthodox,
scholarly millennialism on the one hand, and popular (or folk)
millenarianism on the other is useful for analytical purposes; but the
division is not hard and fast. Those who believed in the millennium
had the option of combining so many variables that a millennialist or a
millenarian could be placed at any point along a continuum of belief.
Millennialism and millenarianism were ways of looking at the world,
rather than specific doctrines. This was at the root of the difference
between the millennialism of seventeenth- and eighteenth-century
divines and scholars (many of them fellows of Cambridge colleges),
and the popular millenarian tradition stemming from the radical sects
of the English Revolution. It is the tone and temper of the popular
millenarians, the way in which they used the texts and symbols from
Daniel and Revelation, which is distinctive. They were the
enthusiasts, the fanatics, the come-outers. Their beliefs were derived
from a literal, eclectic interpretation of the prophetic scriptures, and a
divine revelation vouchsafed to them directly. A simplicity, often
crudity, seemed to mark their mentality, for their reliance on the

supernatural enabled them to dispense with many of the limitations imposed by logic and reason. Moderation and gradualness did not commend themselves as virtues, but rather were signs of lack of faith. The basic principles of good and evil in the world were crystal clear, and life was to be lived by the light of this absolute standard, with no compromises.

The largest group of these popular millenarians in Britain were the followers of Joanna Southcott (1750-1814). She was a country woman from Devonshire, who in 1792 began to hear 'voices' which convinced her that she was a prophetess. She prophesied that Christ's second coming was nigh, and claimed that she was the bride of the lamb described in Revelation 19. She wrote down the messages revealed to her, many of them in doggerel, and in 1801 published her first pamphlet, *The Strange Effects of Faith*. Until this time she had failed to convince anyone of the validity of her claims, but in that year disciples began to gather. A key group of them were followers of Richard Brothers, a prophet whom the government had confined in an Islington lunatic asylum since 1795. Brothers was a young naval officer on half pay, who after studying the writings of prophecy, was convinced that the millennium was now due. Furthermore, he identified himself as King of the Hebrews and Nephew of God, and interceded with the Almighty to spare London from destruction by earthquake for its infidelity. Brothers' *Revealed Knowledge of the Prophecies and Times*, first published in London in 1794, went through several editions and was reprinted in America. His followers included Nathaniel Brassey Halhed, an Orientalist and M.P. for Lymington, William Sharp, a noted engraver and radical reformer, three Anglican clergymen, and businessmen in Liverpool, Manchester and Leeds. These transferred their allegiance to Joanna, who began the practice of 'sealing' believers as a sign of their renunciation of Satan. By January 1804 over 8000 disciples had been sealed, and one estimate put the number of converts in London and its neighbourhood at one time at above 100,000. Southcottian chapels were opened in London, Bristol, Lancashire and Yorkshire; a constant stream of publications by Joanna poured forth; and the sealing of thousands 'to inherit the Tree of Life, to be made Heirs of God and joint-heirs with Jesus Christ' went on rapidly. Joanna's doctrine of the Woman reached its tragic climax in 1814 when she announced in her *Third Book of Wonders* that her 'voice' had told her that she would bear a son by a miraculous conception. This would be the fulfilment of an obscure passage in Genesis 49 referring to Shiloh. But although the prophetess underwent an hysterical pregnancy no child was born, and she died of the shock of disillusionment.

After her death Joanna's mantle was taken up by a succession of prophets – George Turner, John Wroe, John (Zion) Ward – who attracted followers in London and the industrial North and Midlands during the 1830s and 1840s. In America the cause of popular millenarianism was maintained by the Shakers, the early Mormons, and the Millerites.

Having established the nature of the millenarian tradition, we now have to ask whether, and if so how, it relates to utopianism. We shall be helped in the first instance by extending our definition of millenarianism. Its traditional meaning was derived from Revelation 20, the events therein being taken in a strictly literal sense. Satan was to be bound fast and the saints would reign with Christ on earth for a thousand years; after which Satan would be released and finally defeated. But millenarianism also has a wider meaning, extending beyond its theological or doctrinal origins. It is a type of salvationism. The search for salvation, variously defined, is a main preoccupation of most religious movements, and millenarianism can be identified by its distinctive characteristics in this respect. Several such qualities appear to be present in most millenarian movements. First, the salvation sought is conceived as being for the faithful as a group – the saints, the true believers – and not as each individual seeking by himself to save his own soul. Next, this salvation is to be enjoyed in a kingdom on this earth, and it is to come soon and suddenly. It will be total in its effects: the present evil world will not be improved, but utterly destroyed, and replaced by a perfect society. Lastly, the change will come about by divine agency, not by human efforts (5).

In their responses to the world, the seekers after salvation react in different ways (7). Some millenarians will withdraw from the world; others will await its divine destruction; and some will adopt the utopian response of seeking to construct a perfect society, free from evil. The utopian does not wait for a divine cataclysm, he is not satisfied with anything less than a complete replacement of present society, and he is too active simply to withdraw from the world. Such a reaction is to be seen among some of the Southcottians, especially those of a radical inclination like William Sharp. For them the millennium was a perfect society in which all the evils of the present world had disappeared. In this respect they were close to utopians whose alternative societies were intended as criticisms of their own. The millenarian was committed to vast changes; he was looking for a complete transformation of the social order, when all things would be made new. If we dig into the history of popular radicalism almost anywhere before 1850 the chances are good that a millenarian reference will be unearthed. The Owenites in the 1830s drew heavily upon millenarian ideas and vocabulary; and early historians of socialism compared the utopian socialists with millenarian sects.

A very different point of contact with utopian thought can be found in the development of postmillennialism. Unlike the premillennialists (or millenarians), the postmillennialists found it easy to assume that the kingdoms of this world will eventually become those of Christ, that through the endeavours of Christians the world will get better, until finally it is worthy to receive Christ at his second coming. In the eighteenth century millennialists increasingly came to equate this doctrine with the idea of progress. The millennium was secularised into a utopia or perfect state of society, to be attained through a gradual and steady march of improvement. Providence was integrated into the concept of natural law (6).

Thus through salvationism, radicalism or the idea of progress (and also perhaps through millenarian community building), the idea of the millennium could lead into or become synonymous with utopia. At a deeper level, however, there was a gulf between the two concepts. The vision of the millennium in Revelation is about the end of time (the last days) and embraces the whole cosmos. Utopia (literally, no-place) is a picture of a perfect place and the society within it, and is thus more circumscribed (1). The eschatological element is missing in utopia. Whereas the millennium will be realised by divine action, utopia is the product of conscious human will. No man can know when or exactly how the millennium will arrive; it has been fore-ordained and will in due course be revealed or unveiled to men.

But in practice many millenarians were not as far removed from utopians as in the theory they might have been. We cannot neatly assume that millenarians were concerned with perfect time and utopians with perfect space. Belief in the imminence of the last days did not inhibit active preparation for the second coming; in fact quite the contrary. Prophetesses and prophets like Joanna Southcott and John Wroe urged their followers to participate by their deeds and decisions in the preparation for Redemption. A great deal of time and ingenuity was expended by millenarians and millennialists in calculating the time of the arrival of the millennium from the prophecies in Daniel and Revelation. William Miller, indeed, convinced his followers that the millennium would begin on 22 October 1844. Again, although in eschatology the emphasis is on the time of the end, millenarians usually had a picture in their minds which located the millennium in specific surroundings. From the rich imagery of Daniel and Revelation they derived a vivid impression of what life in the millennium would be like, amid jewels and gold and angels and beautiful gardens. The perfect society and the New Jerusalem was in effect a holy utopia.

Finally, what was the function of millenarianism, and was it similar in this respect to utopianism? As a type of salvationism, the millennium promised specific gains. Men seek salvation for many reasons and look for it in many forms. One man's concern will be to find salvation from illness, anxiety or grief: another's will be to save the world. Men will seek to be healed, to be recognised as important, to protect themselves from adversity, to change the social order. What they have in common is the hope that through the millennium these things will be realised. There were also psychic benefits. It has often been observed that millenarian movements seem to flourish most in periods of crisis and upheaval, and when feelings of anxiety and insecurity are rife. At such times men look for alternative and more perfect societies. With some qualifications this is true of the late eighteenth and early nineteenth centuries. The early socialist movement of the 1830s and 1840s, for instance, can be interpreted as a secularised form of millenarianism. But although the millennium may be compared with the idea of utopia intellectually, and may indeed offer the same kind of intellectual satisfactions, millenarianism entailed a different sort of commitment from utopianism. The millenarian was searching for meaning, in both personal experience and the world at large, and this usually found expression in a form of eschatology, either apocalyptic or existential (3). The utopian was concerned with social maladies, and proposed a remedy through a perfect society (2). At some points their paths converged, but their goals were not always the same.

References

1. Buber, Martin, *Paths in Utopia*, Beacon Press, Boston 1958.
2. Goodwin, Barbara, *Social Science and Utopia*, Harvester Press, Hassocks 1978.
3. Harrison, J.F.C., *The Second Coming: popular millenarianism, 1780-1850*, Routledge, London 1979.
4. Mannheim, Karl, *Ideology and Utopia* (1936), Routledge, London 1960.
5. Thrupp, Sylvia L. (ed), *Millennial Dreams in Action*, Mouton, The Hague 1962.
6. Tuveson, Ernest Lee, *Millennium and Utopia*, Harper & Row, New York 1964.
7. Wilson, Bryan R., *Magic and the Millennium*, Heinemann, London 1973.

PART II

Features and Impact of
Utopian Thought

7

Economic and Social Innovation in Utopia

Barbara Goodwin

This chapter looks at some of the main economic and social problems with which utopias have dealt, and at the impact which their proposals have had. There is, obviously, a general problem about detecting, tracing or quantifying the impact of utopian ideas except in the simple case where an experimental community is set up, or a revolution takes place, on the basis of a particular utopian theory. Utopias are often written, like allegories, to influence people's ways of thinking, and do not always demand the implementation of the utopian blueprint *in toto* – although I could easily cite a dozen exceptions to this. They contribute to the formation of a climate of opinion; later other, more academic, individuals take up their ideas and turn them into theory or into social policy proposals. The search for 'impact' thus encounters the same problems of causality and indeterminacy which dog the search for any 'chain of ideas', and the best that one can do is make suggestive connections between utopian ideas and social changes.

The attack on inequality

Inequality is the basis of many of the social evils which utopian writers condemn: their attempts to eradicate it lead them to propose dramatic innovations in the economic and social spheres. It is, of course, arguable that all social inequalities rest on economic ones – you need not be a Marxist to agree with this. Some utopians, however, retain social stratifications resting on age, expertise or other attributes while instituting economic equality – among them, More. We therefore need to look more closely at how they view inequality.

First, there is a need for greater precision about what form of inequality is being attacked. There can be inequality of talents and similar attributes, of social status, of moral wealth, of wealth or ownership, of function (given the division of labour) and of needs. These inequalities do not always conspire together, and may indeed conflict; for example, some societies reward untalented people of good social standing by great wealth, and many Westerners criticise the socialist ideal because they think that a system built on the fulfilment of unequal needs will militate against due reward for unequal talents or contributions. Some inequalities are eradicable, others are not and can at best be mitigated. Inequalities resting on birth (status, good family, etc.) can be eradicated, just as the French revolutionaries abolished the nobility, whereas inequalities of basic intelligence can at most be reduced by good education for the less able. We should note that inequalities at the personal level partly cause and are partly a product of inequitable social institutions and that both individuals and society must be changed to bring about greater equality; but many critics of the egalitarian utopian impulse would argue that inequitable institutions are a product of 'human nature' based on the differentiated worth of individuals or on the individual desire for distinction and stratification. The utopian is obliged to dissent from this view if he wishes to achieve greater equality, and hence to argue that individuals are not characterised by great and ineradicable inequalities or by innate desires for inequality. Both points are hard to establish empirically, and must usually be argued by reference to some conception of an untainted, pre-social human nature, which involves familiar problems.

Economic inequality

Most utopians claim to find this invidious because of its results, which are: (1) the poverty or suffering which it engenders; (2) the inefficiency of inegalitarian methods of production (see, for example, the criticisms of waste made by More, Fourier and Saint-Simon); (3) the social consequences, such as class differences and aristocracies of wealth, and the deprivation of chances for self-betterment and social mobility/ for the working classes; (4) the diminution of human dignity for those at the bottom of the wealth hierarchy; and (5) the intrinsic injustice of inegalitarian systems. It is interesting that utopians use (5) as an argument of last resort, since the educated and wealthy audiences to which they addressed themselves usually had vested interests in considering existing societies *just*: the utopians therefore preferred to cite arguments such as (1) to (4) to highlight their shortcomings and analysed injustice in terms of these. This also avoided immediate commitment to a more substantive view of justice. Different arguments have been brought into prominence at different times; the Levellers used a version of (4) (human dignity), contending that all men were equal in the sight of God to try to convince a Christian audience. Saint-Simon criticised French society largely on the grounds of inefficiency when capitalism was just taking root in Europe. Most utopias want to eliminate all the results (1 to 5) of economic inequality, but the way in which they go about this depends on their perception of how that inequality is itself caused.

Of course, there have been utopians who considered that inequality was rooted in human nature to such an extent that the ideal society had to build on it constructively; Plato's 'three-classes-plus-slaves' Republic exemplifies this approach. Utopians who adhere to a *tabula rasa* view of human nature, often supplemented by perfectibilism, have taken the view that people can be made approximately equal by education and/or conditioning; Owen's utopian communities were to be constructed on the supposition that people were (after the right education) approximately interchangeable and had similar and equal needs. More realistically, no doubt, thinkers such as More, Fourier, Saint-Simon and Morris agreed that men had differing talents which must be harnessed to different productive functions, but sought ways to equalise economic rewards or at least to reduce differentials. This will be discussed later.

Economic inequality is fundamentally linked to the division of labour. Rousseau argued that the evils of interpersonal 'dependency' which is inseparable from inequality, became inevitable once joint productive activities began (he cites 'corn and iron' as the beginning of man's downfall); the more sophisticated the economy, the greater the dependence and the inequality, which degrades man's free, independent nature (15, p. 203). Utopian socialists and the anarchists, in particular Godwin, by and large agreed with Rousseau. Yet accepting, as most of them did, the inevitability of the division of labour, they argued that the evils of dependence would be eliminated by the substitution of the dependence of each on all, of the individuals on the whole. A co-operative method of production was the best means to achieve this, where everyone would see his wellbeing as tied up in the success of the enterprise. (This is quite different from capitalist production, which is also co-operative, but under which workers see a direct antagonism between their interests and those of their employers.) The abolition of privately owned capital was, for most of them, a necessary precondition for producing this non-degrading mutual interdependence.

The majority of utopias presuppose the elimination of the major premise of classical economics, namely, *scarcity*. Some argue that if all the 'drones' or parasites were fully employed, there would be an abundance of goods, even with shorter working hours – for example, More (11), Saint-Simon (16) and Chavannes (2). Others assume that efficient industrialisation would multiply the goods produced many times over. More recently, Marcuse has foreseen 'superautomation', which would free most people for most of the time from tedious work and still maintain a high level of consumption. By contrast, other utopians refer to redistribution as the answer, arguing that the present problem of capitalism is merely that some have too much and others not enough, whereas there is really enough to keep all in comfort. (The statistics about redistribution of wealth suggest that this is empirically false; such redistribution would, in any case, destroy the motive force of capitalism.) Similarly, the abolition of 'luxury' is another means proposed by many utopians, especially those sometimes referred to as 'ascetic' or 'communistic', such as More, Mably and Morelly. A major contention is that material abundance would produce more than enough for everyone, so that there could be no social envy or relative deprivation, even if economic inequalities still existed. Questions of social justice would simply disappear, it is hoped. Again, the evidence seems to be to the contrary; in the richest nation in the world, the USA, the drive for acquisition seems not to have abated, nor do complaints of injustice – although this, it might be said, is due to unfair distribution of wealth. In any case, it is quite possible that equalisation of money incomes and other material goods or abundance of such goods would merely clear the way for arguments about injustice in the distribution of positional (non-abundant) goods.

However, it seems that some form of redistribution is essential to the elimination of economic and social injustice, and most utopians have proposed this, though some, especially in the optimistic period at the beginning of industrialisation, hoped that abundance alone would solve the problem and so avoid the need for a social upheaval. Two major proposals for redistribution recur throughout the history of utopianism from More onwards. (1) The 'socialist' solution, which requires the communalisation of all private property (in the sense of 'capital') and distribution according to need. Advocates of this include More, Owen, most anarchists and, most notably, Marx, although many of these retain some element of distribution according to contribution, while guaranteeing minimum needs. (2) The 'improved capitalism' solution, which either takes the form of pure capitalism, with private ownership and production continuing in tandem with a welfare system reducing the worst inequalities and privations, or of state capitalism, or else of 'modified capitalism', with restrictions on land acquisition, capital accumulation and income levels, similar to the sumptuary laws of the past. I shall now examine these two categories of proposal in more detail.

1. *The abolition of private property.* This term is used to refer to capital and land ownership, although some utopians actually wish to destroy the distinction between 'mine' and 'thine' completely and to abolish the very concept of personal possession; in this sense, More was very

radical. Some socialist utopias incorporate incentive schemes for workers, so rewards would still be unequal (see, for example, 4, p. 250); they justify this by reference to different capacities and the need for, and the justice of, incentive schemes. By contrast, those who recommend equal pay or distribution according to need dwell on the innate pleasure of labour which is a source of satisfaction and a reward in itself. (To the latter group belong More, Owen, Kropotkin, Morris and Marx.) The way in which capital, land and wealth are owned clearly makes an important difference to the social organisation of a utopia; a wide variety of suggestions have been made. Marx advocated central government ownership of the means of production (and was roundly condemned by anarchists because of the state domination to which this would lead); Owen wanted communities to own their own land and machinery (the problem with Owenite experiments was partly that they depended on shareholders for their capital, who interfered with disastrous effects); the anarchists suggested producers' associations or ownership by villages. These, then, are the socialist, anarchist or communist utopias; we should note that a lot of so-called communist utopias were written before the full developments of capitalism and so understandably did not raise questions about whether industrial production and investment could continue in the absence of the profit motive – questions which critics of socialist ideals justifiably raise, and which post-industrialisation utopias do not fully answer.

One further point to note about the socialist and Marxist utopias is the abolition of money as a means of exchange. The part which money plays in facilitating capitalist accumulation and emphasising economic inequalities is self-evident, and Marx's critique of money in his early writings is a classic statement of the socialist position (10, p. 180). But I would regard the abolition of money as a consequence of the more fundamental changes which such utopias propose, and not as an end in itself.

For the sake of completeness I should mention the anti-industrial socialist utopias of the nineteenth century, of which Morris's *News from Nowhere* is a prime example, although earlier socialist utopias had also emphasised agriculture. Morris, a declared Marxist, envisaged a craft-based society, largely rural, where private property had been abolished, as had the strict division of labour. The last 20 years has seen a proliferation of living experiments based on similar ideals and in this sense the anti-industrial utopias have been more successful than some others, probably because they can be experimented with on a small scale, without full-scale political and economic change.

2. *Improved capitalism.* Many examples of this can be found among the American utopias of the late nineteenth century, many of which are

reprinted in Negley and Patrick (12). Most express antipathy towards socialism and communism and vehemently dissociate themselves from these doctrines while maintaining that they are nevertheless socially and economically just. The burden of their economic argument is that the ideal can be achieved by better control of industry (possibly via government takeover of key or of the most profitable industries), the elimination of idleness and waste, shorter hours, and the opportunity for everyone to pursue at least two professions (presumably to counter contemporary criticisms of the alienation and monotony of capitalist production.) But specialisation of work and wage differentials remain key features of such capitalist utopias, for nearly all these writers agree that there are natural inequalities and different capacities which necessarily merit differentiated rewards; these inequalities are to be tempered by high minimum wages and welfare provisions – and, of course, by the elimination of unemployment. Restrictions on income and ownership complete the picture of welfare capitalism with a degree of state intervention – although most such thinkers, in the tradition of the USA, still try to minimise the role of the state. This group of utopians express a firm faith in the American way of capitalism; although the writers were in most cases moved to elaborate their ideals by the spectres of poverty, crime and inhumane conditions of work, they consider the underlying principle right and just. Abundance is to be combined with a civilising of the profit motive and most of the social evils will in consequence disappear.

   In the last two centuries, then, there is a clear dichotomy: some utopians wish to improve and perfect the capitalist system, the liberal-democratic utopia, while others seek to abolish its very foundations. These antithetical views concerning the productive process are not reflected directly in opposed opinions concerning consumption. While many of the utopians of both these categories would eschew the consumption ethic (perceived mainly as the enjoyment of luxury by the rich) few of them are, in fact, ascetic – for how could any ideal society which aims at happiness declare that it will curtail consumption? The emphasis on abundance suggests that such utopias might be modern Lands of Cockaygne, one long orgy of affluence, but most such utopias link their promises of plenty with a clear conception of what is necessary and what superfluous to human needs and offer the former, while rejecting the latter. (This, of course, raises the widest questions about the definition of 'needs' and it is interesting to read Marcuse, who while advocating superautomation also attacks 'artificial needs' and the consumer society (9).)

Work in utopia

Along with proposals for economic change the utopians advance a new conception of the role of work. In the Garden of Eden, Arcadia and the many Golden Ages of the world, man, it is said, did not work. The medieval poem, *The Land of Cockaygne*, details the delights of food and of the flesh where no one has to work to eat. This was the workers' utopia, conceived in defiance of the biblical idea – reinforced by their own experience – that work is man's curse. Intellectuals, by contrast, invariably imagined utopias of industrious and diligent workers and presented work as a duty to which everyone (except perhaps the ruling elite) is subject. More's utopians are obliged to work alternately in town and country and idleness is punished. The ascetic, communistic, utopias of the eighteenth century also emphasised the obligatory nature of work, although this was to be minimised by low consumption. The Industrial Revolution brought about two significant changes: first, as has been said, industrialisation held out the prospect of abundance beyond belief, and second, socialist thinkers developed theories of man's creative nature as antidotes to the reduction of factory workers to mere alienated drudges. If indeed man fulfils himself as much through work as through consumption, work must play a central role in any utopia. Fourier's utopian scheme is based on 'attractive labour', on the idea that for every individual there are several kinds of work ideally suited to his temperament, between which he can alternate, doing as many as eight different jobs in one day (4, pp. 271-328). Other utopians, while less radical, emphasised the importance of having more than one profession or skill, and tailored their societies accordingly.

Nineteenth-century utopians were singularly divided over whether industrialisation was a gift or a curse. Some, like Saint-Simon, dreamed of super-industrial societies, run as technocracies. Marx thought it possible to conserve the advantages of industrial production (namely, increased leisure and material plenty) while making work joyous and fulfilling by the abolition of exploitation. On the other hand, there are the thinkers who invoke 'craftsmanship' against industrial slavery and yearn for less industrialised societies based on artisan skills and aesthetic values; among these were Morris and Kropotkin. Twentieth-century utopias have looked to superautomation to free man entirely from alienating labour, but some still dream of a more rural and more integrated way of life, with a less materialistic emphasis. Utopian writings seem permanently divided about whether work is man's natural state or not, and it may be that the concept of 'useful toil' which many advocate is partly a result of the prevalence of the Protestant work ethic and therefore does not constitute a clean break with existing society.

A general problem with all utopias mentioned is whether we can admit that inequalities of talent are important and functional and yet create a society of equals. The hope is, of course, that *differences* need not be perceived as inequalities, and that people in utopia could specialise in their work without being unequal economically or socially. The unresolved questions are (1) whether people would welcome or tolerate a society which lacked these kinds of stratification, and (2) whether such a society could function economically in the absence of incentives.

The impact of utopian economic proposals

If we take the individual proposals made by utopians, particularly those of the nineteenth century, we find that many of them have been partially implemented. Most Western societies have progressive taxation, minimum wages, social security provisions and other welfare services; such policies are intended to reduce inequalities and cater for individual needs. Yet their effects are muted by the capitalist framework within which they operate; poverty and inequality are still rife, although the general standard of living has risen. The merit-based system of distribution has not changed fundamentally. In England, I would submit, we have tacitly acknowledged the socialist ideal to the extent of providing 'to each according to his (minimum) needs' but have not pursued the preceding stipulation 'from each according to his ability', either by providing the opportunities for everyone to fulfil himself, or by making explicit the duty of each person to contribute fully to the economy. In fact, quite the opposite attitude prevails, and people very often search for maximum satisfaction with minimum contribution. The present state of affairs promotes an ethic of passive consumption which, admittedly, has certain advantages, but in no way approaches the utopian socialists' ideal of 'social labour' (6).

One can cite many other partial fulfilments of utopian prophecies: *nationalisation* in Britain took place for a number of reasons (not all of them socialist) but is now being rapidly eroded. Far from governments nationalising the most profitable industries to use their revenues for social purposes, such industries were for a long time run on a non-profitmaking basis (thus providing consumer subsidies which were not necessarily egalitarian) and the present government's policy is to sell the most profitable nationalised industries. We have seen *work-enhancing experiments*, designed to make the workers feel that their interests are identical with those of the company, as well as to make their work more interesting (e.g. the Volvo experiment) and the setting up of *co-operatives* (usually where firms have failed, and so under the least favourable conditions); some countries, such as Germany, have instituted *industrial democracy* (often as an attempt to domesticate the unions rather than for socialist reasons); the present government proposes *job-sharing* (mainly as a means for solving unemployment, and not to increase fulfilment).

There is much talk about what form the leisure society will take after the micro-chip and superautomation have abolished a large number of jobs and functions, but there has been little action and no fundamental rethinking of the nature of work and fulfilment. The fact that we still live in a society with fundamental inequalities, concealed poverty and little work satisfaction is taken by some economists as a reason for abolishing many of these quasi-utopian policies and reverting to a pure market economy; but the real point is surely that they operate within the capitalist system, which is still dominated by the ethic of self-interest and which prevents the reforms from achieving their aims. Many 'utopian' measures have been introduced for far-from-utopian reasons and this limits their thoroughness and effectiveness. Our present state shows the inadequacy of half-measures; utopias are conceived as unified wholes. We can improve society by borrowing ideas from them, but we cannot expect miracles if the structure of society is unchanged. In the economic sphere, we have to some extent solved the consumption problem, thanks to technology, but have done little to reform the production and distribution systems which, utopians would argue, are intimately connected with consumption. It is not surprising, then, that the impact of utopias has been somewhat limited and that the social problems which persist despite the implementation of the policies mentioned have caused some thinkers to reject utopianism altogether, as does Hayek, as a perfidious influence on a system which, left alone, would function ideally.

I will not discuss the self-evident impact of the Marxist utopia in detail here, but clearly this has been the most 'successful' utopia, in that a large number of societies have been reorganised explicitly on the principles it recommends. The impact of socialist utopianism has in fact rebounded- on the inhabitants of capitalist countries through their observation of the inadequacy of communism at work: some people react with a repugnance for anything smacking of socialism, while socialist reformers try to merge the best elements of socialism with a basically capitalist economy. The reasons for the failure of communist societies to attain the socialist dream is too large a topic to embark on here, but is certainly a major factor in the way in which utopianism is often regarded at present – with dislike and suspicion.

Social problems

Almost anything can be included under the rubric 'social'; here there is only space to give one example of the radical social changes proposed by some utopians, and I have chosen the example of the position of women to illustrate the innovatory inclination of utopias.

Women in utopia

The position of women is surprisingly unaffected by economic and social egalitarianism. Many utopians, from More onwards, have been remarkably (or unremarkably, since most of them were men) conservative about women. Marriage is still seen as the paradigm relationship between the sexes, although the 'hypocrisy' of Christian marriage in reality is often decried. While some utopias make divorce easier, others make it harder or impossible and hark back to some notion of the 'ideal marriage', which will take place in the generally ideal conditions of utopia. The romantic ideal of social harmony was evidently extended across the board to sexual relations! All kinds of romantic and chivalrous attitudes invade these utopias once the topic of women is broached, and women are usually still seen as a sex apart, with special weaknesses. In Macnie's *Diothas* (8), where women form part of the electorate, they use their votes to save themselves from seduction by far stricter sexual laws. While Hertzka explicitly mentions the need to free women from economic dependence on men, he nevertheless allocates them traditionally female roles and clearly has a fixed idea of what proper 'femininity' is (7, p. 119). Most utopians do not take the idea of equality to its logical conclusion in the case of women and do not contemplate freeing them from their economically subservient, home-making roles.

Mercifully, however, there are some 'feminist' male utopians. Plato displayed a degree of open-mindedness on the subject unusual for his time in discussing the female Guardians: 'if the only difference apparent between (the sexes) is that the female bears and the male begets, we shall not admit that this is a difference relevant for our purpose, but shall still maintain that our male and female guardians ought to follow the same occupations' (14, p. 208). Owen fulminated against the evils of marriage (in part, admittedly, because it made parents treat their children as property, rather than because of its effects on women); Marx and Engels, as is well known, characterised bourgeois sexual relations as property relations and expected bourgeois marriage to die along with capitalism, but this is a necessary extension of their social analysis rather than a display of broad-mindedness, and their positive proposals for women are few. The most radical view of the women's question before that of contemporary feminists is probably Fourier's. In his *New Amorous World*, Fourier proposed relations of complete equality between the sexes, and completely equal treatment in every social context. In his communities, a woman could choose one man as a lover, another as husband, another as the father of her child (and indeed could have as many relationships as her temperament demanded). The communal upbringing of children would free women from particular domestic duties and they too would enjoy the delights of attractive labour on equal terms with men. (But many utopias which propose communal childrearing do so to remove invidious influences on children or favouritism and to promote equality at an early age, rather than to liberate women.) Fourier's ideal may seem to be a successor to the medieval utopias such as Cockaygne, or Rabelais's *Abbey of Thélème* (published in 1567), where one of the main advantages was that women were not chaste – but I suspect that these latter were not written from a *feminist* viewpoint!

Clearly one of the reasons for the conservatism about women and marriage was the problem of children. Efficient contraception changes the basis of women's role entirely, but there are not many post-Pill utopias written by men. Interestingly, Aldous Huxley's dystopia, *Brave New World*, presents liberated female sexuality as repellant and destructive of proper (romantic) love relationships between the sexes. However, the possibility of feminist utopias has been broached in the last 15 years by writers such as Firestone, Leguin, Lessing and Piercey. There is no standard feminist utopia – but economic independence and freedom from the necessity to bear children, except voluntarily, are important features of all these writers' ideal societies. Most, however, emphasise the close relation between women and the children they choose to have, and their greater capacity to form loving relationships with men when freed from economic necessity and the artificial constraints of marriage.

In the wider context of sexual relations, there is a great divergence of utopian proposals. The popularity of travellers' tales gave Enlightenment thinkers an excuse to criticise the sexual mores of their own societies; the lives of 'noble savages' were often presented as utopian. Diderot graphically describes the customs of free love among the Tahitians in his spoof traveller's tale, *Supplement to the Voyage of Bougainville* (published in 1796) and criticises the artificiality and hypocrisy of decadent Europe in sexual matters. The decline of Christianity and the consequent rejection of the view that man is inherently sinful and his animal instincts bad, enfranchised thinkers to explore and applaud these instincts. The French have often considered the Marquis de Sade a utopian writer (1): each fortified castle given over to sexual experiment is a mini-utopia, although, given that torture features prominently, his inventions do not seem to fulfil the utopian requirement of happiness for all. Sade argued that to deny Nature's demands was itself wickedness: virtue was to give free rein to all our sexual desires, even when these involved harming others. But for Sade, as for Freud, the sexual instinct was fundamentally anti-social, tending to anarchy and the destruction of civilisation.

Perhaps for this reason, Sade's sexual rituals were curiously permeated by rules. This is also true of his contemporaries, Morelly and Restif de la Bretonne, who drew up strict codes of law governing sex and marriage. For example, girls who refused to marry the partner given to them by society would be allocated to blind men or cripples; young men could not sleep openly with their wives until they were 35, but must steal by night into their parents' houses to do so. (Morelly was evidently unsure whether Nature was a prude or a sensualist, as he later wrote the *Basiliade*, portraying a sexually free and sensuous society.) Nearly all utopians from Plato onwards recognise implicitly or explicitly that sexuality is a public, not a private, matter, a revelation which leads either to puritanism (which is usually synonymous with severe restrictions on women viewed, as in the most primitive cultures, as the source of evils which promiscuous sex unleashes) or to curious forms of liberality. Fourier, who falls into the latter category, describes a utopia given over entirely to sexual activity, which is publicly organised so that everyone can achieve the maximum satisfaction of their desires, however bizarre. Specially gifted lovers are obliged to give their favours to the less well endowed for part of the time. For Fourier, sex fulfils the same socialising and unifying principle that work might in an ideal society, bringing people together, generating bonds of love and friendship, while the emphasis on public sexual activity avoids the social disruption which illicit free love might bring about. This appropriation of sex by the public sector has, of course, been viewed as yet another example of the interfering and authoritarian nature of utopian states, and further evidence for this conviction is provided by the eugenicist utopias, from Plato onwards. However, I think that there could be ways of making sexual activity less private and secret which enhance, rather than destroy, sexuality, and that Fourier and modern feminist utopians are seeking these, and are not trying to make the State into chaperone and bedfellow.

The impact of utopian social proposals

The impact of utopian proposals for social change is even harder to chart than that of economic proposals because their social innovations are, as we have seen, so divergent. Many utopian ideas have, however, become common currency and have come to form part of the climate of opinion which slowly brings about social reform. On the question of women, some feminists have undoubtedly drawn on earlier utopian ideas of economic independence and communal child-rearing, but their analysis of the causes of women's oppression is infinitely more sophisticated than that offered by any earlier (male) utopian; but then, utopians propose rather than analyse. With regard to marriage, even today we still display the same conservative reluctance as most earlier utopians to abandon the institution despite increasingly conclusive evidence (*vide* the divorce rate) that lifelong monogamy is an unattainable ideal, and maybe no ideal at all: this is equally true of communist societies. The idea of breeding a pure, superior race, originally advanced by Plato in relation to his Guardians and revived by various other utopians since the interest in evolution and genetics of the nineteenth century, has had devastating social effects in this century in Nazi Germany and South Africa, for example, although the cult of eugenics should not be blamed exclusively on utopian writers. It is surprising that most 'revolutionary' societies have taken a strict line on sexual relations, and often an illiberal line on the role of women, while the unreformed, non-utopian West has moved closer to Fourier's free-love ideal, though in truly liberal piecemeal fashion, and with a great deal of resistance from many quarters.

Recent utopias

Finally, I shall consider briefly some instances of how the experience of attempts to implement utopian ideas may have influenced current utopian thinking. First, the failure of communist societies to achieve anything recognisably utopian has evoked a large variety of responses from socialist idealists. There are the apologists and the revisionists; there was Bloch who re-emphasised the 'hot current', the utopian element in Marx's thought, in his 'philosophy of hope'. There are those who, like the disillusioned French students in 1968, turn back to the utopian socialists whom Marx dismissed for a new, non-Marxist vision of the ideal society. At present there is an emphasis on action, spontaneity and situationism, in defiance of the theories and utopias of the past which have misled us, and this has produced an anti-intellectual, anti-theoretical climate of opinion not conducive to the invention of new utopias. (But maybe this needs some qualification; many utopias *were* written by individuals with scant theoretical apparatus, autodidacts such as Fourier, who simply had visions of the perfect society.) And there are those like Goodman and Marcuse who have tried to build on these dilemmas and write new eclectic and open-ended utopias which reflect the distaste of the young for the 'final solutions' of past thinkers.

Secondly, the observation (rather than the experience) of communist societies in operation has had a profound effect on feminist thinking and has led to the 'socialist feminist or radical feminist' debate. The failure of communist societies to destroy traditional and oppressive attitudes towards women or to give them equal opportunities in the economic or political sphere has led some writers to reject socialism entirely, while others engage in rewriting Marxism to give women their due. The feminist utopias which I have mentioned are founded on 'socialistic' (as opposed to capitalist) principles, but are far more anarchist in their account of social organisation, and justifiably scornful of political structures. But they do invoke some of the virtues which earlier utopians applauded, such as personal integrity, harmony and the resolution of social conflicts by discussion rather than aggression.

To take a final example, there is the phenomenon of Nozick – whom, in other contexts, I would not honour with the label 'utopian'. Nozick can be identified as the most recent adherent to the 'improved capitalism' school of utopians, and he supports and embellishes his ideal with neo-classical economic arguments. His utopian proposal is fundamentally one of reversion to a free-market principle for the organisation of society. Rational self-interest is legitimised and enfranchised and the present obstacles to the free interplay of rewards and talents are to be removed. He envisages a multitude of small communities with free entrance and exit; the individual calculates whether to join or leave a community on the basis of what it offers him and communities likewise accept or reject would-be entrants on the basis of their potential contributions. The utopian nature of this scheme lies not in the quality of the individual communities (all of which appeal to some people and not to others) but in each individual's having the power to choose and to experiment with the Good Life. Utopia is having a choice between utopias. In theory each community would be perfect of its kind, thanks to the operation of the maximising instincts (just as in economic theory each firm produces an optimum level of output) but, given that individuals have different tastes and skills, a variety of communities is needed so that everyone can maximise his/her own good (13).

I think that Nozick was influenced by seeing attempted utopian experiments in two ways: first, positively, by the commune movement of the 1960s which seemed to offer the paradigm setting for maximising personal satisfaction and freedom. Secondly, he was negatively influenced by the attempts to modify capitalism in a socialist direction, attempts which seem, to those of a conservative turn of mind, to distort or destroy all the idealistic suppositions of classical and neo-classical economics and to lead to disaster. In reaction to this, he chooses an ultra-free, free-market society and relies on rational choice theory (closely related to economic consumer theory of choice) to prove that this could produce the optimal solution for everyone. Out of the liberal and mildly socialist developments of America in the 1960s emerged the new Adam Smith of utopian theory.

As I have already suggested, I think that utopians propose rather than analyse. Their relation to social theory is like that of the poet who rhapsodises on the beauty of a garden to the gardener who knows how to create it. Many utopians of the last two centuries were not highly educated or cultured; their visions of the Good Society expressed, simply and almost symbolically, their desire for freedom, justice, democracy and other ideals. It is left to other writers to explicate theoretically the content of these utopias or to turn them into political manifestos. In other words, the impact of utopias is at least a two-stage process, and the utopian needs disciples with different skills. Today, however, with the burgeoning of academic institutions and norms and the general emphasis on professional expertise, we have almost forgotten the first stage, the utopian idea, to concentrate on the second and later stages – theorisation and policy-making. There are lots of highly trained gardeners but no poets to inspire them, so inevitably they concentrate on weeding, watering and pruning.

References

1. Barthes, R., *Sade, Fourier, Loyola*, Editions du Seuil, Paris 1970.
2. Chavannes, A., *The Future Commonwealth* (1892) in Negley & Patrick.
3. Davis, J.C., *Utopia & the Ideal Society*, Cambridge University Press, 1981.
4. Fourier, F.C.M., *The Utopian Vision of Charles Fourier: selected texts*, ed. J. Beecher & R. Bienvenue, Cape, London 1972.
5. Godwin, W., *An Enquiry Concerning Political Justice* (1793) abridged & ed. K. Codell Carter, Clarendon Press, Oxford 1971.
6. Goodwin, B., 'Grande Bretagne: une culture de la passivité', *Esprit* 12, 1979.
7. Hertzka, T., *Freeland* (1891) in Negley & Patrick.
8. Macnie, J., *The Diothas* (1883) in Negley & Patrick.
9. Marcuse, H., *Essay on Liberation*, Penguin, Harmondsworth 1969.
10. Marx, K., *Karl Marx: early texts*, ed. D. McLellan, Blackwell, Oxford 1972.
11. More, Thomas, *Utopia* (1615) trans. P. Turner, Penguin, Harmondsworth 1965.
12. Negley G. & Patrick, J.M., (eds) *The Quest for Utopia*, Doubleday, N.Y. 1952.
13. Nozick, R., *Anarchy, State & Utopia*, Blackwell, Oxford 1974.
14. Plato, *Republic*, trans. H.D.P. Lee, Penguin, Harmondsworth, 1955.
15. Rousseau, J-J., *A Discourse on the Origins of Inequality* (1755) trans. G.D.H. Cole, Dent, London 1913.
16. Saint-Simon, C.H. de, *Oeuvres de Claude-Henri de Saint-Simon*, 6 vols, Paris 1966.

8

Utopias: the Technological and Educational Dimension

W.H.G. Armytage

Eluding constraints

I find it suggestive that the first person to volunteer to have the genital glands of a monkey grafted to him when his own had ceased to function was an engineer, and that the second was a Catholic priest. By so doing both were decisively rejecting the euthanasic practices of the inhabitants of Hythloday's island. They also indicated that all utopias have a time reference, and the time reference of present utopias now includes the engineering of the human frame as well as the natural environment. 'Spare-part surgery' seems a rather inelegant version of Popper's 'piecemeal engineering' but it serves. With one in five previously childless American couples now able to have children and with an artificial heart working outside the body of a Utah patient, the engineering of humans has become a major industry apart from spare-part surgery.

The engineer was seen by Levi-Strauss (22) as always trying to make his way out of, or going behind the constraints imposed by, a particular state of civilisation, while others, by inclination or necessity, remain within them. So engineers have to be utopian: as Lakoff (20) observed, 'in no actual society is scientific or technological knowledge considered to be a sufficient source of moral or legal authority; and since the exercise of power entails considerations of group and national interest, as well as representation and legitimacy, there is little reason to expect the rise of outright technocracy'.

Sixteen years ago I myself outlined the activities of US engineers in Russia in *The Rise of the Technocrats* (1964) as a good example of such 'Eutopeans' in action. For not only did they represent unprejudiced third parties concerned only with the operation of physical laws, but their plans were developed from outside the frame of reference, enabling them, as Buckminster Fuller later (8b) observed, to act as

...entless robots ... jamming ahead with the work, irrespective of persons' feelings or local precedence'.

One can, like Karl Mannheim (26) put this in another way. 'By calling everything utopian that goes beyond the present existing order', he wrote 'one sets at rest the anxiety that might arise from the relative utopias that are realisable in another order.'

This dedication and single-mindedness of engineers was perhaps best expressed by Albert Speer, Hitler's armaments chief, who confessed that he exploited the technicians' often blind devotion to their task. In their 'apparent moral neutrality they were without scruples about their activities' so that 'the more technical the world imposed on them by the war, the more dangerous was their indifference to the direct consequences of their "anonymous activities" ' (37a). Speer's predecessor in World War I, Walter Rathenau, was also a German engineer-statesman whose two books *In Days to Come* (1921) and *The New Society* (1921) bore the imprint of Rathenau's twenty-two years service with the Allgemeine Elektrizitäts Gesellschaft. Unlike Speer, who half-hoped to emulate him, Rathenau formed a Democratic party based on ideas of industrial self-government with employee participation rather than wholesale nationalisation as in England after 1945.

Unfortunately Rathenau was a Jew suspected of internationalism, and he was shot on his way to his office in June 1922. That office was the Ministry of Reconstruction. With his death, it (and the government) disintegrated and the French occupied the Ruhr (18).

Speer was reported in 1981 as still arguing that 'moral sensitivities are being suppressed everywhere and the human factor is being ubiquitously degraded by technology ... obsessed with performance goals, devoured by personal ambition, people still tend to see human events in the technocratic terms of efficiency. This fundamental program still exists unchanged in our achievement society.' Speer reserved the adjective 'utopian' for the schemes of Ohlendorf at the time of the collapse of Nazi Germany.

The quest for efficiency

Efficiency, though energy, is the propulsive E before the Eutopia – or 'better place' – envisioned by the first engineer to figure in what is now called a futopia or scenario of the future: Bulwer-Lytton's *The Coming Race* (1871). This novel so delighted Bernard Shaw in his boyhood that he adopted the power of Vril for his own purposes in *Back to Methuselah* and in *Heartbreak House*.

Shaw had been the employee of an electrical company then seeking rights of way for their lines, so I find it particularly relevant that a later employee of the General Electric Company of America – Kurt

Vonnegut – should have provided a scenario of a society run by computerised robots. Published over 30 years ago, *Player Piano* (1952) is a remarkable extrapolation of the needs of society being estimated, determined, and provided by the Computer EPICAC. Jobs are determined by IQs, and those with low scores are enrolled in the Recreation and Reclamation Corps – known as the 'Reeks and Wrecks'. The founder of Vonnegut's Ilium is a figure like Albert Speer – a war-time director of America's industrial resources who carried over his war-time activities into peacetime.

Player Piano is a computopia. This reminds me that More's *Utopia* was translated into Japanese a hundred years ago – in 1883 – but was proscribed by the Japanese Home Ministry thirty-seven years later because of its dangerous words (42).

The conflict between the father and son as depicted in *Player Piano* had developed by 1963 into Koestler's 'merry civil war' between Eggheads and Engineers. And it was a civil war which the engineers seemingly could not help provoking. 'When you see something that is technically sweet,' said Robert Oppenheimer, 'you go ahead and do it and then argue about what to do about it only after you have had your technical success. That is the way it was with atomic power' (12, p.368).

Or, as Admiral Rickover had framed in his office:

> Our doubts are traitors
> And make us lose the good we oft might win
> By fearing the attempt (33).

That these lines came from *Measure for Measure* makes them all the more apt to an engineer. Even the horrors of Treblinka required technicians and sober bureaucrats to carry them through. The same accent on concentration for efficiency can be found in the utopian fantasies of King C. Gillette, the razor king, who went to great lengths to deny that his schemes for a People's Corporation could be so interpreted. 'As you read these pages' he confessed 'you will no doubt shrug your shoulders and say "A pleasant Utopian dream" ... I ask the reader to withhold criticism until he has read Chapter XI' (11, p. 12).

Utopia transposed in the skies

Buckminster Fuller was, with Desmond Morris, Dr Spock and the two editors of *The People's Almanac*, a respondent in the symposium on utopias conducted by the *Almanac* in the 1970s, in which it listed the leading theoretical utopias, as well as the attempted utopias, throughout history (43). But in the latest edition of the *Almanac*, published in 1981, the utopian section has disappeared and been replaced by eleven 'planets' devised by science-fiction writers over the last two decades, whereas the utopias previously listed were devised over the last two-and-a-half millennia.

It is significant that one of the 'planets' in the 1981 *Almanac* is Frank Herbert's *Dune* (1965) a desert world, reforested, eco-synthesised and terraformed. Such planetary engineering as a prelude to colonisation is already being envisaged. There have been projects for mining the asteroids (30), the reclamation of the Sahara and the redistribution of the waters of Siberia by reversing the flow of the rivers from feeding the Arctic Ocean to Kazakhstan and the now critical Caspian Sea (23). The ecological consequences of the latter may well be disastrous if the polar ice-cap melts as a result. The US Central Intelligence Agency has already pointed this out (14).

Just as the American frontier generated many 'Backwoods Utopias' (as Arthur Bestor called them) so the frontier of space is eliciting the macro-engineering of the infra-structure of tomorrow (4).

Ford or Buddha?

Such projects are what seemingly arouses eggheads like Theodore Roszak (35b) to excoriate what he calls 'the myth of objective consciousness' and to accuse science of 'corrupting the gnosis'. The same criticisms come from those who label the US Army Corps of Engineers as 'public enemy number one' for their role in accelerating the destruction of the United States as a land capable of supplying human life by building dams and flooding farmlands to sustain the 200 million plus inhabitants of the country who consume the equivalent of 4 billion Indians. For though India has 540 million people to the USA's 230 million, the average Indian contributes very little to the destruction of Indian land whereas the American produces from one third to one half of the world's industrial pollution of the ocean.

Statements like this remind me of Aldous Huxley's discovery of the life and work of Henry Ford in a library of a ship travelling between Java and Borneo in 1926. He wrote at the time:

> To one fresh from India and Indian spirituality, Indian dirt and religion, Ford seems a greater man than Buddha. In Europe, on the other hand, and still more no doubt in America, the way of Gautama has all the appearance of the way of Salvation. One is all religion until one visits a really religious country. Then, one is all for drains, machinery and the minimum wage. To travel is to discover that everybody is wrong (16).

Moreover he put his finger on it again when he told George Orwell that *1984* was destined to modulate into the nightmare of a world having more resemblance to that which he imagined in *Brave New World*. 'The change', he went on, 'will be brought about as the result of a felt need for increased efficiency'. Huxley's own protest in *Island* (1962) is actually a utopia, whereas *Brave New World* (1930) is a dystopia.

Walden Two

Ford was utopian too in believing that it was more efficient to have a world at peace than at war. So was B.F. Skinner, whose *Walden Two* (36) was written as a utopia instead of just another scientific paper marred by 'foot and note disease'. In it Skinner indicated what has been undoubtedly the greatest utopian preoccupation of all: education. The production of the new men and the new women of the future has preoccupied utopographers since Plato, particularly in America where the genre has exfoliated. As Dr Leete says in Bellamy's *Looking Backward* (1888), 'to educate some to the highest degree and leave the mass wholly uncultivated' was to make 'the gap between them almost like that between two different species, which have no means of communication'. Leete compared education for the wealthy with its lack of orientation as incentive to putting them 'up to the neck in a bog', the educator 'solacing himself with a smelling bottle'. Nor was Skinner the first American utopographer to depict operant conditioning. Working under the name of Grigsby, Jack Adams in *Negua: or the Problem of the Ages* (13) depicts controlled environments for pregnant mothers to influence the foetus, while similar foetal education was the subject of William Windsor's *Loma* (45). Mothers' clubs exist on M.C. Edson's *Solaris Farm* (1900) with kindergartens from the first to the fourth year. The latter was recently described by Roehmer (34, p. 121) as 'one of the best examples of how Utopian authors might develop a whole personality' and 'break down associations between learning and a classroom environment'.

'A student *fired* by a *desire* for a career in engineering', continues Roehmer (p. 123), 'would *thrive* in Utopia, but what in fact would become of a child fascinated by Latin and Greek?' Roehmer also points out that twenty of the heroes of the 154 or so American utopian novels published in the last twelve years of the nineteenth century were either engineers, inventors, mineralogists or scientists. But it was a psychologist trained in the literary arts who demonstrated that even human behaviour itself was capable of modification through positive reinforcement. The idea was then accepted, and B.F. Skinner was asked to investigate the training of pigeons by his reinforcement techniques for use during the war. His rejected thesis having not only been accepted but published just before the war, Skinner now decided, like Galton, to resort to the strategy of publishing a utopia to indicate how positive reinforcement could improve education. So in 1945 he wrote *Walden Two*. If the name was reminiscent of Thoreau, the theme was reflexive rather than reflective. There was no trial-and-error freedom but rather the same positive reinforcements that he had found, applied to all biological behaviour.

Just as John Henry Noyes established Oneida Community to test, among other things, the eugenic ideas of Francis Galton, so in 1967 a group began to test Skinner's idea of positive reinforcement at Twin Oaks, Virginia. Five years later one of the participants, Kathleen Kinkade (19), published a report on it with a preface by Skinner himself. The experiment had one serious omission: there were no children, and children were the obvious subjects for such operant conditioning.

Bellamy's *Looking Backward* generated a flush of fervent pro and con Bellamy utopias; Skinner's critics took to the professional journals prompting a supporter of Skinner's, Kenneth MacCorquodale (24) to describe their objections as basically those that hereditarians have always used against environmentalists, in Chomsky's case the deep mysterious structures in the human psyche that account for languages. Nevertheless Skinner still supported testing certain fundamental ideas in other small communities which he suggested could be made similarly experimental by monitoring the results of each social change to see how beneficial it is to the individual or the community. Paying attention to the consequence of our actions would be an advance on making changes and assuming that certain outcomes would occur without collecting data to see if they actually did.

For positive and negative reinforcement *can* be studied, provided we realise how ambiguous is the so-called freedom in which people have to choose their own course of action and the dignity achieved by a person who achieves socially admirable goals. Though control can be constructive and produce positive outcomes, it is usually seen as aversive and punitive. Indeed in Skinner's non-punitive utopia, control is maintained by reinforcing good behaviour, what he called 'positive reinforcement'.

Perhaps Skinner realised the analogy between his obedient pigeon and the paraclete when he told an interviewer in 1967: 'If I could do it all over again, I'd never teach those pigeons to play "Ping Pong" ' (15), for the film of the obedient pigeon made it look as if he had the Holy Ghost under his control. It might well have seemed so to others, one of whom in the same year, 1967, described the call to build the city of God on earth as a 'delirious ideal stamped with the madness of logic'. 'I cannot hope', wrote Thomas Molnar (28), 'to rid the world of the Utopian temptation; this would be itself Utopian.' This is perhaps the best endorsement of how permanent the idea had become.

Nay-sayers and yea-sayers

One is reminded of the forecast made fifty years ago by Oswald Spengler (38): 'The accustomed luxury of the white workman in comparison with the coolie may well be his doom. The labour of the white itself comes to be unwanted. The huge masses of men centered in the Northern coal areas are faced with the probability of going under in the competition.'

Critics of technology who make absolute the dilemmas and have no answers short of apocalyptic solutions ('stop the world, I want to get off') reminded Daniel Bell of Goethe, who rejected Newton's optics on the grounds that the microscope and the telescope distorted the human scale and confused the mind. And, as he confessed, it was not an optimistic bias in him, but an optimistic bias in science and technology. Bell discovered five dimensions in what he called the post-industrial society:

(1) the change from goods to service production;
(2) the pre-eminence of the scientific and technical class;
(3) the centrality of theoretical knowledge as the source of innovation and policy formation;
(4) control of technology and technological assessment;
(5) the creation of a new intellectual technology: systems analysis, operational research, and decision-theory.

Because, as he succinctly put it, 'the technocratic mode reduces social arrangements to the criterion of technological efficiency, therefore it relies principally on credentials as a means of selecting individuals for places in society'. These 'entry devices' to the system he described as 'mechanical at worst or specific minimum achievement at best' (3a).

This virtually endorsed Illich's dismissal of much modern education as 'tooling for the environment that the rich countries, socialist and capitalist have engineered', and seemed to justify his case for 'skill exchanges' and 'reference services' rather than schools as we know them (17; 10).

It also reminds us of the real value of the whole school of utopian educational writers from Paul Goodman (*Growing Up Absurd*, 1960) to P. Freiere (7) as 'a spur to debate on the constraints that would-be educational reformers must recognise if their plans are to be more than pious dreams' (32).

The future of the art

Will engineers continue to exhibit the Speer Syndrome in the future? Student engineers were described in a paper read at the American Academy of Arts and Sciences in December 1958 as uncooperative, narrow-minded, materialistic, security seeking, prestige oriented, parochial, authoritarian, ultra-masculine and anti-intellectual. These qualities actually seemed to be strengthened while they were under training (41). A student of the impact of occupations upon values found that engineers came 13th out of 16 other professions graded on an index of faith and trust in people, 16th out of 18 in their concern for people, and of high consciousness in desiring extrinsic rewards for them. Indeed, in Terman's concept mastery tests (designed for capacity to deal with ideas on an abstract level, to think divergently via analogy and converge logically), independent inventors were at the bottom of the scale at 50.8 whereas the highest at 156.4 were creative writers. Electronic engineers and scientists were at 94.5 and military officers at 60.3 (25). The latest utopia sketched by an American, Alvin Toffler (40) (who actually calls it a 'practopia') is not by an engineer. It envisages a future built round the home, which he sees increasing in importance as a work base, where a work-together family unit would inhabit an 'electronic cottage', sometimes expanded to take outsiders as well. Telelectronics will also make possible greater political participation on issues as they arise in the local council's agenda. Yet as Toffler himself says:

> Today it takes an act of courage to suggest that our biggest factories and office towers may, within our lifetime, stand half empty reduced to use as ghostly warehouses or converted into living space. Yet this is precisely what the new mode of production makes possible: a return to cottage industry on a new, higher, electronic basis ...

References

1. Averner, H.H. & Macelroy, R.D. *On the Habitability of Mars – an approach to planetary ecosynthesis* NASA SP-414 Springfield VA: National Technical Information Service, 1976.
2. Asimov, Isaac, *The High Frontier*, Bantam Books, New York 1978.
3. Bell, Daniel (a) *The Coming of the Post-Industrial Society: a venture in social forecasting*, Heinemann, London 1974. (b) 'Science as the image of the future society', *Science* 4, April 1975.
4. Davidson, F.P., Giacolletto, L.J., Salkeld, R. (*et al.*) 'Engineering and the infrastructure of tomorrow', *AAAS Selected Symposia Series*, Westview Press, Boulder 1978.
5. Ehricke, K.A., *Space Light: space industrial enhancement of the solar option*, California Space Global Corporation, La Jolla 1978.

6. Ellul, J., *The Technological Society* (translated by John Wilkinson, introduction by R.K. Merton), Knopf, New York.

7. Freiere, P., *Education for Control Consciousness*, Seabury Press, New York 1973.

8. Fuller, R. Buckminster, (a) *Utopia or Oblivion*, Bantam Books, New York 1972, p. 217. (b) *Critical Path*, St. Martins Press, New York 1981, p. 299.

9. Galtung, J. 'Schooling and future society', *School Review* 83, 1975, pp. 533-68.

10. Gartner, A., *After Deschooling What? Ivan Illich pro and con*, New York Social Policy, 1973.

11. Gillette, King C., *The People's Corporation*, Boni & Liveright, New York 1924, p. 127.

12. Gowing, Margaret, *Britain and Atomic Energy*, Macmillan, London 1964, p. 368.

13. Grigsby, Alcanoan (Jack Adams), *Negua the Problem of the Ages*, Kansas Equity, Topeka 1900.

14. Hallacy, D.J., *Ice or Fire: surviving climatic change*, Harper and Row, New York 1978.

15. Hall, Mary Harrington, 'An interview with "behaviorist" B.F. Skinner', *Psychology Today* 1, 1967, pp. 21-33, 68-71.

16. Huxley, Aldous, *Jesting Pilate: the diary of a journey*, Chatto and Windus. In America published as *An Intellectual Holiday*, Doran 1928, p. 241.

17. Illich, Ivan, *Deschooling Society*, Harper & Row, New York 1971, pp. 172-3.

18. Kessler, Harry, *Walter Rathenau, His Literary Work*, G. Howe, London 1929.

19. Kinkade, Kathleen, *A Walden Two Experiment*, William Morrow, New York 1973.

20. Lakoff, Sanford, 'Scientists, technologists and political power', in J. Spiegel-Roesing & D. de Solla Price (eds). *Science, Technology and Society: a cross disciplinary perspective*, London 1972, p. 371.

21. Leacock, Stephen, *Afternoons in Utopia*, Dodd, Mead and Co., New York 1932, pp. 159-60.

22. Levi-Strauss, Claude, *The Savage Mind*, Chicago 1966.

23. L'Vovich, M., 'Turning the Siberian Waters South', *New Scientist*, 21, 1968, pp. 834-6.

24. MacCorquodale, K., 'On Chomsky's review of Skinner's verbal behaviors', *Journal of the Experimental Analysis of Behaviors* 3, 1970, pp. 83-9.

25. Mackinnon, D.W., 'Fostering creativity in students of engineering', *Journal of Engineering in Education* 52, 1961, no. 2.

26. Mannheim, Karl, *Ideology and Utopia* (trans. Louis Wirth & Edward Shils) Routledge, London 1936, pp. 192-9.

27. Medawar, Sir Peter, 'On the effecting of all things possible', *The Advancement of Science* 26, 1969, pp. 1-9.

28. Molnar, T., *Utopia: the perennial heresy*, Sheed & Ward, New York 1967.

29. Oberg, James E., *New Earths: transforming other planets for humanity*, Stackpole Books, Harrisburg, Pa. 1981.

30. O'Leary, B., *The Fertile Stars*, Everest House, New York 1981.

31. O'Neill, Gerald K. (a) *The High Frontier*, William Morrow, New York 1977. (b) *2081: a hopeful view of the human future*, Jonathan Cape, London

1981, p. 63.

32. Paulston, R.G., 'Social and educational change: conceptual framework', *Comparative Education Review* 21, 1977, p. 390.

33. Pringle, Peter & Spiegelman, Michael, *The Nuclear Barons*, Joseph, London 1982, p. 151.

34. Roemer, Kenneth M., *The Obsolete Necessity: America in utopian writings*, Kent State University Press, 1976, p. 121.

35. Roszak, Theodore (a) *The Making of the Counter Culture*, Doubleday & Co., New York 1969. (b) 'The Monster and the Titan: science, knowledge and gnosis', *Daedalus*, summer 1974, pp. 17-34.

36. Skinner, B.F., *Walden Two*, Macmillan, New York 1948.

37. Speer, Albert (a) *The Third Reich*, Weidenfeld and Nicolson, London 1970, pp. 211-12. (b) *Infiltration*, Macmillan, New York 1981, pp. 81-2.

38. Spengler, Oswald, *Man and Technics*, trans. C.F. Atkinson (1932), p. 102, A.A. Knopf, New York 1982.

39. Steiner, Jean-Frances, *Treblinka*, Simon & Schuster, New York 1968, p. 7.

40. Toffler, Alvin, *The Third Wave*, William Morrow, New York 1980, pp. 210-23.

41. Trow, Martin, 'Some implications of the social origins of engineers', *AAAS*, Dec. 1955.

42. Uyehare, Cecil B., *Left-Wing Social Movements in Japan: an annotated bibliography*, C.E. Tuttle, Rutland, Vermont 1959.

43. Wallechinsky, D. & Wallace, I. (a) *The People's Almanac*, Doubleday, New York 1975, pp. 1418-37. (b) *The People's Almanac*, William Morrow, New York 1981, pp. 345-52.

44. Weart, Spencer R. & Szilard, Gertrude White, *Scientists in Power*, Harvard University Press, 1979.

45. Windsor, William, *Loma: a city of Venus*, Windsor S. Lewis, St. Paul, Minn. 1897.

9

Utopia in Three Dimensions: the Ideal City and the Origins of Modern Design

Robert Fishman

From Filarete's Sforzinda of the 1460s to Le Corbusier's *Ville radieuse* of the 1930s, the great ideal cities of architectural history have formed a special category within the utopian tradition. Like other utopias, the ideal city is a working plan for the total transformation of society in order to achieve a natural harmony – *the* natural harmony – of man, society, and the environment. But one crucial difference divides the ideal city from other utopias. Almost every utopian author devotes at least some attention to the physical setting of the new society, and many provide highly original solutions. For the creators of ideal cities, however, reconstructing the environment is not one task among many in the utopian project. Rebuilding the city, rather, is the first and foremost step in re-forming society. It is the 'master key', in Ebenezer Howard's phrase, from which all other social changes follow. To build the ideal city is to create the utopian society.

Seen in this perspective, the ideal city would appear to be an unusually rigorous expression of the deep-seated belief that has long inspired architects and planners: that their buildings can change society (cynics have called this 'the doctrine of salvation by bricks alone'). Architecture is surely a visionary profession – does any other group devote so much effort and imagination to the detailed depiction of structures that do not exist? But the architectural imagination is usually content to work within the bounds established by the powers that be. Even the most ambitious and socially conscious architectural projects – the workers' housing of Weimar Germany, for example – respect the property relations and political limits of the established order.

The ideal city, however, is a plan for total transformation. It does not challenge the limits imposed by power so much as ignore them.

This is implicit in the mode of presentation favoured for the ideal city. Characteristically – in common with other utopias – it is presented as already complete. Its structures form a perfect whole which gives no hint of development or change. The ideal city has no history; indeed, it is an escape from history.

Invariably, however, there is one conspicuous tie to the realities of the present: an appeal to an all-powerful patron to build the new city. In the number and variety of his appeals, Le Corbusier took this aspect of the ideal city to its extremes. He began in the 1920s by courting large corporations – the plan for Paris is named after the Voisin aircraft and automobile company. At the same time, he proposed a similar plan to Stalinist Russia, and, in the 1930s, to Mussolini's Italy. During the early forties, he believed Marshal Pétain would erect his *Ville radieuse*, but this did not prevent him from presenting the same ideas to De Gaulle after Pétain's fall. Finally, the Indian state of Punjab built a partial version at Chandigarh.

However opportunistic his efforts, Le Corbusier was following a kind of tradition among planners of ideal cities. The French architect Claude-Nicolas Ledoux (1736-1806) put forward his ideal city at Chaux to the governments of Louis XVI, the Committee of Public Safety, the Directory, and Napoleon. And Filarete designed Sforzinda for the everlasting glory of Francesco Sforza, Duke of Milan.

Such ready allegiances might seem to cast doubt on whether the ideal city is a true utopia at all. But these repeated appeals to authority must be understood in their true context. These planners were fond of depicting themselves as intimates of the powerful whose plans proceeded directly from government command. Ledoux, for example, combined his ideal city drawings with the drawings of a salt works he had been commissioned to design, making it appear that both the salt works and the ideal city had proceeded from government commission (7, pp. 191-210). Filarete span out an elaborate fantasy of the building of Sforzinda, showing himself on terms of the closest friendship with the Duke and his family. Le Corbusier often interrupted his treatises on urbanism for long series of endorsements from powerful people, most of dubious authenticity.

These fantasies of power merely reveal that the archetypal creator of the ideal city is in fact an isolated individual, so far removed from power that the very elaboration and perfection of his plans is a kind of substitution for the opportunity to engage in any real building. In this context, the all-powerful patron is the fantasy-counterpart of the isolated, powerless planner. In the utopian planner's imagination, the political leader – whether good or bad – is simply the 'contractor' who erects the city according to plan. Once the city is built, its very structure will produce social harmony without coercion, indeed, without politics. The leader becomes irrelevant, for freedom is built into the very stones of the city.

The appeal to the powerful patron is thus a kind of utopian opportunism. More troubling, perhaps, than this opportunism is the kind of freedom which is supposed to replace politics. The ideal city raises the classic utopian dilemma of whether the freedom of a perfectly planned society is freedom at all. More specifically, we might fear that behind the promise of total architecture that the ideal city offers there lurks the threat of total power.

Such fears would have little meaning if these ideal cities had remained the personal obsessions of a few architects of genius. In fact, many have proved to be enormously influential in shaping our cities and in forming the underlying assumptions of modern planning practice. In this paper I shall examine in detail three such ideal cities: Filarete's Sforzinda; Ledoux's Chaux; and Le Corbusier's *Ville radieuse*. One might assume that these and other ideal cities achieved their impact in spite of their utopianism. I would argue the contrary. I believe it was precisely their total design; their deep connection between aesthetic and social change; and their remoteness from any immediate practical application that led to their eventual influence.

For me, the ideal city occupies a vital position in the evolution of urban design. These utopian plans characteristically emerge when a new social order – political, economic, and aesthetic – is just beginning: the early Renaissance, for example, or the early Industrial Revolution. At this early stage the implications of the new order are almost impossible to grasp. The change is too far-reaching to be easily comprehended in the abstract, but scattered examples of the new architecture appear distorted against the background of the old. A vast gap opens between advanced theory – still only poorly defined – and current practice.

This is the hour of the utopian planner. Isolated from power and thus freed from all considerations of practicality, he attempts to comprehend the new order as a coherent whole: the ideal city. In this laboratory of the imagination the complex interrelationships of the new order can be precisely delineated. Urban form in its relationship to both aesthetic and social order; the individual and society as expressed in the functions and design of the city; the new architecture and the new social hierarchy; the relationship between society and nature – all these vast, vague questions are depicted in comprehensive and compelling designs. In one heroic intellectual leap the utopian planner attempts to close the gap between theory and practice, and to *make real* the new city.

The attempt is, of course, doomed to fail, at least in its utopian aspirations. The ideal city is always premature. In an era when men's minds lag behind the rapidly-changing reality, the ideal city is wholly of its time and thus out-of-step with popular and professional thought.

The fantasy of the all-powerful but all-compliant patron is no doubt necessary here; otherwise the ideal city might never have been conceived at all.

Yet precisely when even the most obsessive utopian planner loses hope of seeing his designs realised, the ideal city takes on a new and true life. It becomes an invaluable starting-point in the education of other architects. It teaches planners to see and understand the city in powerful new ways. Its many original features become the inspirations for relatively small-scale but nevertheless highly valuable projects. It permeates the consciousness of succeeding generations.

The result is not the gradual erection of an ideal city. In making use of the designs, other architects necessarily destroy the unity which is at the heart of the utopian aspiration. The idea of total transformation is discarded first, followed by the concept that aesthetic change must be related to social betterment. Pieces of the new utopia are inserted into the structure of the old cities, making the complicated urban fabric even more diverse.

This is the exact opposite of the utopian image of symmetrical, coherent and orderly cities; but I believe that these fragmentary applications are the truest – if most ironic – fulfilments of the ideal city. The city, in Levi-Strauss's phrase, is a 'social work of art', the product not of a single imagination but of a whole society's complicated and contradictory aspirations over time. This diversity is the ultimate source of urban vitality. Nothing is so deadening as relentless purity, as all the attempts to build totally-planned cities have amply demonstrated. In all its partial applications, the ideal city is necessarily fragmented and distorted, but in losing its purity it enters history. The ideal city does not replace all existing cities; it enriches them.

Filarete's Sforzinda

We can see all these principles in action in the first ideal city, Filarete's Sforzinda. Filarete, the pseudonym of the architect and sculptor Antonio Averlino (*c.* 1400-*c.* 1470) put forward his plan at a crucial moment in early Renaissance culture. The first masterpieces of the new architecture had already been built, but they were largely confined to Florence. In Francesco Sforza's Milan, this 'Florentine style' had little support compared to the 'Lombard' or late Gothic. Filarete wrote his *Trattato di architettura* (1461-64), the work in which Sforzinda appears, to show that the new style was not simply one fashion of architecture replacing another. The real greatness of the Florentine work was that it embodied the true principle of order – political, social, and aesthetic – which could bring harmony and beauty to the whole society. This harmony, although present in individual structures, could only be grasped fully in a complete community. In Sforzinda, the ideal city, the new order could be seen and understood as a total transformation of human life.

This great transformation was based on the re-discovery of the Greek idea that the universe is a harmonious cosmos derived from number. Man, made in the image of God, is also a harmonious microcosm, and the human body, correctly understood, is the source of all true proportion. But if man and the universe are both harmonious, human society is full of conflict; the city confused and irregular; the buildings out of proportion with each other and with true principles. The challenge therefore is to reconstruct the city on the basis of those simple but divinely-perfect forms – the circle and the square – which are the basis of both human and universal harmony. Such a city would be as lucid, stable, and well-proportioned as the universe itself. It would be the home of peace and beauty.

This desire for a city as immutable as a square or circle is an aspiration deeply conditioned by the real disorders of the time. Filarete's target is not merely the dense irregularity of the late medieval city but the constant strife of the factions within it. The wheel of fortune, for ever destroying human aspirations to stability, was an obsessive image, not least at the court of Francesco Sforza. Although he was described by his contemporary Pope Pius II as 'one whom Fortune loved', Pius goes on to observe that the Duke's mistress, 'whom he loved passionately, was murdered by his madly jealous wife; his comrades and friends, Troilo and Brunaro, deserted him; another Friend, he convicted of treason and hanged; and he had to bear the treachery of his brother and his son'. (6, p. 129).

Sforzinda would be a city beyond the reach of Fortune. Designed in harmony with the universe, based on the true proportions of the human body, centralised in plan and efficient in function, it would reveal the glory of the new era.

In design, Sforzinda proclaims its perfect symmetry. Its outline is formed out of the two perfect geometrical forms, the circle and the square. The city is star-shaped, its walls defined by two overlapping squares inscribed within a circular moat approximately 3.5 miles in diameter. From each of the sixteen angles in the wall a street runs directly to the central piazza. Filarete suggested that alternate streets should in fact be canals to ease the passage of heavy goods to the centre.

The straightness of the streets is in contrast even with Leone Battista Alberti's *De re aedificatoria* (1450), which still held to the medieval pattern of gently curving streets which give interesting new views to the pedestrian as he moves through the city. Sforzinda is based on the perspective-street, in which the city is experienced as a series of vistas from a fixed central point. This point is the main piazza, dominated by the Ducal Palace with its adjoining law courts and prisons. Centralised power is, of course, the counterpoint of the centralised plan: everything flows from the Duke as the creator and leader of Sforzinda. But the Duke's power, beyond the show of magnificence on which Filarete dwells with enthusiasm, is largely negative. He defends the city and prevents factional strife.

The real emphasis is on those institutions which incline the citizens toward harmony. The cathedral, which faces the ducal palace, is built on a centralised plan which reproduces the symmetry of the city as a whole. As Rudolf Wittkower has remarked of such churches, 'the geometrical pattern will appear absolute, immutable, static, and entirely lucid' (11, p. 7), precisely the values of the city as a whole. Filarete also gives careful attention to education – he favours the orderly pattern of sequential learning championed in Renaissance treatises. There is even a 'House of Virtue and Vice', where virtuous citizens can pursue knowledge in uplifting surroundings while those inclined to dissipation and fornication can also be satisfied once they have braved such discouragements as a low portal inscribed with the words, 'Here enters the troop of pleasure-seekers who will later repent in grief' (1, p. 247).

Sforzinda, however, is primarily a city of trade and skilled craftsmanship, and Filarete does not neglect the needs of those who make up the vast majority of the thirty thousand inhabitants. Adjoining the central piazza is a merchants' piazza, clearly subordinate to the central realm of church and state but nevertheless ingeniously planned to provide access through the canals. Moreover, midway on each of the sixteen streets and canals that lead from the walls to the centre there is placed a small piazza that serves as the centre for the surrounding neighbourhood. There one can find the parish church, food shops, a tavern, public bath and brothel.

Filarete distinguishes between the houses of merchants, artisans, and ordinary workers, but he has little to say about their internal arrangements. This is partly the aristocratic bias of Renaissance culture, but also, as Filarete observes, the people themselves will best know what to do with them. This is indicative of Filarete's general approach to life in his ideal city. He assumes that people will know best how to lead their lives, and he requires neither close supervision of the productive activity of the city nor any drastic reform in family life or morals. The parish church with its centralised plan stands for the divine nature of man in harmony with the universe, but it also stands within sight of the local brothel. Once the urban framework of true order has been created, then the people can be trusted to build a beautiful city in their own way.

Sforzinda, of course, was never begun, and there is no evidence that Duke Francesco ever took it seriously. But other architects did. Copied in manuscript for the great Renaissance libraries, Filarete's work inspired a whole series of fifteenth- and sixteenth-century ideal cities. The star-shaped city received a new impetus when it was discovered that this form is the most efficient for fortifications. Only one symmetrical, star-shaped city was ever built – Palmanova (1599) – largely for military purposes. Although startlingly similar to Filarete's design, there is no evidence that life in Palmanova was particularly ideal.

More significant, I believe, than these full-scale attempts at an ideal city were the fragmentary, 'impure', partial applications which are always the most fruitful product of the utopian effort. Sforzinda helped to inaugurate that Renaissance obsession with creating regular geometric spaces in the midst of the older medieval urban fabric. Perhaps the best example of the application of Filarete's urban forms is the rectangular piazza at Vigevano, built to Filarete's ideal proportions by Bramante for Ludovico il Moro, the son of Francesco Sforza. Many of Filarete's other innovations achieved wide currency, most notably the straight perspective streets which attained their most noble form in the avenues which Domenico Fontana cut through Rome to connect the pilgrimage churches.

So long as these geometrical techniques did not obliterate the complex, irregular pattern of the medieval city, they added a remarkable vitality to European urban planning. Even in so ungeometric a city as seventeenth-century London, Inigo Jones imported the piazza plan and naturalised it at Covent Garden (1631-5). The squares of London continue to contrast agreeably with the invincible irregularity of the rest of the city. Old and new created a harmony of their own – not the mathematically precise relations of Filarete's dreams but the organic harmony of change over time.

Nevertheless, these partial applications could never lead to the original goal of a complete aesthetic and social transformation. The revolutionary hopes once associated with the geometric city were either forgotten or restricted to a more limited sphere. This restriction can be seen in the career of Palladio (1508-80). His 'ideal city' is depicted in the famous 'perspective street' which he designed as permanent scenery for the Teatro Olimpico of Vicenza. But Palladio could have no illusion that such a mathematically ordered city was anything more than a stage set. He turned instead to the villas which the Venetian aristocracy were building as retreats from the city. In this limited context he could create that total symmetry, order, and union with nature that Filarete had hoped to bring to the whole city. The total transformation of society is reduced to a refuge for the happy few who in their 'gardens, fountains, and such like pleasant places ... attain to as much happiness as can be attained here below' (5, p. 18).

Ledoux's Chaux

The ideal of a total transformation of society based on an ideal city did not reappear again until a new principle of order emerged from the Industrial Revolution. This 'second wind' for the ideal city can first be seen not in England where one would expect it but in the work of Claude-Nicolas Ledoux, member of the Royal Academy of Architecture and 'Architecte du Roi' to Louis XV and XVI.

This eminently respectable architect was in 1773 given the commission to design for the royal monopoly a new saltworks at Chaux in the Franche-Comté. In preparing his plans Ledoux educated himself in the details of manufacturing salt, a traditional process but one now carried out on a truly industrial scale. He designed two large factory buildings where saltwater was evaporated in huge vats. Between the factories he placed the Director's office and residence – a common arrangement at the time – and facing the factories in a semi-circle were support buildings including a residence for workers engaged in the round-the-clock manufacturing process.

The project was completed in 1779, but this was not the end of it for Ledoux. Working on his own, he continued to add new structures, superimposing them on the basic plan so that they appeared to be part of the original commission. A second semi-circle made the factory complex into a large oval, and in the 1780s he continued to add a market, church, houses, and a school. By the time of the French Revolution Ledoux had extended his plan into the countryside with residences for foresters, charcoal burners, engineers, and others who supplied the saltworks with vital water and fuel. The architecture took on a more abstract, geometrical character, unlike anything that would be seen until the modern movement of the twentieth century.

At the same time he added plans for institutions of a frankly utopian character: a 'House of Communal Life', a 'House of Ethics', a 'House of Conciliation', even a 'House of Virtue and Vice' similar in function to the one in Sforzinda. Yet he continued to believe that his plan was practicable and that the saltworks would soon be surrounded by an ideal city, the 'City of Chaux'. In 1804 he published his plans under the title *L'Architecture considerée sous le rapport de l'art, des moeurs, et de la legislation*. The book was printed at his own expense, and two years later he died.

The idea which inspired Ledoux and which provides the leitmotiv for this vast obsessive project is that the industrial process can provide the basic principle of order for a just, harmonious, and beautiful society. The relations of co-operation and subordination which guide the factory are precisely those which must guide society as a whole. Similarly, the careful attention to efficient function must extend beyond the factory walls.

For the architect-planner, this means that these principles of functional use of space within the factory must be applied to the city as a whole. This applies not only to such clearly-defined needs as the market-place and the road system, but also to residences and even to schools and cultural institutions. Le Corbusier said 'The house is a machine for living in,' but the thought was clearly in Ledoux's mind by the 1780s.

This 'functionalism' operates not only through the rational use of space, but also through an aesthetic style that impresses itself on the observer. Ledoux was of course drawing on the Enlightenment theory that all our knowledge comes through the senses. Just as a machine uses power to form raw materials, we are 'formed' by our sense impressions for better or for worse. An effective building must therefore do more than provide efficient space for the functions it is intended to house. It must through its aesthetic impact create the mentality that promotes its function.

To some degree Ledoux used the classical orders of architecture to achieve this: the Doric columns on the gatehouse to suggest strength, for example. But towards the end of his life he concentrated on creating his own 'language of architecture' based on the primary forms to communicate his meaning. The pyramids of the gun foundry suggest strength; the 'House of Conciliation', 'a mighty cube rising on a sturdy podium' (2, p. 519), suggests unity; the ascending forms of the 'House of Ethics' suggest man's ascent to justice. This 'speaking architecture' sometimes seems far-fetched, as when the barrel-makers occupy a house shaped like the cross-section of a huge barrel. Nevertheless, it inspired the most revolutionary architecture of the eighteenth century.

The aesthetics of the individual building are of course applied to the ideal city as a whole. Here it is important to note that this 'factory town' proclaims in its open, park-like design, the unity of man with nature. For Ledoux, the discipline of the machine age must find its complement and fulfilment in the direct access to natural beauty. Each worker and his family, though they live in a workers' residence across from the saltworks, have a private garden where Ledoux imagines them spending most of their leisure hours. Not only the middle-class villas but all the communal institutions are set in fields or landscaped gardens. Even the Bourse, modelled on a Greek temple, is for once put in an Arcadian setting worthy of its archetype.

Chaux is far from democratic or egalitarian. The Director's residence is both the symbolic and literal focus of the city. As Anthony Vidler has observed, a spirit of 'surveillance', in Foucault's sense of observation leading to social control, suffuses Chaux (10, pp. 4-20). Everyone, from the workers at the centre to the woodsmen and charcoal burners on the outskirts, is to be brought into the discipline of the factory system. And behind the Director there is the architect-planner. Far more than Filarete, Ledoux is the organiser and even the moral guardian of the community. He is the hidden Director of his ideal city.

Both in its positive and negative aspects, Chaux initiates the great themes of the early industrial utopias. Robert Owen's 'villages of unity and mutual co-operation', though based on the English experience, arrive at the same solution of the industrial problem – the marriage of town and country – as does Ledoux. Fourier, though he starts from very different premises, also arrives at a small-scale rural community as his ideal. Chaux embodies that dream of the 'first industrial revolution' for an organisation of production that leads to co-operation rather than chaos, and that brings man closer to nature and beauty.

But early industrialisation really meant social conflict and the growth of the factory towns. It is even harder to trace the influence of Chaux than of Sforzinda. Its spirit survived best not in any actual utopian experiments but in those attempts to rationalise and humanise the nineteenth-century city: the urban parks movement; workers' housing; and the planned industrial suburb. Finally, at the end of the century, technological changes made possible the re-birth of the ideal of an industrial civilisation based on planned, decentralised cities in close touch with nature. Chaux found its true descendant in Ebenezer Howard's Garden City.

Le Corbusier's Ville radieuse

With the beginning of the twentieth century, we see yet another fundamental change in society giving rise to a new potential for urban and social order. This was the 'second industrial revolution': the mastery of mass production techniques; the internal combustion engine; electricity and oil; and, in construction, the prospect of a new architecture based on steel, reinforced concrete, and glass.

As in the Renaissance and the first industrial revolution, these vast amorphous changes found focus in the minds of a few planners of genius who foresaw the prospect of a new urban and social order. Frank Lloyd Wright and Le Corbusier, for example, interpreted the new order very differently; but both agreed that the cities of their day were the cancers of society, and that new cities, once built, would provide the environment for the true order they saw as inherent in an advanced industrial society.

I shall confine myself to Le Corbusier in this chapter, because, more than anyone else, his work sums up the whole utopian tradition of the ideal city. Like Ledoux and Filarete, he was an isolated figure who was obsessed with the idea that he had the plan which could initiate a new era in history – if only authority would consent to build it. For Le

Corbusier, this idea was that high-rise construction had made possible a 'city of towers' connected by superhighways. These towers would define a city as centralised and orderly as Sforzinda; but, because they were built *up*, they would eliminate the congestion of the old industrial cities. The towers would free most of the ground for parks and gardens; it would be a 'green city' like Chaux. In such a 'radiant city' – rational, efficient, beautiful – the hitherto insoluble problems of industrial society would find their just and inevitable solutions.

Le Corbusier follows Ledoux in his belief that the industrial process must provide the basis for the social order. But Le Corbusier's concern is not with factories *per se* but with the whole world of distribution and administration to which mass production had given birth. The mastery of administration, he believed, would determine the future of industrial civilisation. His ideal city, therefore, is a city of administration. In its first and most characteristic form, 'The Contemporary City for Three Million People' (1922), the centre is occupied by sixty-story office towers. There the technical, professional, and intellectual leaders of society bring a beneficent order to the whole population. The city is designed to promote the speed, efficiency, and well-being of this elite. Le Corbusier dwelled rapturously on the office towers where executives enjoyed space, light, bracing views, easy access to their colleagues in nearby towers, and the spiritual refreshment of the parks that lie at the foot of the towers. Surrounding the towers of administration are the luxurious high-rise apartments of the elite, also set in the midst of parks. Subordinate office workers and industrial workers live in garden suburbs outside the city – twentieth-century Chauxs – where presumably they would benefit from the wise decisions made by the elite at the centre. Government has withered away – once the city has been built. As in Saint-Simon's prescription, administration has replaced politics.

Yet, for all its emphasis on the most modern techniques of construction and design, the relentless symmetry of the radiant city reminds one inevitably of the Renaissance ideal of the geometric city. This is no coincidence. For Le Corbusier has gone back to the roots of the tradition in his insistence that geometrical regularity is the symbol of expression of man's freedom from the contingent, his triumphant rationality and his point of contact with the deepest forces of the universe. One might describe the radiant city in the exact words that Wittkower applies to the centralised church of the Renaissance: absolute, immutable, static, and entirely lucid. Not only is this 'contemporary city' presented in the Renaissance tradition as a timeless archetype outside history; but, as many critics have pointed out, its geometrical framework is so rigid that it cannot change or expand.

Such an anomalous conception of a modern city reveals, I believe, the deeper connection of Le Corbusier to Filarete and the ideal city tradition. Like Filarete, he worked at a time of profound disorder: 'Cracks and reforms and bursts in the violet air/Falling Towers', as T.S. Eliot puts it. The towers of the radiant city cannot fall. Out of his fears for the destruction of civilisation, Le Corbusier fashioned an image of the modern city which would have the immutable stability of a Renaissance church. I suspect that this fervent affirmation of order is one of deepest attractions of Le Corbusier's urbanism for the 'practical' administrators who have done so much to realise his ideas.

In one final aspect Le Corbusier also embodies my conception of the ideal city: his plans succeed best in small doses. The tower in the park has certainly earned its place in the urban landscape. But whole districts planned according to radiant city principles – as Le Corbusier himself first proposed for the centre of Paris in 1925 – have proved to be disasters. His urbanism, though 'unfashionable' is perhaps in its most fruitful and productive period, as architects and planners learn to assimilate it as one element only of a complex urban fabric.

We are now in an era of assimilation and eclecticism in which the hopes for total urban transformation which accompanied the rise of the modern movement seem as meaningless and irrelevant as Sforzinda must have seemed a half-century later. As compensation we have gained a better appreciation of the diverse cityscape, the 'structural discontinuities and multiple syncopated excitements' as Colin Rowe puts it, of our 'collage cities' (9, pp. 66-91). This post-modernism, combined with the collapse of revolutionary ideologies in the course of the twentieth century, tempts me to conclude this paper with an announcement of the demise of the ideal city.

But such an announcement might well be premature. If my analysis of the conditions which give rise to the ideal city is correct, then we can hope for a new period of creativity soon. For the advanced industrial nations have already entered a 'third industrial revolution' based on microchips, the computer, and the 'information revolution'. Like the early periods of the Renaissance and the previous industrial revolutions, this profound change now seems too complicated to be understood. In places like 'Silicon Valley' south of San Francisco one can sense the emergence of a decentralised city based on new techniques of production and new attitudes toward nature. The material both for a total transformation of the city and for a corresponding re-form of society are surely there, but action is paralysed because the 'new order' cannot yet be seen with any precision.

This is precisely the moment when an individual of genius can direct social change by giving us an 'ideal type' of the new society – an

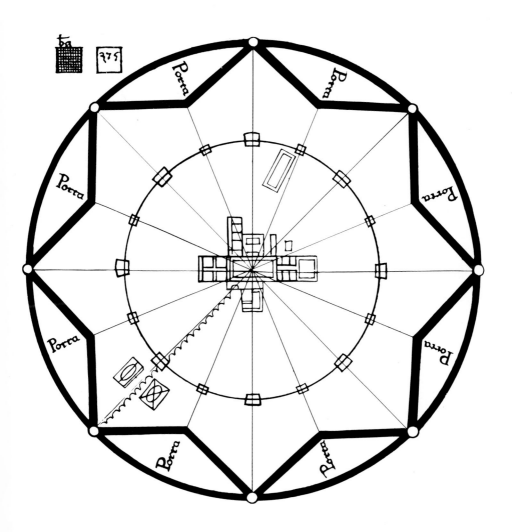

1. Filarete's groundplan of Sforzinda illustrates the Renaissance ideal of perfect geometry embodied in an ideal city. From each of eight gates (*porta*) a street runs straight to the central piazza; midway to the centre it crosses a smaller piazza serving the local district. Alternating with the streets are eight canals which run from the walls to the central piazza for the transport of heavy goods.

2. Claude-Nicolas Ledoux's 'Shelter for the Rural Guards' at Maupertuis. Here Ledoux takes up the Renaissance belief in perfect geometrical forms as the most appropriate for an ideal city and gives it a far more radical application than

3. Ledoux's cannon foundry surrounded by public buildings and residences. Geometry ensures industrial efficiency, and the smoky world of production is set in a landscaped world of open space.

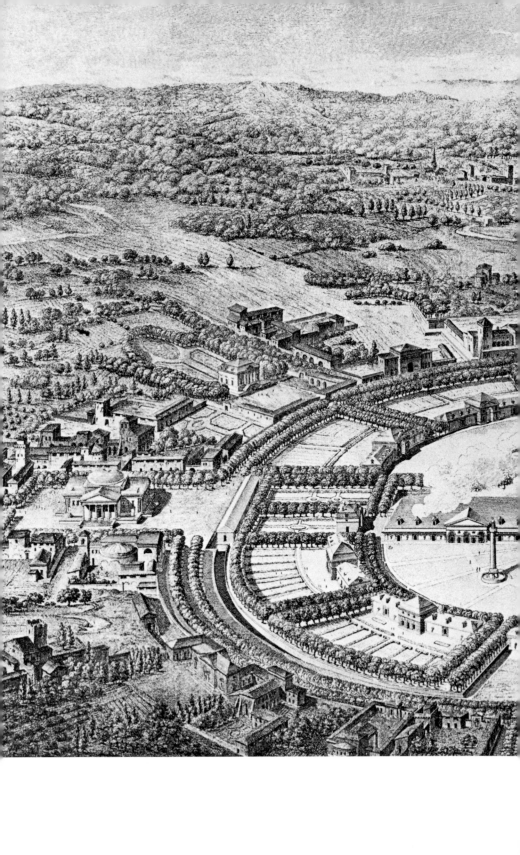

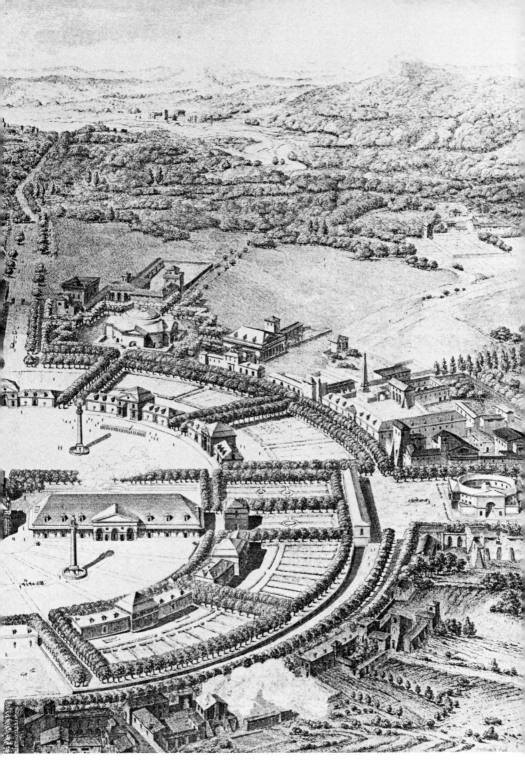

4. Ledoux's City of Chaux. In the centre of the oval are the Director's House and two flanking saltworks which were the heart of Ledoux's 1773 commission; these buildings and the gatehouse and workers' residence along the oval in front of the central group were the only parts of Chaux actually commissioned and constructed. The rest of the 'City of Chaux' represents Ledoux's plan for an ideal industrial city.

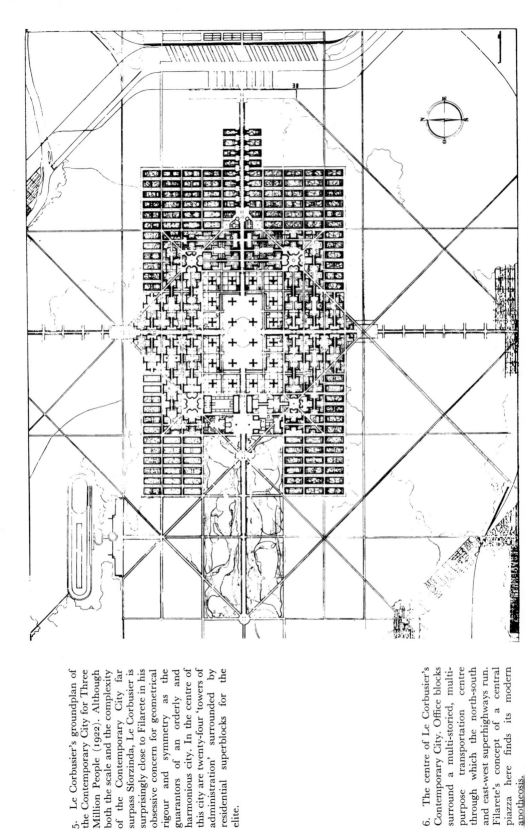

5. Le Corbusier's groundplan of the Contemporary City for Three Million People (1922). Although both the scale and the complexity of the Contemporary City far surpass Sforzinda, Le Corbusier is surprisingly close to Filarete in his obsessive concern for geometrical rigour and symmetry as the guarantors of an orderly and harmonious city. In the centre of this city are twenty-four 'towers of administration' surrounded by residential superblocks for the elite.

6. The centre of Le Corbusier's Contemporary City. Office blocks surround a multi-storied, multi-purpose transportation centre through which the north-south and east-west superhighways run. Filarete's concept of a central piazza here finds its modern apotheosis.

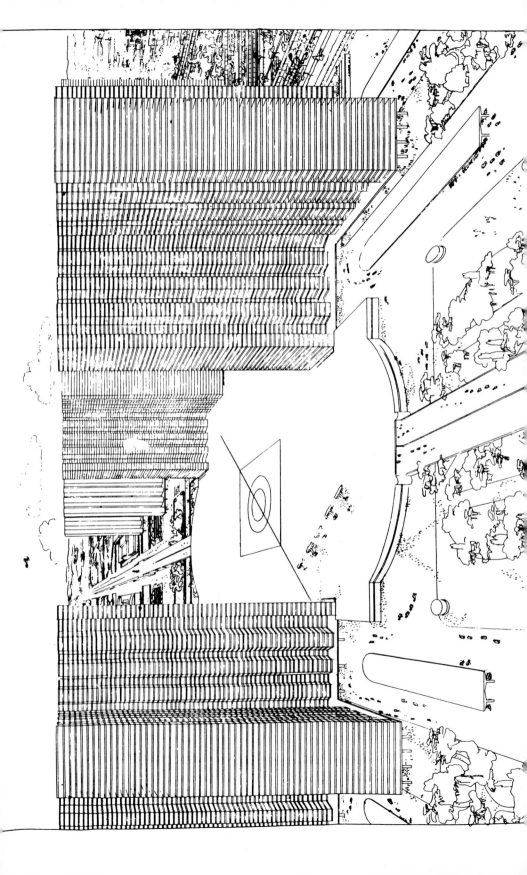

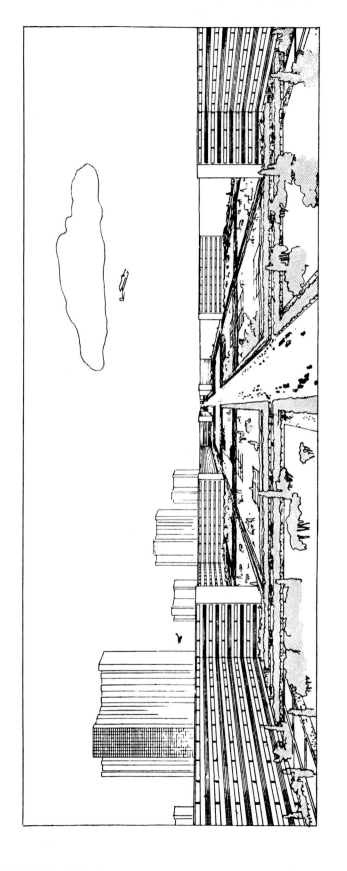

7. Residential superblocks for the elite in Le Corbusier's Contemporary City. Through the superblock Le Corbusier achieves both high density and open space reminiscent of the landscaped areas in which Ledoux placed his residences.

ideal city. One might argue that this 'third industrial revolution' is so complex that even the greatest architect-planner would not be able to master its meaning. Nevertheless, I suspect that somewhere on a computer terminal the quest for the ideal city is beginning again.

References

1. Filarete, *Filarete's Treatise on Architecture, Being the Treatise by Antonio di Pierro Averlino, known as Filarete* (1464), ed. J.R. Spencer, New Haven, Conn. 1965.
2. Kaufman, Emil, 'Three revolutionary architects', *Transactions of the American Philosophical Society* 42.
3. Le Corbusier, see especially *Urbanisme*, Paris 1925, and *La Ville radieuse*, Paris 1933.
4. Ledoux, Claude-Nicolas, *L'Architecture considerée sous le rapport de l'art, des moeurs, et de la legislation*, Paris 1804.
5. Palladio, Andrea, *The Four Books of Architecture*, New York 1959.
6. Pius II, *Memoirs of a Renaissance Pope*, New York 1952.
7. Herrmann, W., 'The problem of chronology in Claude-Nicolas Ledoux's engraved work', *Art Bulletin* 42.
8. Rosenau, Helen, *The Ideal City in its Architectural Evolution*, Routledge, London 1959.
9. Rowe, Colin & Koetter, Fred, 'Collage city', *Architectural Review* 158.
10. Vidler, Anthony, 'Architecture, management and morals in the design of a factory community at the end of the 18th century', *Lotus International* 14, 1977.
11. Wittkower, Rudolf, *Architectural Principles in the Age of Humanism*, 1962.

10

In England's Green and Pleasant Land

Roger Gill

The focus of this chapter is the strategy underpinning the County of London Plan and the Greater London Plan prepared by Patrick Abercrombie and published in 1943 and 1944 (1; 2). These plans provided a solution to the problems of the metropolitan region and will be referred to as the London Plans. They are seen in this chapter as the culmination of a British movement within which an emerging picture of an ideal environment was continually enriched by contact with utopia.

The main elements of the strategy were dispersal, containment, *rus in urbe*, and community enhancement. Dispersal involved the decanting of $1\frac{1}{4}$ million people from the centre of London to expanded towns and New Towns beyond the existing urban fringe, in order to spread the population more thinly on the ground. The old residential densities at the heart of the city were reduced to 136 persons per acre, although 100 persons per acre would have been preferred, and a much lower figure was specified for the new areas, that of 30 persons per acre (2, ch. 8).

Containment was a device for preventing sprawl. The London Plans reinforced the policy started before the war of stopping the outward expansion of London by creating an encircling belt of land, the Green Belt, permanently reserved for agriculture and recreation (2, para. 11). Each New Town across the Green Belt was given a maximum size (2, app. 11). But containment was not just a negative idea; it was made a positive policy for encouraging a sense of belonging by giving physical bounds to all the communities:

> Dominating the aim of both [plans] is the community idea – at one end the community of the Capital of the Empire, at the other the communities of simple people whose work and existence happen to lie

within this imperial metropolitan region – the proposal is to emphasise
the identity of the existing communities, to increase their segregation,
and where necessary to reorganise them as separate and definite entities
(2, paras 73, 75).

Four kinds of community were listed. First, the old borough; secondly,
the sprawling suburb of inter-war development only just built but in
need of treatment: 'In addition to the elimination of high density
pockets, the whole area requires working over with great detail and
care in order to carry out the Community Principle ...' (2, para. 28).
The third kind of community was the old town in and beyond the
Green Belt, and the fourth the proposed New Town. The London
Plans also divided the communities into Neighbourhood Units,
varying between 5000 and 10,000 people, built around their schools
and local centres.

Rus in urbe was the bringing of the country into the town; the goal
being to mirror the Green Belt around London by making green
girdles around every community, and the long-term task to knit the
girdles and the remaining wedges of open country reaching in from the
Green Belt, to create a continuous park system with a network of
footpaths, riverside walks, bridle-ways and green lanes (2, paras 39,
40).

The origins of the strategy

By 1914 the form of the strategy had emerged in the writings and
actions of the founding fathers of planning in this country, Ebenezer
Howard, Patrick Geddes, George Cadbury, W.H. Lever, Joseph
Rowntree, and Raymond Unwin. The year 1914 is thus a good point at
which to assess the growth of the strategy before tracing the flow of
ideas forward to 1940 and then backwards to More and his Utopia.

Containment and dispersal were key themes in Howard's Garden
City thesis. The Garden City was a settlement covering 1000 acres with
a maximum population of 30,000 set in a belt of permanent
agricultural land. The land was to be owned in time by the community,
and the town was to be largely self-contained for jobs, activities and
services. Howard pictured a swift transformation of the urban pattern
in these islands as people moved out of the industrial cities to live and
work in Garden City clusters, and the industrial conglomerations were
forced to restructure themselves along the same lines (18).

The industrial villages of Port Sunlight, built by Lever in 1888,
Bournville, started by the Cadbury family in 1875 but restarted as a
major project in 1894, New Earswick, begun by Joseph Rowntree in
1902, and the Hampstead Garden Suburb, built by Henrietta Barnett
from 1905, were compelling demonstrations of the advantages offered

by planned small communities and by dispersal in the sense of low density development. Raymond Unwin and Barry Parker, the designers of New Earswick and the Hampstead Garden Suburb, combined the diagrams produced by Howard and the traditions of the industrial village movement in the first Garden City of Letchworth (1904), and in doing so established a model for residential development used for the next half century.

The *rus in urbe* component was also well developed by 1914. Cadbury believed that it was impossible to improve social conditions in the smoke and grime of crowded industrial areas: 'the only way was to bring men out of the cities into the country and to give every man his garden where he can come into touch with nature and thus know Nature's God' (13, p. 21). Howard wrote in a similar vein about returning people to the land, 'that beautiful land of ours with its canopy of sky, the air that blows upon it, the sun that warms it, the rain and the dew that moisten it, the very embodiment of divine love for man …' (18). However, the green wedges and park system prescribed by Abercrombie more probably came from Geddes. Unlike Marx, who refused to speculate except on rare occasions about the future society arising from the present, Geddes painted many pictures of his Eutopia. In one of them he described a two-pronged attack on the industrial city, one moving down from the uplands to drive wedges of open country into the paleotechnic sprawl, and the other moving outwards from the centre to clear away dereliction and leave space for recreation and for 'tree-planted lanes and blossoming hedgerows'. These actions would give a better form to the cites that 'must now cease to expand like inkstains – once in true development they will repeat the star-like opening of the flower, with green leaves set in alternation with its golden rays' (14, pp. 355-8). Abercrombie was a disciple of Geddes. He once wrote about his teaching as '… a vital idea – a divine inoculation, that goes on spreading its influence without exhausting its original élan' (6, p. 252).

The community enhancement component was not quite so well formulated by 1914 as the others. Although Bournville and the other villages were communities in the sense of an environment in which people lived and worked and enjoyed common facilities, and although the diagrams for the Garden City show the whole divided into six wards, there were few pointers to the putative benefits to be gained from living in the neighbourhoods of the London Plans. A further encounter with utopia was needed to expand the component.

This came through the work of a small group of men who formed the Regional Planning Association of America in 1923. Lewis Mumford, Stuart Chase, Clarence Stein and Henry Wright were among the founder members. Mumford claimed that they blended the civic ideas of Geddes and Howard (Geddes was present at the first meeting), the economic analysis of Veblen, the sociology of Cooley and the educational philosophy of John Dewey (26). Their thinking led to the town of Radburn, the cradle of the neighbourhood unit concept, and the Greenbelt towns of the New Deal. In Stein's view the important feature of Greendale, one of these towns, was the belt of natural green around the town which guaranteed its 'integrity' and brought country folk and town folk within walking distance to know each other as friends and associates. The limitation of size was essential, 'because only so can the neighbourly character be sustained – and the common interest of all in their common affairs be kept alive' (32). At Greenbelt a very determined effort was made to engineer a community of equals. An early aim was to minimise social stratification. Residents were selected to lessen differences in income and social background, and emphasis was given to co-operation and participation in work, play and management. In an early ruling the administration warned that anyone with an income rising above 2000 dollars a year would be required to leave town (11).

Mumford was the passionate advocate of neighbourhood, and by 1940 the concept offered a sure method of enhancing community life. There were some minor modifications to the other components between the wars, but the task undertaken by Abercrombie was the translation of the developed ideal model into practical plans and policies for Greater London, which in turn served as a model for all town and country planning in the immediate post-war period.

Looking backwards from 1900

Howard acknowledged Edward Bellamy, James Silk Buckingham and William Wakefield as influences in his book, but clearly there were many others, among them Bernard Shaw, the Webbs, and B.W. Richardson with his utopia of Hygeia (31). Howard may have attended meetings of the Fellowship of the New Life, and the primary generators of the Garden City thesis were possibly found in the activities of the many small reform groups concerned with the 'land question' (27c and d). Raymond Unwin was nurtured in the same reform circles. His mentors were John Ruskin and William Morris. Geddes also gained his vision of a society based on co-operation and fellowship from Ruskin (3; 20). Armytage in *Heavens Below* gives a definitive account of the vision held by Ruskin and Morris, Kropotkin, the disciples of Tolstoy, and a host of minor utopians and communitarians; a vision that grew from the 'Heyday of Experiment' in the middle of the century with connections to St Simon, Fourier, the American religious communities, Buckingham and the Owenite Apocalypse. Howard's Garden City, according to Armytage, was a revised version of the old gospel (3).

Alongside this continual utopian infusion the ideal model was being moulded by two respectable groups of reformers. The first group comprised the precursors of Lever, Cadbury and Rowntree, the founders of earlier industrial villages. The second group contained members of various learned societies concerned with social reform, particularly the members of the Social Science Association. A few of the many attending the annual meetings of the Association (1857-1884), were Gladstone and Joseph Chamberlain; the Christian Socialists, Maurice, Ludlow, Kingsley and Thomas Hughes; Robert Owen, J.S. Mill and Octavia Hill; William Morris and Ruskin; representing the industrial village builders were Akroyd and Titus Salt; and two men from West Yorkshire almost certainly known to Akroyd, Henry Solly and James Hole (7).

Hughes, Hole and Solly belonged to a short-lived body, the Society for Promoting Industrial Villages, formed in 1885 (4). The society was helped financially by Cadbury and Alfred Marshall the economist, a keen supporter of dispersal and development planning (28). Solly at the last meeting of the Social Science Association made a strong plea for dispersal; Hole many years before in 1864 had suggested the building of model villages to relieve congestion and misery (16), and he may have been following J.T. Danson who five years earlier made a detailed case for moving the mass of city dwellers to new settlements along the railway lines (8).

A number of industrial villages appeared in the first half of the nineteenth century; Saltaire built by Titus Salt from 1851; Akroyd's village of Copley started in 1849; Bromborough Pool built by the Wilson family (Price's Candles) around 1854; and Bessbrook in Ireland. Bessbrook, started by the Richardson family, was directly inspired by William Penn's proposals for the colony of Pennsylvania (5; 9), and Bessbrook was inspected by George Cadbury when 'the prospect of an ideal suburb was shaping in his mind'. Bournville also had an indirect link with Owenism. In the early archives of Cadbury Brothers there is a small leaflet produced by the Model Parish Mission proclaiming an intention to build a model village with a factory, in a rural area having easy access to a railway (22). John Cadbury was one of several grocers passing on to the mission some of the profits from selling cocoa. Ironville in Derbyshire, started around 1800, and Mellor in Cheshire, started about 1790, were two further industrial villages designed to provide a good environment and to promote moral and social well-being (25; 34).

The industrial village as it is traced back through the eighteenth century becomes more and more utopian in offering a planned alternative to existing society. The ferment of dissent in the seventeenth century and the millennial dream finally turned inwards, but one outcome was the flurry of small villages built and guided in the main by Quaker families. These were practical experiments in good works, little welfare states well in advance of their time. They offered good housing; gardens; small-holdings; insurance against sickness, unemployment and old age; co-operative shops and mills; free education and free medical care – but also paternalism (15; 30). The steady stream of experiments ran from 1700 to Robert Owen and eventually to the post-war New Towns.

Rus in urbe, containment and community, were also prominent themes in the 'systematic' colonisation propounded by William Wakefield, a programme with utopian dimensions (24). The first colony of South Australia (1834), and the first settlements in New Zealand at Wellington, Nelson, and New Plymouth, had support from Bentham and his circle. For his last two ventures Wakefield tried to bind his communities together around one religion, having noted the success of the American religious communities. He helped the Free Church of Scotland to develop the Province of Otago with its capital, Dunedin (1844), and members of the Oxford movement to found an ideal See of the Church of England in Canterbury with its capital, Christchurch, three years later (21). The instructions given to the leader of the Wellington expedition convey the scope of Wakefield's vision:

> In forming the plan of the town you should make ample reserves for all public purposes, such as a cemetery, a market-place, wharfage, and probable public buildings, a botanical garden, a park, and extensive boulevards. It is indeed desirable that the whole outside of the town, inland, should be separated from the country section by a broad belt of land, which you will declare that the company intends to be public property on condition that no buildings be ever erected on it (27a).

The country belt goes back a little further in the history of Australia. In 1809 Governor Macquarie of New South Wales was given instructions on the layout of townships including the reservation of common land, and in 1792 an earlier governor had reserved all land within a specified distance of Sydney (27a). The scent gets cold at this point. It is possible that the concept came from America, as William Light, the Surveyor to the South Australia expedition, was instructed to study the planning of American towns (letter of Instruction from the Commission). Many years earlier *rus in urbe* was manifest in William Penn's plan for Philadelphia. Although the grid pattern is standard, Penn wanted each house to be set in a plot of at least half an acre to give a green country town; a fundamental change from the towns of Europe (19).

Osborn in his search for the origins of the Garden City jumped from the decade before Howard's book was published to Wakefield, to More and the Renaissance ideal city, and then to Classical Greece and the

Levitical cities of Palestine (27d). More is far enough back however to demonstrate the age of some aspects of the London Plans, and the continuity of the themes.

More's Utopia can be seen as a direct inspiration. In the book the capital town is divided into four parts, each with a shopping centre. The same description applies to Philadelphia with the centre arranged around an open square. The plan of Adelaide in South Australia follows closely the pattern of Philadelphia. Other parts of Utopia are redolent of the Garden City concept; the 54 towns all built to the same plan, the spacing of the towns at a minimum distance of 24 miles apart and a maximum of one day's walk, the limitation of each town to 6000 households and the colonisation of a new settlement once the population threshold is reached. The description could also be used to give an impression of the first generation New Towns in this country, particularly if coupled to a comment made by Andreae about his own utopia of Christianopolis: 'things look much the same all around, not extravagant nor yet unclean' (17).

Some conclusions

If the substance of the previous section is reasonably accurate, the solution for the industrial city found in the London Plans originated in utopia; but always the utopian input was modified by a set of filters that blocked the unworldly to give the ideal output.

The industrial village at least by late Victorian times had become an instrument of radical reform; but when Port Sunlight, Bournville and New Earswick were accepted as models for city expansion, the three main strands of the early industrial village movement – work, welfare and environment – were unravelled, each the responsibility of some other person or body. When Letchworth arose so swiftly after the publication of Howard's book, one of the key ideas, the gathering of increases in land value for the community through regular adjustments of the rentals, was dropped (10). Stein, in his account of Greenbelt, omits the social aim of minimising differences in status (32).

The ideal plan served two prime functions. One was to provide a 'practical vision' of a better but realisable future which reform groups, spearheaded by the Town and Country Planning Association, could use for propaganda. Canon Barnett made the point in his *Ideal City* that action would not be taken 'until cityzens are captured by the thought of what their city might be' (23).

The second function was to present planners with a working model. Even today it is difficult to imagine a search for a solution in a 'soft' problem area taking place without some prior overall view of what the solution should be. Forty years ago the working model was the strategy of the London Plans, which embodied the conventional wisdom of the profession (12), although at that time the conventional wisdom was being challenged in turn by the new utopia portrayed by Le Corbusier.

The dangers of blindly accepting the ideal are obvious. Particularly when untested it may be far from optimal, as was the case when the architectural utopias of the modern movement were used in the reconstruction of our city centres just over two decades ago. The danger of resisting the ideal is the possibility of rejecting the good, for the environment designed by the idealists of the British tradition has invariably been better than the environment designed and built by 'practical' people.

Robert Godley, Wakefield's agent for Canterbury, will be given the last word: 'I often smile when I think of the ideal Canterbury of which our imagination dreamed. Yet I see nothing in the dream to regret or be ashamed of, and I am quite sure that without the enthusiasm, the poetry, the unreality – if you will – with which our scheme was overlaid, it would never have ben accomplished' (21).

References

1. Abercrombie, P. & Forshaw, J.H., *County of London Plan*, MacMillan, London 1943.
2. Abercrombie, P., *Greater London Plan*, H.M.S.O. 1944.
3. Armytage, W.H.G., *Heavens Below: utopian experiments in England 1560-1960*, Routledge, London 1961.
4. Ashworth, W., *The Genesis of Modern British Town Planning*, London 1954.
5. Bessbrook Centenary Booklet, *Bessbrook 1845-1945*.
6. Boardman, P., *Patrick Geddes: maker of the future*, North Carolina University Press 1944.
7. Creese, W.L., *The Legacy of Raymond Unwin: a human pattern for planning*, M.I.T. Press 1967.
8. Danson, J.T. 'Propositions and inferences, with statistical notes touching the provision of country dwellings for town labourers', *Journal of the Royal Statistical Society* 22, 1859.
9. Fell Smith, C., *Reminiscences of Friends in Ulster*, 1925.
10. Fishman, R., *Urban Utopias in the Twentieth Century*, Basic Books, New York 1977.
11. Form, W.H., 'Status stratification in a planned community', *American Sociological Review* vol. 10.
12. Galbraith, J.K., *The Affluent Society* (1958) Penguin Books 1962.
13. Gardiner, A.G., *Life of George Cadbury*, London 1923.
14. Geddes, P., *Cities in Evolution*, Williams and Northgate, London 1915.
15. Grubb, I., *Quakerism and Industry before 1800*, London 1930.
16. Harrison, J.F.C., 'Social reform in Leeds: the work of James Hole, 1820-1895', *The Thoresby Society*, monograph III, 1954.
17. Held, F.E. (ed.), *Christianopolis*, O.U.P. 1916.
18. Howard, E., *Tomorrow: a peaceful path to real reform* (1898), reissued in

Osborn, F.J. (ed.), *Garden Cities of Tomorrow*, Faber and Faber, London 1946.

19. Janney, S.M., *Life of William Penn*, 1852.

20. Kitchen, P., *A Most Unsettling Person: an introduction to the ideas and life of Patrick Geddes*, Victor Gollancz, London 1975.

21. Marais, J.S., *The Colonisation of New Zealand*, O.U.P. 1927.

22. Marsh, W., Robinson, W.W. & Carus Wilson, W., *The Model Parish Mission*, c. 1850.

23. Meller H.E. (ed.), *The Ideal City*, Leicester University Press, 1979.

24. Mills, R.C., *The Colonisation of Australia*, London 1915.

25. Mottram, R.H. & Coote, C., *The Butterly Company through Five Generations*, 1950.

26. Mumford, L., introduction to Stein, C.S., *Towards New Towns for America*.

27. Osborn, F.J. (a) 'Country belts', *Town and Country Planning* 13, 1944.
(b) *Green Belt Cities: the British contribution*, Faber and Faber, London 1946.
(c) Letter to author 1959. (d) & Whittick, A., *New Towns: their origins, achievements and progress*, Leonard Hill, London 1977.

28. Pigou, A.C. (ed.), *Memorials of Alfred Marshall*, London 1923.

29. Price's Centenary Booklet, *Price's of Bromborough 1854-1954*.

30. Raistrick, A., *Two Centuries of Industrial Welfare*, London 1938.

31. Richardson, B.J., Presidential Address to Health Section, *Social Science Association Transactions*, 1875.

32. Stein, C.S., *Towards New Towns for America*, M.I.T. Press, 1957.

33. Unwin, G., Hulme, A & Taylor, G., *Samuel Oldknow and the Arkwrights*, Manchester University Press, 1924.

34. Unwin, R., 'Regional planning', a paper read before the RIBA and published in Creese, W.L. (7).

11

Collectivism, Community and Commitment: America's Religious Communal Utopias from the Shakers to Jonestown

Donald E. Pitzer

The Shakers and Jonestown are points at opposite ends of the American religious communal spectrum. Within that spectrum can be found the most constructive achievements and the most destructive events of the communitarian tradition in America. Lessons emerge all along this continuum which I will treat under the general categories of collectivism, community and commitment.

Defining commune

For the purposes of my remarks I will take commune to mean a small, voluntary social unit partly isolated from the general society in which the members share an economic union and lifestyle in an attempt to implement, in part at least, their ideal religious, philosophical, economic, social and/or governmental systems. Because communes are social microcosms they are highly attractive subjects for social and philosophical investigation. The best estimates suggest that about 600 communal societies were formed in English colonial America and the United States from Plockhoy's Commonwealth in 1663 until 1965 (4a, pp. 235-43; 12, pp. 173-234; 14, p. 3). The communal explosion since 1965 is a new order of communitarian social phenomenon which has produced some 100,000 such social units, mostly small, urban and short-lived (22, pp. 3-24). Perhaps one-third to one-half of the 600 before 1965 were sectarian, but not more than one-fifth since. However, because religious communes tend to be more populous,

* The Colston Lecture

longer lasting and more intentionally visible, they are much better known than their secular counterparts. To make the study all the more colourful and confusing, commune is but one name by which these religious and secular groups are known. We find them as communal societies, co-operatives, collectives, colonies, cults, intentional and utopian and experimental communities, tribes, families and fellowships.

American religious utopias: praised and condemned

Often organised effectively under charismatic, authoritarian leadership, religious communal utopias have reached greater extremes of achievement and disgrace than secular ones in America. They have attracted more members and lasted longer. Ann Lee's Shakers emigrated to America from Manchester in 1774 and established twenty-four settlements in nine states with tens of thousands of adherents (1). Fourteen lasted more than a hundred years, and two continue in Maine and New Hampshire after nearly two centuries. George Rapp's Harmony Society had 1200 disciples between 1805 and 1916 (2a). Forty-two American Benedictine monasteries since the 1840s have had thousands of monks and nuns. Since 1874, 35,000 Hutterites have lived in more than 165 colonies (42; 19; 47).

Sectarian communes have been recognised for accomplishments in the fine arts, architecture, education and religious philosophy. Musical composition has flourished from the Ephrata Cloister Baptists, Moravians, Shakers, and Harmony Society to the Society of Brothers, Hippies at Stephen Gaskin's Farm, Jesus People U.S.A. and International Society for Krishna Consciousness. The Ephratans, Shakers, Harmonists, Jansenists, Society of Brothers and Hare Krishnas have excelled in graphic arts and printing (18; 43; 50; 20). Innovative architecture has marked Shaker buildings, Katherine Tingley's Theosophical Point Loma, Thomas Lake Harris's Spiritualist Fountain Grove and the Hare Krishna's New Vrindaban Palace of Gold (31; 34; 54; 17; 23; *Brijabasi Spirit*, April 1981).

Progressive co-educational schools were set up by the Ephrata Baptists, Shakers, Mormons, Transcendentalists of Brook Farm, Oneidans and Theosophists (7; 6). From George Rapp, Joseph Smith, Christian Metz and Barbara Heineman to Clarence Jordan, Eberhard Arnold, Sun Myung Moon and Bhaguwan Shree Ragjneesh, sectarian utopians have added to American religious literature.

If Americans have praised religious communities more than secular ones, they have also condemned them more soundly. Departures from accepted standards regarding sex, the family, military service and the sanctity of life have evoked public outcries and even violence. Alleged and actual sexual practices at John Humphrey Noyes's Oneida,

Harris's Fountain Grove, in Moon's Unification Church and, especially, among Smith's Mormons have drawn attack (6; 17; 53). Harmonists suffered and two Hutterites died for their pacifism (26; 44; 47).

The most justified denunciation was reserved for the Reverend Jim Jones's San Francisco-based People's Temple. The suicide-massacre of more than 900 men, women and children in their Agricultural Project at Jonestown, Guyana, on 18 November 1978, brought the darkest elements of religious authoritarianism and commitment of members to their most destructive and inhumane levels in the annals of American communal history. But it also must be remembered that the public harassment Jones endured for his liberal racial views in his early ministry in Indianapolis, Indiana, helped fire the apprehensions and hatreds which later became his apparently psychotic paranoia. In 1960 alone, Jones's multi-racial family which included seven adopted black, white and Asian children suffered threatening phone calls, explosives put in their yard and stones thrown at their house. Jones's name was forged on anti-black letters sent to civil rights leaders (28; 26; 27; 46).

The utopian nature of communitarianism

Communitarianism is an awkward word referring to the method of non-violent social change in which communal societies become the working models of the perfect systems which the communalists think the entire world will soon adopt either by divine intervention (as anticipated by most religious communities) or by reasoned choice. Eras in which large numbers of communes are formed should alert us to periods of fundamental social, political, economic and religious tension and transition. This is because communitarianism offers distinct advantages as an alternative to individualism, gradual reform by legislation and violent political revolution. Communitarianism is immediate, non-violent and humanitarian. It can mean voluntary escape, isolation and collective security. It is flexible enough to implement a utopian design or to be inventively experimental. And it promises imitation by the world at large.

For these reasons and because communal living constantly beckons to the downtrodden, discontented and dissenting as well as to the visionary as the most natural struture of primitive societies, communitarianism is a perpetually recurring social phenomenon. Nevertheless, historians of communitarianism in America, like weathermen, have been poor prophets of the next cycle. When Arthur Bestor, Jr. wrote his *Backwoods Utopias* in 1850 he treated the communitarian faith in the past tense, assuming that an industrialised and partly socialised United States would not produce new waves of

communal fervour. Everett Webber titled the last chapter of his 1959
Escape to Utopia: the communal movement in America 'The Song is Done'
and concluded the book with the words, 'it seems unlikely that we
shall again see any great promulgation of the village commune. The
song is surely done' (58, p. 419). Mark Holloway's *Heavens on Earth:
utopian communities in America, 1680-1880* (18) leaves the impression that
little of communal significance lay beyond 1900 and, of course, was
powerless to predict the great counter-culture revival of communes
beginning in the mid-1960s. But Holloway did protect himself by
titling his epilogue 'The Idea Persists'. And it may be reassuring to
note that a few historians, including Robert Fogarty and Laurence
Veysey (57), are fleshing out the story of American communities so
well after 1880 that except for the bursts of commune building by the
Shakers in the 1790s, the Fourierists in the 1840s, the Socialists in the
1890s, and the hippies in the 1960s, the history of American
communalism resembles a continuous river more than a wavy ocean.

The utopian roots of American religious communes

Communitarianism provides the communal link to utopianism. The
titles of the three books just mentioned strongly imply that historic
American communal societies have also been utopian experiments.
Most of the other major works in the field reinforce this association
of communes with utopianism. The following titles will serve as
examples: Victor Calverton's *Where Angels Dared to Tread: socialist &
communist utopian colonies in the United States* (1941), John Egerton's
*Visions of Utopia: Nashoba, Rugby, Ruskin, and the 'New Communities' in
Tennessee's past* (1977), Richard Fairfield's *Utopia: U.S.A.* (1972),
Robert Hine's *California's Utopian Colonies* (1953), Charles LeWarne's
Utopias on Puget Sound, 1885-1915 (1975), Gairdner Moment's *Utopias:
the American experience* (1980), and Peyton Richter's *Utopias: social ideals
and communal experiments* (1971).

Although we may be wrestling with the classic chicken or egg
question if we try to determine whether religious millennialism or
secular utopianism came first, we *can* assert that those communal
societies which are truly communitarian in purpose are the
materialisation of utopian thought in secular and religious forms.
They seek the immediate implementation of preconceived ideas and
ideals, experiment with new ideas, and strive for perfection while
escaping an evil and self-destructing world. And, all the while, they
await a general Utopia. Arthur Bestor argues that America's historic
communitarian efforts were 'Patent-office models of the good society
...' (4b). If we agree that no nation has ever achieved the utopian
ideal, we might also recognise that, however briefly, in communal
societies, and in communal societies *alone*, human relations and

institutions have approached the realisation of utopia as 'now here' rather than 'no where'.

The historic roots of modern Western religious communes lie deep in the utopian vision and communal examples of the Essenes and other communitarian groups of the Middle East in the century before and following the birth of Christ. This vision, largely drawn from even more ancient Persian beliefs, focused upon apocalypticism, millenarianism, chiliasm and a rigorous eschatological interpretation of history. Taken together, these concepts direct all personal and collective attention, values and activities toward the imminent collapse of the contemporary world order and the cataclysmic formation of the Kingdom of God on earth. So compelling and influential is this set of religious utopian ideas that Kenneth Rexroth does not overstate the case when he maintains that 'these outstanding characteristics of the Essenes were to remain the distinguishing marks of almost every communalist sect from then on, and were, in a secularised form, to be perpetuated in the revolutionary movements of the nineteenth century, utopian, communist, anarchist, and socialist' (47, p. 15).

Except for the more recent communes and monasteries of Far Eastern origin which draw heavily upon the promises of self-purification, enlightenment and ultimate escape from reincarnation into the 'utopia' of Nirvana, the prospect of regaining the Paradise lost in the Garden of Eden has been the single most powerful motivating force in American religious communities. Often emphasising the idea that their followers are Chosen People of the end times, analogous to the Hebrews of Bible times, most sectarian communal leaders have constantly commended to their congregations their interpretations of the millennial passages of the Books of Isaiah, Jeremiah, Ezekiel, Daniel, Revelation and the sayings of Jesus.

Ann Lee taught that she and all Shakers were agents in God's post-millennial plan by which Christ's spirit would permeate the globe, ultimately redeeming everyone (1). Millenarianism was also an essential doctrinal element in Magister Kelpius' Woman In The Wilderness community, Rapp's Harmony Society, Smith's Latter-Day Saints, Noyes's Oneida and David Berg's Children of God (18; 2a; 33; 56; 55; 38; 36). The lesson to be derived from communal millenarianism is not only that it can be an unequalled engine for religious organisations, but also that its end results may be frustration, division and the breakdown of the community. The interpretations which they placed upon the biblical passages and the 'signs of the times' failed Kelpius, Rapp, Smith, Noyes, Berg and many other charismatic communal figures. The Ephratans, Zoarites, Inspirationists, and Hutterites were wise to minimise the urgency of the second coming in favour of emphasis upon Christian collectivism and community as worthy ends in themselves.

Lessons of collectivism from American religious utopias

First-century Christian communism and its broader implication of a community of believers stand second only to millennialism as an impetus for American religious utopias. Jesus himself set the example by the common treasury of his disciples. Pure communism was already in use among the Essenes and may have served as a source of Christian ideas on the subject. Four centuries later St Augustine's *City of God* added his blessing to communistically organised Christian monastic communities. The Benedictines made cenobitic monasticism the standard form in Europe after the sixth century. The Waldenses, the Hutterites and other heretical sects before and during the Reformation carried the tradition of communistic, communal sharing forward. Although necessity itself drove many of these and subsequent religionists in America to a common purse to ensure group survival, all justified their communalism as an effort to reproduce the divinely ordained economic arrangement of the early church as described in Acts 2:44-5 and Acts 4:32-5:

> All that believed were together, and had all things common: And sold their possessions and goods, and parted them to all men, as every man had need.

> And the multitude of them that believed were of one heart and of one soul: neither said any of them that ought of the things which he possessed was his own; but they had all things common. ... Neither was there any among them that lacked: for as many as were possessors of lands or houses sold them, and brought the prices of the things that were sold. And laid them down at the apostles' feet: and distribution was made unto every man according as he had need.

The instant punishment by death of Ananias and Sapphira after they lied to Peter about giving all their resources to the community reinforced the importance many have attached to the practice of Christian communism (Acts 5:1-11).

By a literal application of this clear and simple formula, religious communes in America have proved the economic viability of collectivism. When they have screened their members well and combined their commitment to millenarian goals with leadership from capable men and women of wide practical experience, they have been extremely successful. Community of goods, wholesale purchasing, frugal life styles, dormitory and apartment-like housing in large buildings that anticipated the economies of row houses and condominiums, hard work for long hours in the common cause, and reputations for honest business transactions and fine products have paid high dividends. Prosperity, in fact, has often threatened the very spiritual fibre of religious communities.

When the Ephrata Cloister became too prosperous to suit its founder Johann Conrad Beissel, in 1745 he closed its mills, cancelled its contracts for exports, fired its outside employees, uprooted its orchards, ousted its best businessmen and nearly killed the community in the process. After 1825, when the Harmony Society built its third town whose name, Economy, implied the materialistic, if still utopian, direction in which it was moving, its profits grew so rapidly that its business agent Frederick Rapp sought advice as to how to disguise the fact. He did not want to corrupt the faithful who nevertheless went on to become collective millionaires.

Religious utopias were the first social entities in America beyond the family or partnership to demonstrate that collective economic ventures could succeed. In a land where individualism and private enterprise were championed, they became objects of curiosity for businessmen, reformers and utopians. Hundreds made visits to examine their economic systems first hand. The Shaker settlements and the Harmonist towns were of special interest because they were the first to show that collective economies could be effective for large populations making their living from agriculture and light industry. Frederick Evans, a free-thinking, deistic, socialist reformer from Leominster in England, came to the United States in 1820 and was so attracted by the Shaker success that he joined them at New Lebanon in 1830. Evans managed to turn the Shaker movement itself toward more active participation in secular humanitarian crusades such as emancipation of the slaves as he became the leading Elder and chief Shaker spokesman of the 1830s. Robert Owen, that wealthy cotton spinner who had conducted famous educational and social experiments in his New Lanark, Scotland, milltown and who would sire communal socialism in the United States, corresponded with and visited the Shakers and Harmonists to learn their collective techniques. Then he brought New Harmony, Indiana, from George Rapp's Harmony Society and attempted the first major secular communal experiment in the United States from 1825 to 1827. The radical English reformer Frances Wright learned communalism from the Harmonists and Owen. Her short-lived Nashoba, Tennessee, communal experiment to free American slaves through their earnings at the community in the late 1820s was formally predicated upon the economic success of the Moravians, Shakers and Harmony Society (4a; 8).

Edward Bellamy went to Utah in 1883 to observe the highly successful co-operative economy of the Mormons. It was nearly five decades since Joseph Smith had announced the unique 'United Order' plan for the Latter-day Saints at Kirtland, Ohio, in 1831, but the obligation of fellow saints to co-operate with each other in the building of the community and the church was still very strong. The United Order, the earliest communal economic arrangement suggested by an American, was a curious blend of co-operation and capitalism. Each head of a Mormon family was to 'consecrate' all possessions to the bishop and to receive in return an 'inheritance' which he was to use to sustain his family through private enterprise. Although the strict practice of the United Order was soon abandoned by most Mormons for the more practical 10 per cent tithe, elements of Smith's intentions continued into the latter part of the century and may have contributed to Bellamy's most influential utopian novel, *Looking Backward, 2000-1887*, which he published five years after his Utah visit. The book pictures the social and political transformation as the United States nationalises all industry and its people become animated by Christian brotherhood by the beginning of the twentieth century. The Nationalist Clubs that sprang up across the nation in support of Bellamy's ideas are reported to have 'respected Mormon economic doctrines as representative of advanced social planning' (5, p. 152).

Many other religious, as well as secular, communes have thrived on collective economies. Oneida supported itself by the manufacture of animal traps and the Roman Catholic St Nazianz Colony of Father Ambrosius Oschwald in Manitowac County, Wisconsin, after 1854 by agriculture. Today the Hutterites are doing well on agriculture and chicken farming, the Koinonia Farm in Georgia on processed pecans, the Society of Brothers on manufacturing wooden toys, God's Valley led by Daniel Wright near Bedford, Indiana, on lumbering, and the International Society for Krishna Consciousness on incense and book sales.

In the late nineteenth century, the spiritualist Thomas Lake Harris and theosophist Katherine Tingley were the first communal leaders to introduce the substitution of massive donations from new members and outsiders for internal collective industry as the economic base for religious communes. George Baker, known as Father Divine, utilised the same idea in his black-oriented communal Peace Mission Movement. Beginning in New York City in the 1920s, his 'Heavens' fed, clothed and sheltered thousands of destitute blacks during the Great Depression and spread to urban centres across the country (15; 25). Jim Jones learned his lessons in fund raising by consulting George Baker himself. It was the technique of soliciting members' gifts from property to social security cheques which led him from selling monkeys door-to-door to sustain his congregation in Indianapolis in 1953 to a surplus of millions of dollars when tragedy struck at Jonestown.

More importantly for our consideration, Americans are once again becoming aware not only of the financial success, but also of the generally attractive humane qualities of communal collective economies past and present. Work is lightened by comradeship. The

Harmony Society was noted for marching to the harvest fields with its band leading the way. Furthermore, collective enterprise has usually meant security within the group, insurance in the labour of one's brothers and sisters against the vagaries of illness, injury and old age, and rotation of jobs to avoid boredom and to learn new skills. It has always put working with technology on a human scale rather than on one of giantistic proportions. Sometimes it has included a diversification of jobs and leisure activities for women, as at Oneida and Brook Farm where nurseries and kindergartens existed. Possibly best of all, from the viewpoint of the outside society, collective economies have realised full employment.

Through their collectivism religious communal utopias have become the supreme expression in human society of the universal principle in nature that co-operation is at least as important as competition for growth and survival. Astronomer Carl Sagan expressed the principle eloquently in his 1980 *Cosmos* television series and book (51, p. 33).

Lessons of community from American religious utopias

Perhaps the most constructive element of American religious utopias and the most urgently instructive for modern man lies in the intangible realm of community – that indefinable network of social relations characterised by the mutuality and emotional bonds of human personalities and spirits. Since a survey in 1955 uncovered ninety-four different meanings for community in the literature of the social sciences, I shall not attempt to be more specific (16). 'Attunement' is the term preferred by the spiritual Sirius community near Amherst, Massachusetts. As a 1978 offshoot of the group at Findhorn, Scotland, Sirius uses 'attunement' to imply the universal awareness and positive relationship which one can have with oneself and all life forms.

To the twentieth-century urbanised, industrialised, secularised society, so impersonal and so frightfully capable of self-destruction, the religious communal heritage holds out plans for survival. The plans are expressed in working models of human relations based on affection rather than intimidation, care rather than exploitation and understanding rather than disregard. In their finest hours, sectarian and, often, non-sectarian communities alike, have offered the humanising, stabilising and healing effects of face-to-face human relationships. Wounded egos have been repaired, individual worth and dignity restored, self-respect renewed, and the loving warmth and reassuring security of family feeling re-established.

George Rapp captured the sentiment of such an environment when he described his New Harmony community as one where those who occupy its peaceful dwellings are so closely united by the endearing ties of friendship, confidence and love, that one heart beats in all, and their common industry provides for all. Here, the members kindly assist each other, in difficulty and danger, and share with each other, the enjoyments, and the misfortunes of life; one lives in the breast of another, and forgets himself; all their undertakings are influenced by a social spirit, glowing with noble energy, and generous feeling, and pressing forward to the haven of their mutual prosperity (45, p. 66).

From the perspective of a young student in the Brook Farm school, John Sears later wrote that 'there was no prejudice against cards or chess or any other game so far as I know, but no one cared for any form of amusement that separated two or four from all the others. I imagine that even courting, the divine solitude of two, must have been handicapped by this persistent penchant for all being together' (52, pp. 102-3). Sears was also impressed by the community-enhancing function of conversation at Brook Farm.

It was only in the mid-nineteenth century, as industry and the rise of the city split American society, separating forever the community aspect (*Gemeinschaft*) from the market aspect (*Gesellschaft*), that the normal community spirit of religious communes stood out in unusually bold relief (3). As the world of *Gesellschaft* threatened to invade every niche of *Gemeinschaft* with its rationality, individual self-interest, functionalism and impersonality, even the nuclear family seemed like a utopian retreat (21; 30). And the 'extended families' of communal societies became all the more enticing as sanctuaries from the harsh realities of the world, except for those who actually forsook communes during this era for the lure of lucrative jobs and excitement in the city. John Humphrey Noyes envisaged his Oneida community acting as a yeast by projecting the sincerity of the 'family union beyond the little man-wife circle to large corporations' (40b).

Even in 'utopian' circles, however, individuals are less than perfect and conflicts do occur. Therefore the Ephratans, Shakers, Oneidans, Benedictines, Hutterites and others developed techniques to ameliorate disputes and lovingly to give members the admonition of leaders and comrades in a reconciliatory process that in some communities anticipated modern group therapy. In various communities this included daily or weekly oral or written confessions and periodic appearances before the entire congregation. At Oneida, Noyes made this a major feature known as 'mutual criticism' supported by all the necessary biblical justifications and, by most reports, very successful (40a).

Lessons of commitment from American religious utopias

Commitment is ironically the tower of strength and the Achilles' heel of religious communal utopias. Commitment holds the key to their constructive solidarity and their destructive authoritarianism. At the radical end of the communal spectrum where religiosity becomes cultism, commitment can be transformed into blind obedience with annihilation of personality, reason and life itself, as at Jonestown (10; 11; 41; 59).

It may be easy to see that commitment is potentially dangerous. But to recognise that the commitment to Jim Jones and his People's Temple movement was different only in degree, not in kind, from that seen in most religious communal utopias as well as in many institutions and political regimes in the larger world is more difficult (29; 39; 60). Nevertheless, even Shaker loyalties and practices run uncomfortably parallel to those of the People's Temple. Both groups put their complete trust in a charismatic leader whose life they believed to be infused with the miraculous. Both relinquished all goods and their use to the communal organisation. Both followed regimented daily schedules under close surveillance. Both internalised their leaders' negative opinions about the outside world. Both permitted their sex lives to be altered by fiat of the founder whom they delighted to call Mother or Father. The most committed in both groups abandoned their right to future progeny; one through celibacy, the other through suicide.

The difference lies in the willingness of Jones's disciples to pursue their commitment to him and his cult in the face of his own degeneration into unspeakable perversions and, more importantly, in the face of their own best moral judgments, humane sensitivities, and sane reason. Many who had joined the People's Temple to share in the noble causes proclaimed by Jones in his early ministry in Indiana and California – inter-racial Christian fellowship, communal-style care for the needy, social activism for civil rights, and personal salvation – were desperately disappointed by the increasingly bizarre behaviour of Jones as time progressed.

Unlike Mother Ann, Father Jones faked healings before his congregation, and, by 1964, claimed to be divine. In his Indianapolis Temple he threw his Bible to the floor saying that too many were looking to it rather than to him. By the 1970s Jones had constant bodyguards. His interminable sermons, sometimes lasting through the night, were filled with his impassioned harangues against the Ku Klux Klan, the Federal Bureau of Investigation, the Central Intelligence Agency and other threats from the outside, real or imagined. Parents watched as their children were beaten unmercifully at Jones's San Francisco Temple for minor infractions of his rigid code of conduct. Both men and women in the cult were sexually abused by 'Father' although he had others whipped before the congregation for alleged immoralities. One reason for the fateful, and partly misguided, visit of United States Congressman John Ryan and his party to Jonestown in November 1978 was to gather facts regarding a young boy, John Stoen, whom Jones claimed to have fathered on a former member. She was then suing for John's custody in California. Jones had often tested the loyalty of his closest aides by giving them a drink and then telling them they had drunk poison. By the time Congressman Ryan arrived, he apparently had rehearsed what he called the 'white night' of mass protest suicide with his congregation more than once and had threatened to invoke it if the Stoen case was not halted. During the last years of the People's Temple a few members such as Grace and Timothy Stoen did leave under the threat of violence (and some of these 'deserters' *have* died violent deaths since the Guyana massacre), but most simply had invested too much, had become too dependent upon the community and followed on to the isolation of Guyana and their own destruction.

Unwittingly perhaps, Jim Jones utilised a disturbing facet of human nature which also surfaced in a now-famous psychological laboratory experiment at Yale University conducted by Stanley Milgram (37). He discovered that more than 60 per cent of his subjects, regardless of age or socio-economic and educational background, would administer what they thought to be highly injurious and probably lethal electric shocks to other subjects because they had answered questions incorrectly. Milgram concluded that this obedience in the commission of an act which, on their own, the subjects would have considered unreasonable, immoral or inhumane was based on their submission to the authority they associated with the experimenter in his grey lab coat, the university and the cause of science itself. Therefore, although many of the subjects protested as the experiment proceeded, they transferred the moral responsibility to the symbols of authority and excused their own involvement. This is closely akin to the attitude of Adolf Eichmann in attributing his responsibility for the deaths of hundreds of thousands of civilians to the fact that he was merely obeying the orders of his Nazi superiors. Lieutenant William Calley, who was convicted of murdering innocent women and children at My Lai during the United States' occupation of Vietnam, admitted his actions but justified them on the grounds of obedience to his commanding officers. The victims at Jonestown can be seen taking the next logical step and becoming willing to destroy even themselves on the suggestion and responsibility of their demented authority-figure and his supposed mandate from heaven. Not since the 1000 Jewish Zealots at Masada defied the Roman tenth legion in A.D. 73 by taking their own lives has the world been so stunned by this phenomenon.

Rosabeth Moss Kanter's sociological study of ninety-one known communal utopias in the United States from 1780 to 1860 identified the specific commitment mechanisms at work in the eleven groups that survived more than twenty-five years (24a). Significantly, she found that this longevity was enjoyed only by *religious* communities. The secular communes which tended to champion freedom of thought and action, egalitarianism and democracy failed to generate the philosophical cement and commitment necessary to endure over time. This fact is worthy of further study with respect to the stability of democratic institutions and societies in general. However, we might speculate in passing that all societies must develop a unifying mystique of manifest destiny based upon widely accepted values, common cultural usages and divine or cosmological sanction in order to be self-sustaining.

Kanter isolated six commitment-mechanisms which she termed sacrifice, investment, renunciation, communion, mortification and transcendence. These were the processes by which communities sought to meet their needs for continuance, cohesion and control. Kanter found that the number and kind of commitment-mechanisms used contributed to the community's ability to maintain itself and to satisfy its members.

The progressively authoritarian and personally restrictive qualities of these mechanisms are important for our consideration. For continuance (the securing and retaining of members), successful communities have proselytised by an appeal to rational thinking: 'sacrifice' the few benefits of the world to receive the 'investment' of the many blessings of the communal fellowship. For cohesion (loyalty within the group), communities have used internal emotional ties to induce members toward 'renunciation' of relationships and attachments to people and things on the outside in favour of the unequalled 'communion' of the communal family. For control (the complete adoption of group values and authority by its devotees), communities have moulded members' wills to the group's own system of moral values through a process of 'mortification' in which the disciples give up their inner privacy by confessing all weaknesses, failures, problems and doubts. 'Transcendence' occurs as the power of the charismatic leader and his divinely-ordained movement becomes the source of meaning for the true believers. Eventually, the ideology of the group becomes the members' only means of interpreting life and the universe. The members may be required to take vows and oaths and to undergo periodic tests of loyalty. They may wear a uniform, shave their heads, change their names and otherwise lose their personal identity. Ultimately they may become totally loyal to their leader and his commands. The very meaning of their own lives becomes bound up with the mission and survival of the group.

Evidence of control-commitment can be found in most religious communal utopias past and present. Let one example from John Humphrey Noyes' Oneida suffice. When he was ready for volunteers to begin the eugenic experiment he called 'Stirpiculture' in 1869, fifty-three young women of the community signed the following pledge:

1. That we do not belong to ourselves in any respect, but that we belong first to God, and second to Mr. Noyes as God's true representative.

2. That we have no rights or personal feelings in regard to childbearing which shall in the least degree oppose or embarrass him in his choice of scientific combinations.

3. That we will put aside all envy, childishness, and self-seeking, and rejoice with those who are chosen candidates; that we will, if necessary, become martyrs to science, and cheerfully renounce all desire to become mothers, if for any reason Mr. Noyes deem us unfit material for propagation. Above all, we offer ourselves 'living sacrifices' to God and true Communism.

Thirty-eight young men at Oneida sent Noyes a similar statement (49, p. 338). During the ten years that followed, Noyes, a man in his sixties, sired no fewer than nine of the fifty-eight children born to the eugenic effort.

American religious utopias from the Shakers to Jonestown, therefore, have employed commitment-mechanisms. Sometimes their moderate usage with careful humanitarian safeguards has produced the laudable achievements which I enumerated in the beginning. At other times, the abuse of commitment-mechanisms has contributed to the most damnable exploitation. As individuals and nations, we can learn from this experience of the communal societies never to relinquish our right to judge all institutions, ideas, actions and leaders, regardless of the authority they claim, on the basis of our own best moral, rational and humane standards.

Conclusion

If the urgency of a spiritual revival is as critical for the survival of Western civilisation as Arnold Toynbee concluded in his monumental *A Study of History*, or if the choice for the modern world is indeed between utopia and oblivion, as Buckminster Fuller proclaimed in his 1969 book *Utopia or Oblivion*, mankind might well heed the lessons of collectivism, community and commitment tendered by American religious utopias. Young people in the 1960s seemed to sense that intentional community was a means to security, sanctuary and a *raison d'être*, that is, an alternative environment in which to humanise an otherwise depersonalised society. This, it may seem to reasonable minds, would be a commodious atmosphere for reflection upon universal values, renewal of the spirit and planning for the future.

We might find Kenneth Rexroth's observation in 1974 just as compelling nearly a decade later:

> The present relation of man to his environment and man to man has become so unlike the optimum necessary for the evolution of the species that humanity as we know it cannot endure. In such a situation a demand for readjustment is as instinctive as the reaction of an invertebrate animal subject to electric shock. This is what all the schools and tendencies of the libertarian and communal tradition have in common, a primary emphasis on man as a member of an organic community, a biota, in creative, non-exploitative relationship with his fellows and his environment (47, p. xiii).

> Today we realise that social change must move toward a rather clearly envisaged future or it will move toward disaster. It is either utopia or catastrophe (47, p. xv).

References

1. Andrews, Edward Deming, *The People Called Shakers: a search for the perfect society* (1953), New York 1963.
2. Arndt, Karl J.R. (a) *George Rapp's Harmony Society 1758-1847* (1965), Associated University Presses, Cranbury, New Jersey 1972. (b) *Harmony on the Connoquenessing, 1803-1815: a documentary history*, Harmony Society Press, Worcester, Mass. 1980.
3. Bender, Thomas, *Community and Social Change in America*, Rutgers University Press 1978.
4. Bestor, Arthur, Jr. (a) *Backwoods Utopias: the sectarian and Owenite phases of communitarian socialism in America, 1663-1829*, University of Pennsylvania Press 1950. (b) 'Patent-Office models of the good society: some relationships between social reform and westward expansion' (1951), *American Historical Review* 58, April 1953, pp. 505-26.
5. Calverton, Victor F., *Where Angels Dared to Tread: socialist & communist utopian colonies in the United States* (1941), Bobbs-Merrill, New York 1969.
6. Carden, Maren Lockwood, *Oneida: utopian community to modern corporation*, Johns Hopkins Press, Baltimore 1969.
7. Curtis, Edith R., *A Season in Utopia: the story of Brook Farm*, Nelson, New York, 1961.
8. Egerton, John, *Visions of Utopia: Nashoba, Rugby, Ruskin, and the 'New Communities' in Tennessee's past*, The University of Tennessee Press, Knoxville, Kentucky 1977.
9. Fairfield, Richard (ed.), *Utopia U.S.A.*, Alternatives Foundation, San Francisco 1972.
10. Feinsod, Ethan, *Awake in Nightmare – Jonestown: the only eyewitness account*, W.W. Norton, New York 1981.

11. Flanery, Michael, *The Why of Jonestown*, First Edition Books, Pittsburgh 1980.
12. Fogarty, Robert S., *Dictionary of American Communal and Utopian History*, Greenwood Press, Westport, Connecticut 1980.
13. Fuller, R. Buckminster, *Utopia or Oblivion* (1969), Overlook Press, New York 1973.
14. Gardner, Hugh, *The Children of Prosperity: thirteen modern American communes*, St Martin's Press, New York 1978.
15. Harris, Sara, *Father Divine*, Macmillan, New York 1971.
16. Hillery, George A., Jr., 'Definitions of community: areas of agreement', *Rural Sociology*, 20, 1955, p. 118.
17. Hine, Robert V., *California's Utopian Colonies* (1953) Yale University Press, New Haven 1966.
18. Holloway, Mark, *Heavens On Earth: utopian communities in America, 1680-1880* (1951) Dover, New York 1966.
19. Hostetler, John A. & Huntington, Gertrude, *The Hutterites in North America*, Holt, Rinehart and Winston, New York 1967.
20. Isaksson, Olov, *Bishop Hill: a utopia on the prairie*, L.T. Publishing House, Stockholm 1969.
21. Jeffrey, Kirk, 'The family as utopian retreat from the city: the nineteenth-century contribution', *Soundings* 60, 1972. pp. 21-40.
22. Jerome, Judson, *Families of Eden: communes and the new anarchism*, The Seabury Press, New York 1974.
23. Kagan, Paul, *New World Utopias: a photographic history of the search for community*, Penguin Books, Harmondsworth, Middlesex 1975.
24. Kanter, Rosabeth Moss (a) *Commitment and Community: communes and utopias in sociological perspective*, Harvard University Press 1972. (b) *Communes: creating and managing the collective life*, Harper & Row, New York 1973.
25. Kephart, William M., *Extraordinary Groups*, St Martin's Press, New York 1982.
26. Kilduff, Marshall & Javers, Ron, *The Suicide Cult*, Bantam Books, New York 1978.
27. Knerr, Michael E., *Suicide in Guyana*, Belmont Tower Books, New York 1978.
28. Krause, Charles A., *Guyana Massacre*, Berkley Publications Corporation, New York 1978.
29. Lane, Mark, *The Strongest Poison*, Dutton Press, New York 1979.
30. Lasch, Christopher, 'The family as a haven in a heartless world', *Salmagundi*, 1976, pp. 42-55.
31. Lassiter, William L., *Shaker Architecture*, Bonanza Books, New York 1966.
32. Manuel, Frank E. (ed.), *Utopias and Utopian Thought*, Beacon Press, Boston 1965.
33. Manuel, Frank E. & Fritzie P., *Utopian Thought in the Western World*, Harvard University Press 1979.
34. Meader, Robert F.W., *Illustrated Guide to Shaker Furniture*, Dover, New York 1972.
35. Meisel, Anthony C. & del Mastro, M.L., *The Rule of St. Benedict*, Doubleday, Garden City, New York 1975.

36. Melton, J. Gordon, *The Encyclopedia of American Religions*, McGrath, Wilmington, North Carolina 1979.
37. Milgram, Stanley, 'Some conditions of obedience and disobedience to authority', *Human Relations* 18, 1965, 57-76.
38. Moore, Thomas, 'Where have all the children of God gone?' *New Times*, October 4, 1974, pp. 32-7.
39. Naipaul, Shiva, *Journey To Nowhere: a new world tragedy*, Simon and Schuster, New York 1981.
40. Noyes, John Humphrey (a) *Mutual Criticism* (c. 1868), Syracuse University Press, 1975. (b) *History of American Socialism* (1870), Hillary House, Atlantic Highlands, New Jersey 1961.
41. Nugent, John P., *White Night: the true story of what before and after Jonestown*, Rawson, Wade, 1980.
42. Peters, Victor, *All Things Common: the Hutterian way of life*, Harper & Row, New York 1965.
43. Pitzer, Donald E., 'Harmonist folk art discovered', *Historic Preservation* 29, Oct.-Dec. 1977.
44. Pitzer, Donald E. & Elliott, Josephine M., 'New Harmony's first utopians, 1814-1824', *Indiana Magazine of History* 75, Sept. 1979, pp. 224-300.
45. Rapp, George, *Thoughts on the Destiny of Man*, Harmony Society Press, New Harmony, Indiana 1824.
46. Reston, James, Jr., *Our Father Who Art in Hell: the life and death of Jim Jones*, Times Books, New York 1981.
47. Rexroth, Kenneth, *Communalism: from its origins to the twentieth century*, The Seabury Press, New York 1974.
48. Richter, Peyton E., *Utopias: social ideals and communal experiments*, Holbrook Press, Boston 1971.
49. Robertson, Constance Noyes, *Oneida Community*, Syracuse University Press, 1970.
50. Rose, Milton C. & Mason, Emily, *A Shaker Reader*, The Main Street Press, New York 1977.
51. Sagan, Carl, *Cosmos*, Random House, New York 1980.
52. Sears, John Van Der Zee, *My Friends at Brook Farm* (1912), AMS Press, New York 1975.
53. Stegner, Wallace, *The Gathering of Zion: the story of the Mormon trail*, McGraw-Hill, New York 1964.
54. Thomas, Samuel W. & James C., *The Simple Spirit: a pictorial study of the Shaker community at Pleasant Hill, Kentucky*, Pleasant Hill Press, Harrodsburg, Kentucky 1973.
55. Thomas, Robert D., *The Man Who Would Be Perfect: John Humphrey Noyes and the utopian impulse*, University of Pennsylvania Press 1977.
56. Tod, Ian & Wheeler, Michael, *Utopia*, Harmony Books, New York 1978.
57. Veysey, Laurence, *The Communal Experience: anarchist and mystical counter-cultures in America*, Harper & Rowe, New York 1973.
58. Webber, Everett, *Escape to Utopia: the communal movement in America*, Hastings House, New York 1959.
59. White, Mel, *Deceived*, Fleming H. Revell, Old Tappan, New Jersey 1979.
60. Yee, Min S. & Layton, Thomas, *In My Father's House*, Holt, Rinehart and Winston, New York 1981.

PART III

The Uses and Necessity of
Utopian Thought

12

Uses of Utopia

Alasdair Morrison

I

In this chapter I ask what best case can be found for utopia, given my own preconceptions about the world and about the kind of political theory which that world makes most appropriate. I start with utopia as a form, often a literary form, in which a society other than the present one is described as a whole, with the implication or assertion that it is either the best or at least a better society. As such this chapter is essentially critical, so far as present society is concerned, and in one way or another is intended to be. There are of course other ways of criticising present society, but it is distinctive of utopia as a form that it does so by counterposing an account of a society in which things are different.

Utopia can serve as a mirror for society, a mirror in which it can see its own defects more clearly. More's original *Utopia* is to be seen in this light. The tone is serious, but hardly dramatic. The intention is clear enough, but the argument is not forced upon the reader. More does not raise his voice above the conversational level proper among civilised men. It is very much a book to be read at the appropriate level of courtesy: it has its ironies and its convictions, but any evidence of passion is submerged under the calm and conventional surface of the fictitious narrative. To register in this way civilised convictions (or at least civilised doubts) and to invite civilised readers to ask questions themselves is both legitimate and socially useful.

Utopia can constitute a thought-experiment, an extended hypothetical speculation, where the eventual judgment is left open. Even in More's case it is not clear that he was in any sense *advocating* the replacement of English institutions with utopian ones. There can be an element of mere play here, even in what seem the most savage satires. The eventual politics of a Swift or a Butler cannot be too simply deduced from the particular imaginative games which they invite us to join.

One side of the speculative value of individual utopias is in what they *say*, in the sense of which problems they select or highlight, which values they overturn, which institutions they deflate or abolish. Some topics – wealth, for instance, and sex and community size – recur quite often in a way which is itself significant. But societies vary in their characteristic defects, so that what the mirror needs to show will not necessarily be the same in every case, even though some features apear repetitively common to all – perhaps because all are human. As Horsburgh (3) points out (although working to a somewhat looser concept of utopia): 'Commonly, a utopian policy seeks to give practical form to only one value – or at the most two or three – and the result is a tremendous gain in clarity and forcefulness.'

But a second valuable speculative possibility in regard to particular utopias lies in the examination of where they break down. If they are imaginary, are they possible? And if they are not possible, why is that so? Which particular assumptions does the utopia make which are at variance with what the world will permit? If utopia is a theory, it is open to testing, and it would be an error to suppose that only attempted implementation is admissible as a test. Past experience and what in general we reliably know about ourselves and our world can be called in evidence too. But the specific test in a particular case may leave us wiser.

Yet we cannot stop at mere speculation, mere mirror gazing, mere intellectual sport. The subject matter is too important. The criticism and the reflection is supposed to produce some results, even if the author may have no very clear idea either of what results he will achieve or even of what he wants.

So far as the effect on the individual is concerned this indeterminacy is unavoidable. Two steps (roughly) are involved, and both are steps in the dark. When I say two steps, this is because, however reservedly, I am interposing belief (or something like it) between the reading of the book and any subsequent behaviour. How a given text will affect a reader's beliefs or perspectives will vary from reader to reader and is in effect for the most part unknowable. How his beliefs or perspectives will affect his actions is similarly obscure. This is a thicket full of philosophical brambles into which we should go no further here. Even the language is uncertain. However we conceptualise what is involved, empirically the effect remains indeterminate.

Considerations such as these remind us that utopia is not alone among what is written in having, and being intended to have, practical effects on its readers. Utopia is art. It has an expressive as well as a communicative function, and it needs to be seen in perspective among the whole range of imaginative writings of other kinds. How, for instance, does one compare More's *Utopia* with such writings as *The Vision of Piers Plowman, Coriolanus, Gulliver's Travels, Prometheus Unbound, War and Peace, Brave New World*, or *Animal Farm* and *1984*? There is a clear sense in which all are subsumable under one improvised genus: serious works of literature commenting on the human condition in a specifically (although not exclusively) political light. And they use the resources of literary art – if in various forms – to do so. They aim to convey a message, to move.

We are dealing here, to use traditional terms, with rhetoric, defined by Aristotle himself as 'the power to see the possible ways of persuading people about any given subject'. Rational argumentation has a place in rhetoric, but it is emphatically not the whole of it. People are, after all, people. Yet it is right to be concerned about the place that rational argumentation is to have in the effort to persuade. Plato's *Ion* is perhaps tangentially relevant here: for Ion's ability to move his audience by his recitals and expositions of Homer is not matched, as Socrates discovers, by any proportionate understanding of the physical and human world. But Plato – in some ways the ur-utopian – is relevant more generally. What he does in the *Republic* is instructive. I know of no work in which the problem of the relation between rhetoric and rational argument is more subtly explored. And at the centre is a city 'painted in words'.

We should perhaps remind ourselves that a city painted in words is not actually a city at all. Plato himself makes that quite clear. It is an imitation, and he is not even clear what 'imitation' involves. But the ideal city is not a city – it is only words, either on the page or (perhaps primarily) in the air. So comparison with actual cities is a problem.

The interesting thing about the *Republic* is its shape, which has been (in my view) frequently misunderstood. Book One is filled up with scene-setting and with unsatisfactory desultory dialectic, in which the level of rational argument is (to say the least) uneven. But at the start of Book Two everything takes a different turn. Glaucon and Adeimantus, fine young men plainly caught in a real difficulty – they *want* to do the right thing, but have been knocked off-balance by what they hear around them – appeal to Socrates for what is in effect help. Dialectics are dropped, and the construction of the ideal city begins. Socrates cannot resist their appeal, and he turns to what is, in the largest and grandest sense, rhetoric in order to meet it – something which even Thrasymachus acknowledges.

I think we see in this early example how utopia can be used. Whatever else Glaucon and Adeimantus forgot on the walk back from Piraeus, they would remember Socrates' city painted in words.

II

So we are led to consider the social or public dimension in the formulation and communication of ideas. And of course in relation to utopia it is something of a relief to reach this point, since historical experience shows utopia to have been not just the private inspiration of individuals but the collective obsession of masses. The ideas of utopia have had a collective effect well beyond any individual effect they may have had, and these collective effects are not readily, or indeed at all, reducible to strictly individual terms. The ideas of utopia have given rise to, or have been associated with, movements which have burned quite brightly across the political sky. This has been so whether or not the authors of utopia have themselves either intended or participated further in the results of their imaginings or prophecies.

What is required now is some account – however loose – of how human society works and what place ideas, including ideas of utopia, play in that process. We need to refer again to the (evolving) flesh-and-blood world, in which the human species confronts its physical environment, and try to place utopian ideas in that setting. If, after all, they have no use in that setting, they really have no use at all.

The mere fact of change is obvious. It is quite general, even if no particular pattern is necessarily evident. Nothing could be more obvious or more banal than the changes which have in all sorts of ways swept across the human world, perhaps in rising waves, over the past few hundred years. To understand this change (or concatenation of changes) is very hard; it is indeed (in my view) impossible to do so unless one takes two constants – the geographical world and the human animal.

Against that background it is easy enough to characterise the practical problem: how to cope with change, knowing that the specific changes which change generally consists of are very largely themselves the outcome of antecedent human activity. Within the geographical-biological fixed frame the social or cultural processes continue to evolve. The population thickens and redistributes itself. In such a situation there is a literally endless problem of mutual adjustment: how to re-balance interests, adjust relationships, reconstitute institutions, reimplement in the new situation what have been called eternal values, satisfy in new specific circumstances more or less constant human needs. It is a profoundly collective business.

The solution of this continuing problem involves, but is not solely composed of, the development of new specific ideas in the social and political field. It *involves* that development, because we are (after all) what we are. But equally it is not composed *exclusively* of such development because (again) we are what we are.

Now it seems to me that this is where utopia comes in. For there is plainly a case to be made for some scouting ahead. If (to use another image) we think of the future as breaking on us like a succession of waves, then there is a good case for trying to use our abilities and our experience to try to work out in advance what might be behind the wave which has either just washed our feet from under us or is just about to hit us. Utopia and futurology are siblings, even if their procedures (and their personnel) differ. There is absolutely nothing wrong in trying to work out what might be going to happen or what might be possible in a future which could be quite different from our present – as long as one stays within the parameters of the possible. Quite the contrary: few intellectual exercises are more necessary if we are (as they say in Scotland) to be spared. Speculation does not have to be idle speculation.

Although I think he exaggerates the utopian's role, Horsburgh (3, pp. 127-38) is very much to the point when he says: 'But there is another and still more fundamental role which the utopian is called upon to fill, namely, that of introducing new values into the life of the community. It seems fairly clear that this part alone, of the many that he is called upon to play, is one for which he has no understudies.'

It is not reasonably to be expected that in the evolving process described above there will be, generally or at any particular time, any agreement either about what the problems are or about what ought to be done. People have different experiences; they have different interests. So it is natural to *expect* partiality in people's ideas and in their perspectives. They will have different priorities and agendas. There will be a certain kind of specialisation, so far as both diagnosis and prognosis are concerned. One will get some sort of social dialogue. It is inconceivable that in a complex society faced with continuous and massive change anything like unanimity on the important questions will be forthcoming.

To say that a social dialogue (quite probably confused) will take place is not to reduce history to that dialogue. Nor do I wish to advance here any special causal theory of how the great historical engine is powered. But at least I am certain that the dialogue referred to comes into it, and that the outcome is not entirely indifferent to the dialogue. The dialogue makes a difference, because (again) we are what we are.

So far as utopia is concerned, its place in this story is not hard to identify. Wherever utopian ideas originate, they are, as stated earlier, essentially critical of the existing order. If they catch on, therefore, it is likely to be because they express the aspirations of the currently disadvantaged: the toads under some harrow. It does not matter that the ideas themselves may be formulated by someone quite other – typically some intellectual by the standards of the day. Nor does it matter that the disadvantaged may not be the *most* disadvantaged. For example, as Sorel (6) points out, 'liberal political economy is one of the best examples of a utopia that could be given'.

Such a broad indication of the historical role of utopian ideas in the public realm is enough here. It is obvious enough and in line with what Mannheim (5) and many others have said. There is an abundant and fascinating detailed literature which records the histories of particular utopian projects, experiments and movements. The variety is great, even if some broad patterns do repeat themselves.

III

In the public realm, now, there arises the question whether (and how) any utopian scheme is to be put into effect. For utopia can, and often does, generate both enthusiasm and determination. It attracts supporters who will not be content with thought-experiments: they want the real thing. That indeed is what utopia is *for*: it is an inspiration and a goal. But this is where the major difficulties, both intellectual and political, begin.

It will be helpful to start with what is from most points of view the easiest general case – the case of the small community utopia. There have been many of these, and though many of the experiments have been short-lived, some have survived. Survival must be counted as one criterion of success. Survival does at least show that the theory behind the experiment falls within the range of human possibility, although it does not prove that the resulting community is the best sort of human community or indeed that it is necessarily a particularly good one. Other criteria would have to be used to judge that. Some arguably very bad social systems have, after all, lasted a long time. On the other hand, if the experimental community withers or collapses, that does not in itself prove that the utopian theory behind it is faulty. The failure may cast doubt on the theory and suggest a case for re-examination, but it remains possible to argue that it was some other factor in the situation which led to the failure. We have not shown that the project is humanly impossible, only that it was impossible in these circumstances.

This sort of communitarian experiment is surely both legitimate and interesting, even if one is not personally inclined to commit oneself to anything of the kind, and even though some of them have looked very odd and ill-conceived. Huxley (4) puts it very well:

> For anyone who is interested in human beings and their so largely unrealised potentialities, even the silliest experiment has value, if only as demonstrating what ought not to be done. And many of the recorded experiments were far from silly. Well planned and carried out with skill and intelligence, some of them have contributed significantly to our

knowledge of that most difficult and most important of all the arts – the art of living together in harmony and with benefit for all concerned.

Community experiments of this kind have, so far as utopian theory is concerned, two striking merits: they have to specify their practical implications in considerable detail, and the experiment itself is voluntary for those involved in it. But the motives of the participants may be mixed, and the costs may in the end be sadly high and even eventually involve a considerable waste of spirit. Huxley gives a grim list of the sort of impracticality which can lead to failure, and it illustrates well the ways in which the world will not be mocked:

> Except in a purely negative way, the history of Llano is sadly uninstructive. All that it teaches is a series of Don'ts. Don't pin your faith on a water supply, which, for half the time, isn't there. Don't settle a thousand people on territory which cannot possibly support more than a hundred. Don't admit to your fellowship every Tom, Dick and Harry who may present himself. Don't imagine that a miscellaneous group can live together, in closest physical proximity, without rules, without shared beliefs, without private and public 'spiritual exercises' and without a magnetic leader. At Llano everything that ought not to have been done was systematically done. A pathetic little Ozymandias is all that remains to tell the tale.

The communities which last are those that avoid that kind of impracticality. But other conditions must be satisfied as well, of which the most pressing concerns the relationship with the outside world. No community is an island, entire unto itself, and only in certain specialised types of location can long-term integrity be given much of a chance. It may be a matter of physical isolation, or it may require the compliance of a neighbouring or encircling social system prepared not to interfere. Such conditions are relatively rare, certainly rare enough by far to ensure that the community prescription must remain exceptional and that it cannot become universal for all men. There is a real sense in which such communities cannot help being dependent, if not actually parasitic, on the world outside with its other ways of living.

It is natural, then, to move on to the next stage and to ask whether the assumptions made about the wider world may not be unnecessarily gloomy. Can we not envisage a transformation of the wider world in parallel with the transformation achieved inside our utopian community? Can we not have a utopia for the wider world? Of course we can design such a utopia. It has been done many times, often enough as an extension of the ideals of the community utopia. But there are two great areas of difficulty and of controversy, corresponding to the two great merits seen above in the small community case, which show conclusively what a profound error it is to think of the wider world as if it were politically the same as the smaller world – only bigger.

To put the matter briefly, it becomes, first, shockingly hard to specify in anything approaching the required detail what the implementation of the utopia would entail in practical institutional terms. Nor is this something to which utopian theorists, perhaps understandably, have given enough attention. Sometimes, indeed, like Marx, they have expressly declined to do so. To do so would, paradoxically, be utopian. Secondly, the wider utopia cannot plausibly be represented as voluntary. At least in any period of transition compulsion will be needed. I will say a little more about each of these difficulties in turn.

IV

The wider world itself needs to be specified more clearly. For there is a good deal of variety among utopian writers both in the attention they have given to the wider world itself and in the scope of wider world which they have taken into view. For some – More himself, for instance – the question does not really arise. The visions and the political programmes of most of the English writers in the seventeenth century were addressed to and limited to England. A diffuse cosmopolitanism, devoid of much detail, characterised much eighteenth- and nineteenth-century thought. Where the problems of international relations were confronted – by the Abbé de Saint-Pierre, Rousseau, Kant, Saint-Simon – the focus was very much on Europe, with the rest of the world left pretty much as a blur. Fourier's fanciful structure of caliphates and so on looks more authentically global, even if it sits fairly loosely on the real world of geography and politics.

Strictly speaking utopia *requires* attention to be paid not merely to the wider world but to the world as a whole. It is no real criticism of writers in earlier centuries that they operated with a conception of the wider world which was either limited or left indeterminate. But nowadays there is less excuse. One does not have to be a *dependencia* theorist in good standing to sense the extent to which human problems have become global problems. As Goodwin and Taylor (2), for instance, observe:

> In the countries of the Third World the standard of living is so miserably low that, looking at global society *as a whole*, Western man must surely recognise the need to radically improve global conditions through the implementation of some kind of plan of utopian dimensions.

Unfortunately the problem is even worse than such a statement suggests – and the statement is itself their only reference to the global perspective. It is tempting to think only of social or moral questions in the world order, and to frame one's utopia accordingly. But geopolitical and strategic factors are also involved, whose institutional accommodation poses daunting difficulties not only to the will but to the intellect. Clark and Sohn's *World Peace Through World Law*, a utopian project deriving from the Anglo-Saxon constitutional tradition, illustrates well enough the depth of the difficulties which face us. Will and understanding – and power – have to come together on a very large scale indeed, and it would be sad if some 'utopian' attempt to force the pace by mobilising mass enthusiasm for some emotional short-cut were to trigger off exactly the explosion which we want to avoid.

Whatever conception of the ideal we have at the global level, the practical implications in institutional terms are of extreme complexity and difficulty. And it is not surprising that few people have tried to spell out at all adequately what in practice a future world order might look like. Yet by the standards of my earlier argument this should be high on the utopian agenda at this time.

If, however, we withdraw from the global problem, things are still not easy. At any level above the community, considerations of scale and complexity make the task of specifying in practical terms what utopia requires much more difficult. Certainly this is so if perfection (or anything like it) is the goal. It is not too difficult to conceive of alternative sets of imperfect institutions. We have, after all, quite a range to choose from. It is also possible to evaluate comparatively the merits in human terms of alternative sets. But none of the viable sets which we know of is a simple magnification of what can in favourable circumstances be achieved at the autonomous community level.

It is tempting, partly because of this inherent difficulty, to stop at the abstract ideal, but always that ideal has to be turned into actual proposals for change, and the utopian task is less than half done if that responsibility is dodged. Sorel (6) is on the right lines when he says:

> A utopia is … an intellectual product; it is the work of theorists who, after observing and discussing the known facts, seek to establish a model to which they can compare existing society in order to estimate the amount of good and evil it contains. It is a combination of imaginary institutions having sufficient analogies to real institutions for the jurist to be able to reason about them; it is a construction which can be taken to pieces, and certain parts of it have been shaped in such a way that they can (with a few alterations by way of adjustment) be fitted into approaching legislation.

One sees here the speculative element discussed earlier, but one sees also the practical: a utopia based on reality in some detail lends itself not merely to the purposes of change but to constructive change. And it is significant that Sorel's account does not point to the imposition on society of some total blueprint, but to partial modifications of society *in the light of* the alternative blueprint. We touch on a major controversy here. On my left (no doubt) Barbara Goodwin; on my right (for instance) Sir Karl Popper.

I want to make just two points, the first of which is to ask whether at the intellectual level the argument has not become over-polarised. It seems to me rather obvious that there are times when it is right to override individual wishes and interests in order to secure some general good. It seems to me also sensible to make such decisions not in isolation but carefully in the context of the whole web of social practices and values – if this means thinking 'totally', so be it. It also seems to me to be desirable, especially at some moments, to think *imaginatively* about alternatives. I am not sure where in this Popper would disagree. Is, for example, the sort of process described above by Sorel to be counted as utopian engineering or piecemeal engineering?

On the other hand, if we are to take seriously statements made by Goodwin and Taylor (2) in their chapter 9, it is not clear how far we have moved. For instance:

> Elster's criticism of the utopians who dogmatically cling to their ideal in the face of changing contours and possibilities is sound, but his rejection of utopian thinking in general on these grounds is not ... The political thinkers who draw on utopian ideas do not use them as blueprints which must be followed to the letter, but as suggestive devices which help us decide in which directions change should take place.

Such an approach to the use of utopia ought to go some way towards defusing the intellectual tension which utopia often generates. They say a little later:

> What these experiments and the experience of history make clear is that all utopias, although conceived as totalities, are in constant need of revision, since utopian thinkers cannot possibly predict all sources of human dissatisfaction, or all social and technical developments.

This all sounds very reasonable even if, or perhaps because, it makes revisionism sound respectable. But does this version, with its suggestions that the utopian blueprint is constantly in need of modification in the light of experience and that the function of the blueprint may only be to suggest directions for partial change, really catch the whole spirit of utopia? I am not sure that it does. And if in the controversy about 'totalitarianism' (and so on) we are faced not only with two different strengths of informed and responsible pragmatism but also with differences in temperament, then some of my worst fears would revive, and I might fly to Popper for refuge. In my book Robespierre, for instance, stands as an Awful Warning, some kind of a political monster. I am not certain in what sense even his intentions were good.

V

Utopia in itself may not be dangerous, but that does not mean that some utopians may not be. The reason can be traced back to the two difficulties which utopia faces in the larger than communitarian context, mentioned at the end of part III of this chapter. The first of these I have discussed: the difficulty of specifying in the larger context what the practical implications of utopia are. I shall in a sense return to that shortly. But the second difficulty was that utopia in the larger context can no longer be voluntary. We then have problems about the degree of compulsion to be used and equally severe problems about how compulsion is to be organised and exercised. These are areas where differences of temperament may show and where both individual and social psychology may have some fairly sinister insights to provide. Some people, to put it bluntly, are happier than others when it comes to knocking other people about for what is supposed to be their own good, and there is absolutely no warrant for supposing that their motives are necessarily what they think they are, nor what they are publicly claimed to be.

In the appeal which utopia has for its proponents and adherents it is the abstract ideal element which leads. The vision of community, of harmony, of peace, of brotherly love, of perfect justice – these call out to people whose lives may well lack such experiences, often to a spectacular extent. They are probably not greatly interested in and certainly not as moved by the particular institutional forms which the ideals are to entail – although the picture is admittedly more complicated than that suggests. But social movements not only have certain characteristic dynamics, they also exhibit characteristic structures, which we ignore at our peril. This is not something about which it is wise to be innocent or, worse still, to pretend to be innocent.

In the case of utopia in particular its appeal to intellectuals and the nature of that appeal needs to be studied, since it is characteristic of utopia that intellectuals, whose own position in society is distinct from that of the majority, should be the main originators and proponents of the utopian programme. Of course that is almost a truism: that is what intellectuals are for. They are the articulate ones, the originators and exchangers of ideas. They deal in ideas as financiers deal in money. In a way beyond the experience of most people they are at home in the realm of abstract thought. But that does not mean that their judgment in practical matters is uniformly impeccable. Still less does it mean that they do not remain heir to all the temptations that flesh is heir to. They may even develop some interesting specialised ones of their own. Suffice it to say that the role of intellectuals in utopian politics has been a prominent one, and that there have been some unfortuate results. The total appeal of a utopian conception, making, as it were, everything clear, can have an almost aesthetic appeal for the abstract mind, to which details, contradictions, dilemmas and compromises – whether with other people or with some other aspect of recalcitrant reality – are uncongenial. (Sorel, in the passage quoted above, was concerned to distinguish utopia from myth. But myth and utopia have points of similarity.) To sum up, the great gulf between the rational men and the Yahoos is in one way or another with us still; and the Yahoos had better remain on their guard.

But if an argument about the degree of compulsion which is proper or wise in the implementation of utopia is one thing, advocacy of what is impossible is something else. It is no doubt true that impossibility in human affairs is, strictly speaking, hard if not impossible to prove. 'The bounds of possibility, in moral matters, are less narrow than we imagine,' says Rousseau. Yes indeed. But that does not mean that they are infinite. Nor does it mean that we cannot come by a reasonably reliable idea of where the bounds in fact lie. We should not neglect either human necessities or human potentials. But we need to take reality at least as seriously as we take our aspirations. A sense of limits is something we cannot very well do without. As it is, over-ambitious ideas of what human beings might be like have often enough been the pretext on which some of their number have treated the rest as they should not be treated. And, quite generally, the motives of anyone who proclaims, especially from a public platform, that something which is palpably impossible is inevitable and/or imminent call for particular scrutiny.

That rather negatively said, I would like to right the balance by quoting Goodwin and Taylor (2):

> Underlying all forms of utopianism is the conviction that optimistic, imaginative thought and action are capable of bringing about a change towards not only a new social existence, but a better one.

That seems to me to be a necessary belief and a true one, even if we fail in the end. But if we must be open-minded about what the future can be like, we cannot afford to be empty-headed about it. Nor, even though it is fair to insist that utopia should not be condemned as a whole because of some excesses, should we seek to legitimise every aspect of utopian thought under cover of its undeniable positive potential. If utopia has its uses, it also has its abuses.

References

1. Clark, G. & Sohn, L.B., *World Peace Through World Law*, Harvard University Press, 1958.
2. Goodwin, B. & Taylor, K., *The Politics of Utopia*, Hutchinson, London 1982.
3. Horsburgh, H.J.N., 'The relevance of the utopian', *Ethics* 67, 1956-7, pp. 127-38.
4. Huxley, A., 'Ozymandias', *Adonis and the Alphabet*, Chatto and Windus, London 1956.
5. Mannheim, K., *Ideology and Utopia*, Routledge, London 1936.
6. Sorel, G., *Reflections on Violence* (1925), translated by Hulme & Roth, Collier, New York 1961.

13

Marxism and Utopianism

Steven Lukes

What is the relation of Marxism to utopianism? In attempting to answer this question, we face at least three central difficulties.

The first, and least interesting, is the definitional problem of what, for these purposes, is to count as Marxism. The textual legacy bequeathed by Marx and Engels has proved, to say the least, an ambiguous inheritance in this as in other respects – a fact whose significance is only magnified by the bibliocentric character of Marxism, whether as an oppositional or a ruling ideology. The dominant interpetation within mainstream Marxism – in the Second and Third Internationals, within Trotskyism and in many social-democratic variants – has been largely 'scientific' and 'anti-utopian': as Milan Šimečka rightly observes in this volume (14, p. 170), it has for over a hundred years 'striven to differentiate itself from utopias by means of a scientific veneer, and it cannot be denied that it has had some success in this ...'. But utopian countercurrents have always existed, finding their most eloquent recent expression in the thought of Ernst Bloch, for whom Marxism discovers 'concrete' rather than 'abstract' utopia in 'the not yet [*noch nicht*] actual objective real possibilities in the world' (7, p. 55; 2, p. 727). I shall deal with this first difficulty here by focussing almost entirely upon what Marx and to some extent Engels wrote. Just because it *is* so bibliocentric, Marxism's distinctive positions on this topic can all be traced back to readings and misreadings of their writings, so it is essential at least to begin with them. And indeed, as I shall argue, they exhibit a structure of thought which has had important consequences throughout the history of Marxism.

The second difficulty is also definitional, but more interesting: what is to count as utopian? This is a problem area into which I do not propose to enter here except to observe that the term poses peculiar problems of definition which are only magnified when considered in the context of Marxism. For it is not only a matter of defining the term's referential scope (here Professor Davis's narrower definition within a taxonomy of types of ideal society is of particular interest). Its proper application is also subject to dispute, since what counts as 'utopian' will depend on where (and how) the boundaries between the real and the ideal, and between the feasible and the merely possible are drawn. For I take it that utopians are devisers of schemes of ideal societies that are doubly unrealistic, contrasting with existing evils, and unrealisable within existing parameters. Typically, many so-called 'utopians' (such as Saint-Simon and Kropotkin) have described and even thought of themselves as 'realists', and some self-styled utopians have been thought of by others as realists. Is 'utopian' an external category, relying upon the observer's judgments concerning the boundaries indicated, or an internal category, relying upon the observer's interpretation of the actor's judgments? And if the latter, are such interpretations based on explicit statements or implicit assumptions (so that someone may be utopian because, although claiming to be a realist, and not a utopian, he is offering a persuasive utopian redefinition of 'realism')?

The problem is only compounded in relation to Marxism, which offers a theory of the social basis and historical role of utopian thinking, which it both embraces and rejects as anachronistic: its self-understanding is scientific and revolutionary and thus anti-utopian, and yet that self-understanding may well seem severely deficient, obscuring the utopian aspects of Marxism from its adherents. Yet that judgment itself presupposes boundary judgments of the sort indicated that are arguably implicit in Marxism itself. Bloch saw a kind of concrete utopianism as implicit in Marx. As he wrote:

> Marx ... explains the dialectics of history which leads to tensions, utopias and revolutions, in a materialistic way for the first time. He grounds and corrects the anticipations of utopia through economics, through immanent revolutions of production and exchange ... The abstract utopias devoted nine-tenths of their space to painting the future and only one-tenth to critical, often purely negative analysis of the present ... Marx devoted more than nine-tenths of his writings to the critical analysis of the present, and a relatively small space to designations of the future ... Genuine *designations* of the future are lacking ... because Marx's whole work serves the future, and indeed can only be understood and carried out in the horizon of the future, not indeed as one that is depicted in an abstract utopian way, but as one that takes effect in and out of the past as well as the present. (7, pp. 56-7; 2, pp. 724-5)

Which leads me to the third difficulty: the very complexity of Marxism's relation to utopianism, to which the rest of this chapter is devoted. The thesis I shall argue for is two-fold. First, that Marx adopted and Marxism inherited a view that was both anti-utopian and utopian, and that this was not mere ambivalence but a theoretical position, a kind of anti-utopian utopianism, distinctive of Marxism. Secondly, that Marxism's anti-utopianism has weakened and subverted its utopianism, to the considerable detriment of Marxism itself, both in theory and in practice.

I

Attacks by Marx and later Marxists on utopians – notably Owen, Saint-Simon and Fourier, but also the Babouvists and the Germans, such as Weitling and the hapless Herr Duhring – are too well-known to need repetition here. They produced 'fantastic pictures of future society, painted at a time when the proletariat is still in a very undeveloped state and has but a fantastic conception of its own position' and corresponding to 'the first instinctive yearnings of that class for a general reconstruction of society' (12g, p. 62). Marx's and Engels's main critical attention was focussed on Owen, Saint-Simon and Fourier, and it is as well to recall, with the Manuels, that their evaluations of these three, which range from contempt to generous praise, 'swayed with the subject under discussion and the political exigencies of the times' (10, p. 702). What is worth accentuating here is the positive: the reasons for which they valued all three and were decisively influenced by them.

Engels stated the most positive general appreciation in 1870:

> German theoretical Socialism will never forget that it stands on the shoulders of Saint-Simon, Fourier and Owen, three men who despite their fantasies and utopianism are to be reckoned among the most significant minds of all times, for they anticipated with genius countless matters whose accuracy we now demonstrate scientifically. (5a, p. 541; 10, p. 702)

'We delight', he wrote elsewhere, 'in these stupendously grand thoughts and germs of thought that everywhere break out of their phantastic covering' (5b, pp. 119-20); and in the *Communist Manifesto*, Marx and Engels say of the famous trio that they 'attack every principle of existing society. Hence they are full of the most valuable materials for the enlightenment of the working class' (5b, p. 63). Marx saw their utopias as 'the anticipations and imaginative expression of a new world' (12e, p. 172).

In Owen they especially valued the practical determination to prove the virtues of co-operation, harnessing the abilities of all through the direct social organisation of labour based on the factory system, and his commitment to the working class. For Marx, he was one of those 'really doughty natures who, once having struck out on a revolutionary path, always draw fresh strength from their defeats and become more decisive the longer they swim in the flood tide of history' (12a, XXI, p. 530) while Engels saw his *New Moral World* as 'the most comprehensive project of the future communist community, with its groundplan, elevation, and bird's-eye-view' (12a, XIX, p. 289). What united them with Saint-Simon and his followers has been well described by the Manuels: 'an endlessly dynamic prospect founded upon the boundless expansion of science and technology, exploitation of the inexhaustible natural resources of the globe, and the flowering of human capacities' (10, p. 707). And from Fourier they took the notion of a community of richly diverse needs, as essential to many-sided individuality within a genuinely reciprocal community (though they balked at Fourier's interest in sensual and sexual experimentation). In short, the Manuels are absolutely right to see these three utopian socialists as having 'left an indelible stamp on the banderole of the *Critique of the Gotha Programme*' (10, p. 701) whose inscription was intended to describe communism's higher phase (Marx's and Engels's utopia): 'From each according to his abilities, to each according to his needs.'

So far I have sought to show that Marx and Engels were anti-utopians and utopians. Their anti-utopianism was a general critique of such fantasising as premature and pre-scientific, that had become in their own time reactionary and dangerous; their utopianism a specific acceptance of the Utopian Socialists' visions of the future which they synthesised and incorporated into their own vision of human emancipation. That vision was without doubt the vision of an ideal society, contrasting with pre-human, alienated, class societies, whose realisation was only feasible through the destruction of existing parameters. It is instructive, however, to see that it was precisely not, in their eyes, a utopia in Professor Davis's sense: a 'bureaucratic, institutional, legal and educational' order, accepting 'the bases of the problem from which politics arises' and containing 'organisational forms and practices which will guarantee the just distribution of finite resources and contain the anti-social proclivities of men and women' (4, p. 10). On the contrary, it was an order in which the conditions which call forth politics and principles of distributive justice, notably scarcity and conflicting interests, would have withered away – as would the state, bureaucracy and law. In Professor Davis's terms, their vision of emancipation was a peculiar synthesis of Cockaygne (abundance), the perfect moral commonwealth (in which, however, the morality of duty would wither away) and the millennium (Engels wrote of the vocation of socialists to risk their lives in a 'last holy war that will be followed by the millennium of freedom' (7, p. 230n; 12a, I, 2, 225)).

Marx and Engels were not anti-utopian in the sense of vesting high hopes in the future: few have held higher hopes than they did. But they did criticise the Utopian Socialists for drawing up utopian *blueprints*, just because in doing this they laid claim to a type of knowledge, social forecasting, that could not be had *now*: this was, as Lenin said, 'to indulge in idle guesswork about what cannot be known' (18a, p. 458). As Marx wrote, while communists should 'lay stress on far-reaching aims', none the less 'the thing to be done at any definite, given moment of the future, the thing immediately to be done depends of course on the given historical conditions in which one has to act' (12e, p. 408). Engels made the same point in discussing the goal of abolishing the distinction between town and country:

> To be utopian does not mean to maintain that the emancipation of humanity from the chains which its historic past has forged will be complete only when the antithesis between town and country has been abolished; the utopia begins only when one ventures, 'from existing conditions', to prescribe the *form* in which this or any other antithesis of present-day society is to be resolved. (5c, p. 628)

Secondly, they saw the very project of speculating about the ideal society as 'utopian' and thus both anti-scientific and anti-revolutionary. Indeed, for them 'utopian' was an antonym of both 'scientific' and 'revolutionary': the early utopians had speculated about the ideal society just because they were not (and could not be) clearly aware of the future latent in the present, and so failed to identify with the class that would bring it into being. (Later utopias, such as those constructed by Duhring 'out of his sovereign brains', were simply 'silly, stale and reactionary' (12a, XIX, p. 190; 12e, p. 376).) As Marx wrote,

> Just as the economists are the scientific representatives of the bourgeois class, so the *Socialists* and the *Communists* are the theoreticians of the proletarian class. So long as the proletariat is not yet sufficiently developed to constitute itself as a class, and consequently so long as the struggle itself of the proletariat with the bourgeoisie has not yet assumed a political character, and the productive forces are not yet sufficiently developed in the bosom of the bourgeoisie itself to enable us to catch a glimpse of the material conditions necessary for the emancipation of the proletariat and for the formation of a new society, these theoreticians are merely utopians who to meet the wants of the oppressed classes, improvise systems and go in search of a regenerating science. But in the measure that history moves forward, and with it the struggle of the proletariat assumes clearer outlines, they no longer need to seek science in their minds; they have only to take note of what is happening before their eyes and become its mouthpiece. So long as they look for science and merely make systems, so long as they are at the

beginning of the struggle, they see in poverty nothing but poverty, without seeing in it the revolutionary, subversive side, which will overthrow the old society. From this moment, science, which is a product of the historical movement, has associated itself consciously with it, has ceased to be doctrinaire and has become revolutionary (11b, pp. 116-17).

Here Marx is saying, in quasi-Hegelian fashion, that, with the forward movement of history, a vantage-point becomes available from which the self-transformation of capitalism into socialism becomes increasingly visible. Adequate knowledge of this process, though not of the shape of the future society, becomes available to the scientific observer. And Marx wrote that the only appropriate response to such scientific knowledge is a revolutionary one: such an observer can only become a partisan theoretician of the proletarian class. Lukacs, among later Marxists, stated this aspect of Marx's thought with maximum force and clarity:

> ... since the ultimate objective has been categorised, not as Utopia, not as *reality which has to be achieved*, positing it above and beyond, the immediate advantage [of revolutionary classes and parties] does not mean abstracting from reality and attempting to impose certain ideals on reality, but rather it entails the knowledge and transformation into action of those forces already at work *within* social reality – those forces, that is, which are directed towards the realisation of the ultimate objective. Without this knowledge the tactics of every revolutionary class or party will vacillate aimlessly between a *Realpolitik* devoid of ideals and an ideology without real content. It was the lack of this knowledge which characterised the revolutionary struggle of the bourgeois class ... The Marxist theory of class struggle, which in this respect is wholly derived from Hegel's conceptual system, changes the transcendent objective into an immanent one; the class struggle of the proletariat is at once the objective itself and its realisation (9, pp. 4-5).

The knowledge that that theory expresses is the knowledge of a self-transforming present, not of an ideal future.

But, one must ask, how can one have the one kind of knowledge (of the self-transforming present) without the other (of the shape of future society)? How can scientific observers know that 'what is happening before their eyes', that the result of 'forces already at work within social reality' is the 'realisation of the ultimate objective', the emancipatory transformation of capitalism into socialism, unless they also know, or at least have good reason to believe, that the 'new society', latent in the old, will take a form that *is* emancipatory, thus justifying their support for the proletariat's struggle? In other words, to assume that they do know the former is to assume that they know, or have good reason to believe, the latter.

Marx and Engels failed to see the force of this objection, for various reasons. If they had done so, they would have seen the inescapable need both to specify possible futures as closely as possible, indicating which are more or less feasible, and to set out the grounds for supporting the struggle for one of them, by showing how it could realise values that would justify that support – a need that was all the greater, since the future they envisaged was currently unfeasible. Instead of this, they fixed upon one such future, which they conceived as possible, but unfeasible without revolutionary transformation, believing that its realisation depended in part upon the prevalence within the revolutionary class of an anti-utopian mentality: that it could only be delayed by the very attitudes such questions embodied and only hastened by refusing to face them.

They failed to see the objection and these corollaries for at least three reasons. First, they assumed a teleological philosophy of world history, alongside or rather behind their causal-cum-intentional explanations, according to which the goal of world history is the resolution of all 'the antitheses of present-day society' (11h, p. 155) and communism 'the solution of the riddle of history [which] knows itself to be the solution' (ibid.); and they interpreted world history and current events in the light of that goal. Consider, for example, Marx's notorious remarks about the British in India:

> England, it is true, in causing a social revolution in Hindoustan, was actuated only by the vilest interests, and was stupid in her manner of enforcing them. But that is not the question. The question is, can mankind fulfil its destiny without a fundamental revolution in the social state of Asia? If not, whatever may have been the crimes of England, she was the unconscious tool of history in bringing about that revolution. Thus, whatever bitterness the spectacle of the crumbling of an ancient world may have for our personal feelings, we have the right, in point of history, to exclaim with Goethe:
>> Sollte diese Qual uns qualen
> Da sie unsre Lust vermehrt,
> Hat nicht Myriaden Seelen
> Timur's Herrschaft aufgezehrt? (11c, I, p. 351)

Thus they made the rash and strange assumption that 'mankind only sets itself such tasks as it can solve (11c, I, p. 363), supposing thereby that success in the task of building socialism was somehow historically guaranteed.

Secondly, they thought that the evils of capitalism were so blatantly obvious and the possible future so probable *and* obviously desirable that speculation about the latter was unnecessary. Just as emancipation had followed slavery, so human emancipation would follow wage slavery. To ask whether and why was, for them, a question that simply did not arise.

Thirdly, they saw such speculation as counter-revolutionary: as open to endless possibilities of disagreement, wasting revolutionary energies and inclining those who engage in it to fruitless appeals to society as a whole or to the goodwill of leaders and statesmen. Marx, it is said, wrote to the English positivist Beesley in 1869 that 'The man who draws up a programme for the future is a reactionary' (10, p. 698). The revolutionary, by contrast, avoids such disagreements, concentrates his energies and focuses his political activity by 'taking note of what is happening before [his] eyes' and becoming 'its mouthpiece'.

These, then, were the reasons that inhibited Marx and Engels, and their followers, from reflecting seriously and systematically upon their utopia. In the second part of this chapter, I turn to consider the nature of that utopia more directly, and the consequences of that inhibition for both theory and practice.

II

The Marxist utopia is full communism, or human emancipation.

What, then, does emancipation promise? What are the distinctive virtues embodied in the realm of freedom? As we have seen, Marx and orthodox Marxism systematically avoid explicit answers to this question as 'utopian'. Yet the Marxian views of justice and injustice, exploitation and the unfreedom of alienation all presuppose an ideal of freedom. They all employ a radical critical perspective, the standpoint of 'human' society, or the realm of freedom, that cannot be adopted unless it is answered, unless some content is given to 'communism'. In what follows, I shall focus (unless otherwise indicated) entirely upon communism's higher phase, the lower being still 'a communist society, not as it has developed on its own foundations, but on the contrary, just as it emerges from capitalist society, which is thus in every respect, economically, morally and intellectually, still stamped with the birth marks of the old society from whose womb it emerges' (11g, II, p. 23). To continue this favourite metaphor of Marx's, we are concerned here with communism full-grown and mature, unmarked by its origins (or, one might add, by whatever obstetric methods were used to bring it into being).

In such a society, principles of justice, and more generally of *Recht*, are assumed to have withered away: they have, in Engels's words, been forgotten in practical life. By what principles or standards, then, is this society to be judged superior? What kind of morality is the 'really human morality' that it embodies? Is it intuitionist? Much of Marx's and Marxist writings could be seen in that light: frequent appeal is made to the reader's sense of indignation, sympathy, and also his sense of what is 'worthy of human nature'. Yet it is an elementary Marxist thought that moral intuitions will be prime candidates for class-related bias: there seems to be no good Marxist reason to suppose such intuitions to be universally shared, even by fully reflective agents, let alone to appeal to them in practical reasoning. Is it deontological, then, say Kantian? There is, as the neo-Kantians saw, much to support this view in the canonical texts – as, for example, in Marx's condemnation of capitalist exchange relations as social relations in which 'each becomes a means for the other' (11a, pp. 136-41), and more generally in his frequent talk of the 'slavery', degradation and indignity inherent in capitalist relations. Or is it, perhaps, utilitarian? Here too there is much support in what Marx and later Marxists have said. Communism will be not only more efficient and productive; it will abolish misery, unhappiness and frustration: as Lenin said, working people's lives would be eased and their welfare maximised (8b, p. 411). Or is it rather perfectionist, couched in teleological Aristotelian terms of the realisation of distinctively human potentialities and excellences? There is much evidence to support this interpretation: as, for example, Marx's claim that the 'calling, vocation and task' of human beings is to 'develop themselves and their capacities in a manifold way' (12f, p. 292).

Marx was no moral philosopher and he did not discuss the differences between these different kinds of morality. I suspect that if he had done so he would have responded that under communism they all come to one anyway: that communism will at one and the same time embody what (Marx held) is intuitively essentially 'human', respect human worth or dignity and maximise both welfare and self-development. Certainly, there is within the Marxist tradition no discussion of the possibility of conflicts between these various ideals. Rather than pursuing these rather recondite questions any further, I shall simply assert that, if we are here concerned with the question, 'What makes the realm of freedom really (rather than formally) free?', it is the teleological, Aristotelian, perfectionist Marx we must follow. For the freedom that capitalism denies and communism promises is systematically couched in the language of 'species powers', potentiality, and self-actualisation.

In the self-transforming and self-realising process of emancipation, one factor is crucial: free time. As Marx wrote in the *Grundrisse*: 'free time – which is both idle time and time for higher activity – has *naturally* transformed its possessor into a different subject' (11d, p. 712). He stressed this again in what is perhaps his best-known text on the subject:

> In fact, the realm of freedom actually begins only when labour which is determined by necessity and mundane considerations cease; thus in the very nature of things, it lies beyond the sphere of actual material production ... freedom in this field can only consist in socialised man, the associated producers rationally regulating their intercourse with nature, bringing it under their common control, instead of being controlled by it as by the blind forces of nature; and achieving this with the least expenditure of energy and under conditions most favourable to, and worthy of, their human nature. But it none the less remains a realm of necessity. Beyond it begins that development of human energy which is an end in itself, the true realm of freedom, which, however, can blossom forth only with this realm of necessity as its basis. The shortening of the working day is its basic prerequisite (11e, III, p. 799).

There is, as Heller notes, a somewhat different possibility sketched out in the *Grundrisse* where, in a visionary anticipation of automation, Marx writes of a future in which

> Labour no longer appears so much to be included within the production process itself; rather the human being comes to relate more as watchman and regulator to the production process itself ... [the worker] steps to the side of the production process instead of being its chief actor. In this transformation, it is neither the direct labour he himself performs, nor the time during which he works, but rather the appropriation of his own general productive power, his understanding of nature and his mastery over it by virtue of his presence as a social body – it is, in a word, the development of the social individual which appears as the great foundation-stone of production and of wealth ... As soon as labour in the direct form has ceased to be the great well-spring of wealth, labour time ceases and must cease to be its measure, and hence exchange value must cease to be the measure of use value (11d, p. 705; 6, p. 104).

But note that in this vision too, it is the time for free development that is crucial, only here that development takes place in the form of scientific understanding and technical control, enjoyed for their own sake as a 'vital need', within the production process itself. For, in general, Marx held that

> free time, disposable time, is wealth itself, partly for the enjoyment of the product, partly for the free activity which – unlike labour – is not dominated by *the pressure of an extraneous purpose which must be fulfilled*, and the fulfilment of which *is regarded as a natural necessity* or *a social duty*, according to one's inclinations (11i, III, p. 257).

And here we come to what is, I believe, the heart of the matter. It is emancipation from the pressure of 'extraneous purposes', from 'what is regarded as a natural necessity or a moral duty' that is the key to Marx's conception of 'real' freedom. This, I believe, is why Marx thought that

> Communism differs from all previous movements in that it overturns the basis of all earlier relations of production and intercourse, and for the first time treats all naturally evolved premises as the creation of hitherto existing men, strips them of their natural character and subjugates them to the power of the united individuals ... The reality which communism creates is precisely the true basis for rendering it impossible that anything should exist independently of individuals, insofar as reality is nevertheless only a product of the preceding intercourse of individuals (12f, p. 81).

But if this is a correct interpretation, then a host of questions crowd in upon us. What makes a purpose count as 'extraneous'? Not (unless Marx is saddled with a purely subjective, phenomenological notion of alienation) whatever the agent counts as such. But what, then, are individuals' authentic, non-extraneous purposes? Marx imagines a world in which the question does not even arise, because its answer is both not in doubt and correctly understood, both obvious and true (a world, therefore, free of moral scepticism). And *are* there not natural necessities which human activity (including labour) must fulfil as a prerequisite of social co-operation in general and (as both Weber and Durkheim thought) of a complex modern social order in particular? As for social *duties*, is their disappearance conceivable, even in a world inconceivably more abundant and altruistic than our own?

Further, wider questions also arise. Marx's vision is of 'the free development of individualities ... the general reduction of the necessary labour of society to a minimum, which then corresponds to the artistic, scientific, etc. development of the individuals in the time set free, and with the means created, for all of them' (11d, p. 705). But what does 'the free development of individualities' for all mean? That all should have an equal *opportunity* to develop whatever manifold capacities (or rather, relevant 'human' capacities) they severally have? Or that all would *in fact* realise such capacities, achieving, therefore, different levels of achievement in any one capacity and of success in developing and integrating several? Or does it mean that a maximum level of 'artistic, scientific, etc. development' will be achieved in 'society' as a whole? Whichever interpretation is the right one, it seems undeniable that it evokes a *distributive* principle, even if this is not a principle of distributive justice (in the Hume-Rawls sense), for it specifies how resources should be allocated to achieve the result in question, indicating who should get what. In fact, the three interpretations invoke three different distributive principles: (1) equal (and unlimited) access to the (external) means to self-development (the maxima of such development varying across individuals), i.e. a version of the *equality of opportunity* principle; (2) application of whatever means (including resources) are needed to achieve universal maximal self-development, i.e. a version of the *equality of results* principle (so that all are equally maximising their respective potentials); and (3) whatever distribution of resources and application of means are needed to achieve maximal artistic, scientific, intellectual, etc. development in 'society', which says nothing about equality but makes both the proper distribution and social policy depend on what that desired outcome requires.

Yet further questions arise here. First, what is to be the initial criterion of development itself, what is to count as a capacity realisation, and how are specific capacity realisations to be traded off against many-sidedness and both against the integration of the sides into a meaningful life-plan? Secondly, which of the principles suggested seems most likely, as an interpretation of Marx? Does not 'the free development of individualities' mean, precisely, autonomy or *self*-development, i.e. not merely the abstract possibility but the reality of individuals' choosing *non*-development? This suggests interpretation (1). But Marx usually writes as though he favours interpretation (2) – and he almost certainly did not distinguish between (1) and (2). But (2) poses extreme difficulties in application. It is a principle specifying who should get what, but one in which the *who* and the *what* are interdependent: the identity of agents is affected by some of the means in question (from special schools for the gifted to genetic engineering). If the principle is carried beyond a certain point (set by some limit to how far any given self may be altered), selves are being transformed, even created. Depending on the technical possibilities (and under communism these would surely be very great), (2) could come to mean the application of whatever means are needed to achieve universal *and equal* maximal self-development. Sometimes Marx and Marxists have suggested that this is what is meant. But often they have suggested that they favour interpretation (3), and most probably assume that (3) would coincide with (2) and (1). But would it? Take first (3) and (2). This is most unlikely, since scientific and artistic *achievement* must surely involve some succeeding where others fail. Although the latter may in some sense realise their capacities, to say that they do so as the former do is either to delude or to mock them. And perhaps some (considerable?) measure of such failure is a precondition for maximum success overall? What then of (3) and (1)? Here perhaps distributive justice re-emerges after all, since maximal scientific and artistic development may well require the concentration of resources among the most talented, and not all resources could be so abundant for this not to be a real issue (e.g. education and training).

Aside from these distributional questions, there are others. How is the 'free development of individualities' to be *co-ordinated*? In particular, is there not a contradiction between the image of *community* or even community of communities, on the one hand, and that of society as a gigantic factory, on the other? For Marx was also the author of the idea, taken up by Kautsky and Lenin, that society as a whole could be organised on the basis of the division of labour, socially controlled and regulated, rather than being subject to 'competition, ... the coercion exerted by the pressure of ... mutual interests' (11e, I, p. 356; 13, p. 13). Selucky has suggested that Marx's community-concept applies to the political sphere and his nation-wide factory concept to the economic sphere, and that the two are in conflict:

> Since economic base and superstructure are to be in structural accord, one is facing a dilemma: either to accept and introduce Marx's centralised society-type organised economy and to revise Marx's concept of the decentralised community-type polity, or to accept and introduce the decentralised community-type polity and to revise Marx's concept of the centralised society-type organised economy (13, p. 87).

Lenin, Selucky suggests, did the former, and the Yugoslavs, in their market-based socialist economy, have sought to do the latter. Is any other solution possible?

And what of decision-making? How are the allocation of resources and the assignment of functions to be decided upon? By all, but by what methods: participatory or representative? Marx was undoubtedly committed to the ideal of direct democracy. His early conception of such democracy involved a Rousseauesque critique of the principle of representation and the view that true democracy involves the disappearance of the state and thus the end of the separation of the state from civil society, which occurs because 'society is an organism of solitary and homogeneous interests, and the distinct "political sphere" of the "general interest" vanishes along with the distinction between governors and governed' (3, p. 44). This view reappears in Marx's writings about the Paris Commune, which he admired for holding every delegate 'at any time revocable and bound by the formal instructions of his constituents: so instead of deciding once in three or six years which member of the ruling class was to misrepresent the people in parliament, universal suffrage was to serve the people, constituted in Communes ...' (11f, p. 520). Partly because this was his view, he never addressed the procedural issue of what forms collective choice or decision-making should take under communism, whether at the lower or higher stage. And how seriously is the withering away of conflicting interests to be taken? The more seriously, the less will constitutional protections be needed, and the more Rousseauesque will communism be (whatever that might mean in a complex industrial society).

Finally, and most deeply, *who* are the individuals who are to be united under communism, and what kind of unity do they attain? Do they come with attachments, commitments and loyalties, their identities shaped by local, regional, national, historical experiences and memories? Or are they the ultimate fruits of Enlightenment individualism: individuals who, once their class situation has withered away, are free of 'extraneous purposes', 'natural necessities' and 'social duties', with nothing existing 'independently of them'? Is the unity of communism a *community*, rooted in particularity and marked off from others? Or is it the unity of freely associating sovereign choosers, combining to attain 'the full development of human mastery over the forces of nature, those of so-called nature, as well as of humanity's own nature' (11d, p. 488)?

To none of these questions do Marx or the Marxist tradition give determinate answers. That is because Marxist anti-utopianism has systematically inhibited their pursuit. And the consequences of that inhibition have been disastrous in two respects.

First, in *theory*, Marxism has failed to clarify its ends and to explore the institutional and political forms that could embody them. It has thus precisely failed in that elucidatory endeavour that Professor Alexander identifies as the philosophical function of utopian thinking (1, p. 41).

Secondly, and far more disastrously, by trusting in what Lukacs called the immanence of the ultimate objective, by believing that the ends would somehow call forth the appropriate means, it has almost totally failed to bring social and political imagination to bear upon real-life problems – such as the distribution of resources, social policy, economic, social and industrial organisation, political and constitutional structures, nationalism and regionalism. On none of these has Marxism had anything distinctively constructive to say. Instead, it has given birth to the deformed world of 'actually existing socialism', so vividly evoked in Šimečka's paper (Chapter 14 in this volume), in which the final irony has been the eventual destruction of the very ideal of communism as an object worthy of allegiance or even serious attention.

References

1. Alexander, Peter, 'Grimm's Utopia', Chapter 3 in this volume.
2. Bloch, Ernst, *Das Prinzip Hoffnung* (1954-59) in *Collected Works*, Surkamp Verlag, vol. 5.
3. Colletti, Lucio (ed.), Karl Marx, *Early Writings*, Penguin, Harmondsworth 1975.
4. Davis, J.C., 'The History of Utopia', Chapter 1 in this volume.
5. Engels, Friedrich (a) *The Peasant War in Germany* (1850), in Marx-Engels, *Werke*, vol. 7. (b) *Socialism: utopian & scientific* (1892) in Marx & Engels, *Selected Works* in 3 vols, 1970, vol. 3. (c) *The Housing Question* (1873/1887), in Marx & Engels, *Selected Works* in 2 vols, 1962, vol. 1.
6. Heller, Agnes, *Karl Marx's Theory of Needs*, St Martin's Press, New York 1974.
7. Hudson, Wayne, *The Marxist Philosophy of Ernst Bloch*, Macmillan, London 1982.
8. Lenin, V.I. (a) *The State and Revolution* (1917) in *Collected Works*, Lawrence & Wishart, London 1960- , vol. 25. (b) Speech at First Congress of Economic Councils in *Collected Works*, vol. 27.
9. Lukacs, G., *Tactics and Ethics*, New Left Books, London
10. Manuel, F.E. & F.P., *Utopian Thought in the Western World*, Blackwell, Oxford 1979.
11. Marx, Karl, (a) *Economic & Philosophical Manuscripts of 1844*, Foreign Languages Pub. House, Moscow n.d. (b) *The Poverty of Philosophy* (1847), Progress Publishers, Moscow 1978. (c) *Preface to a Contribution to the Critique of Political Economy* (1859), in Marx & Engels, *Selected Works* in 2 vols, 1962. (d) *Grundrisse* (1859) translated by M. Nicolaus, Penguin, Harmondsworth 1973. (e) *Capital* (1867), Foreign Languages Pub. House, Moscow 1962. (f) *The Civil War in France* (1871), in Marx & Engels, *Selected Works* in 2 vols, 1962, vol. 1. (g) *Critique of the Gotha Programme* (1875), in Marx & Engels, *Selected Works* in 2 vols, 1962, vol. 2. (h) *Early Writings*, ed. & translated by T.B. Bottomore, C.A. Watts, London 1963. (i) *Theories of Surplus Value*, Lawrence & Wishart, London 1972.
12. Marx, Karl & Engels, Friedrich (a) Marx-Engels, *Werke*, Dietz, Berlin 1956-65. (b) *Collected Works*, Lawrence & Wishart, London. (c) *Selected Works* in 2 vols, Foreign Languages Pub. House, Moscow 1962. (d) *Selected Works* in 3 vols, Progress Publishers, Moscow 1970. (e) *Selected Correspondence*, Progress Publishers, Moscow 1975. (f) *The German Ideology* (written 1846, pub. 1932) in *Collected Works*, vol. 5. (g) *The Manifesto of the Communist Party* (1848) in *Selected Works* in 2 vols, 1962, vol. 1.
13. Selucky, R., *Marxism, Socialism, Freedom*, Macmillan, London 1979.
14. Šimečka, Milan, 'A World With Utopias or Without Them?' Chapter 14 in this volume.

A World With Utopias or Without Them?

Milan Šimečka

Socially speaking, there is nothing quite so depressing as a defeated, written-off utopia. Abandoned by its erstwhile supporters, it stinks like an empty railway-carriage shunted into a siding which, unventilated for weeks, reeks of tobacco smoke, remnants of food, and human sweat. Such a utopia is an embarrassing reminder of defeat and the fallibility of man's intelligence, a monument to the wreckage of dreams, and such monuments make a sad sight. Rarely do people speak respectfully of failed utopias – on the contrary, they tend to evoke embarrassment and irritation, those sentiments which are brought on by a guilty conscience.

Defeated utopias usually leave behind their grieving bereaved – their philosophers, priests, prophets and fellow-travellers. It does not take much imagination to realise how they must feel. All we have to do is to don for a while the garb of a contemporary of such a failed utopia. Here in Bohemia, for instance, the habit of a radical Hussite preacher who, at the end of the long civil war, gazes upon the ruins of Tabor, that city which was to be the new Jerusalem. Not an enviable experience.

I have often toyed with this kind of fantasy, conscious of a malicious regret that the majority of authors of utopian visions had not lived to see their caricatured realisations in practice and were thus saved from inhaling the stench of their decomposition. How I would have liked to have stood next to, say, Rousseau in the midst of a howling mob – the Rousseau so admired by all French revolutionaries – and watched the decapitation of Danton, Robespierre or Babeuf on the guillotine. It would have been interesting to use the occasion for a discussion of equality, to inform Rousseau of the brief history of the Empire, and then to lend him a Balzac novel to read.

And how instructive it would be if Karl Marx could be transported

* Translated by George Theiner.

by some time machine to present-day Czechoslovakia, where his theories have come so strangely to be realised, and if he could be forced to attend a political schooling lesson where, his teeth clenched, he would have to listen to a speaker reporting on the declining milk-yield of our cows. Or, better still, if he were to be interned together with the Solidarity leaders in Poland, thus having plenty of time to reflect on the future of the classless society and the empire of freedom.

Everything that remains following the defeat of a utopia is full of strange paradoxes, reminding us more forcefully than anything else of the tremendous gulf between man's actions and the ideas matured in the brains of select individuals.

Perhaps in other parts of the world the debris of old utopias mean little to people; in Eastern Europe, however, they give rise to emotion. For my part, I have never been able to view failed ideals without feeling sad and depressed. No doubt this is partly due to the fact that I live inside one such moribund utopia, inhaling its nostalgic smell. It never ceases to affect me, even though I was not present at its beginnings and did not experience its bloody fanaticism and eschatological faith at first hand, thus being saved the worst traumas which afflict the two generations before me.

'Real' socialism – that is, the political-economic system in power in the countries which like to call themselves socialist – is one such stale, moribund utopia, defeated by the normal course of events. But the citizens of the post-utopian states are not aware of this, believing – and the official propaganda does its best to confirm this belief – that the existing conditions represent the realisation of the original intent. And while the socialist system is unthinkable without the original utopian formula, its theory remains implacably hostile towards all utopias. For a hundred years now it has striven to differentiate itself from utopias by means of a scientific veneer, and it cannot be denied that it has had some measure of success in this, given the universal respect in which science has been held in the last century. Hundreds of thousands of propagandists are to this day trying to prove – in the face of Marx himself – that ideology can be a science and science an ideology.

But old utopias penetrate the original roots of society, and buried deep down like a dangerously taut spring there is the eternal tension between the utopian promises of the past and the caricatured present. With the result that the entire realisation of socialism continues to represent both the fulfilment and betrayal of the old utopia, unable to escape dependence on it for all its propagandist claims as to its scientific character.

In some of its details real socialism is incredibly similar to the marginal details of the old utopias. Unfortunately, it is these very details which show these utopias to have been mistaken. Even a superficial acquaintance with our East European utopias convinces us that it is only their worst aspects that come to be realised. Thus for instance, in the social hierarchy of real socialism, we have lost Plato's tolerant wise men and philosophers, say in the role of district Party secretaries, while retaining with great exactitude the class of 'guardians', attired in police and army uniforms. From Campanella's Sun State there have not survived the incorruptible officials and judges, administering the State under the triumvirate of Wisdom, Power, and Love; we have, however, faithfully copied the 'work brigades', by means of which our citizens are forced to work in the fields to save the harvest or to clear away rubbish on our housing estates. Contrary to what Thomas More supposed, no one in the socialist system disdains gold. On the contrary, the socialist state is quite ready to make even ideological concessions for the sake of gold and foreign currency. It would seem that all we have managed to realise of More's utopia is tranquillity and order at all costs.

Yet all this is as nothing compared with what happened to Marx himself. It is easy to see that we can hardly quote anything from the many pages of his *oeuvre* dealing with the sins of the state bureaucracy, police, censorship, class superiority, nationalism, etc, without running the danger that the socialist state will see this as an attack upon itself; while those few sentences he devoted to the need for dictatorship of the proletariat for a transitional period retain their vitality to this day. Anyone who has seen at first hand the workings of a manufacturing enterprise in a socialist economy will not be reminded in the least of Marx's vision of socialist labour in *Das Kapital*. Everything is different.

It is as though utopias were incapable of translating any of their great ideals into real life – nothing but idiocies. Harmony is nowhere to be seen, nor equality, while justice has to be sought with a lamp in broad daylight; and though the politicians promise people happiness from morning till night, they are in no position to provide it. Wells's real-life samurai take bribes, and the 'new man' standing on the threshold of communism frequently drowns his sorrows in vodka. Starving nations are buying arms and no one is able to guarantee peace.

All the indications are that utopias are nothing but the instrument of a historical deception, the bait set out for the desperate, a false rainbow beneath which the people is easily to be led into a new slavery. The question arises whether utopias actually contain the seeds of their eventual downfall, whether any and every attempt to put them into practice will inevitably produce a caricature of their original intentions.

There can be no doubt that there is something inherent in all utopias which leads to an outcome wherein their good intentions pave the way to hell. Being as a rule the fruit of elite aspirations and minority dreams, they automatically provoke attempts to inculcate forcibly the minority's ideals in the majority. Attracted by the lure of an abstract good, they easily succumb to the view that the end justifies the means, thus taking a direct part in the history of violence, dictatorships and slaughter in the name of a better future.

Utopias are the products of the human brain, to take Koestler's definition of the human brain as a superstructure over the animal. Utopias are a symptom of all man's unnatural endeavours, a product of the 'unnatural animal', the being which has rebelled against Nature, which attempts to subjugate and change it. Utopias are an expression of transcendence, in the same way as religion. And that is why they fail when they are introduced to the natural world, which is on the whole ruled by the natural requirements of the human being – in particular material requirements – and which resists a purely 'intellectual' transformation. Utopias find their way barred by all the natural human attributes like selfishness, aggressiveness, greed, social apathy, all the purely instinctive motivations, and so on. Since all utopias give expression to a human desire to outstrip natural limitations and achieve an ordering of the life of society which would correspond to the sum of all human experience, their enemy is bound to be stupidity and the inability of mankind enthusiastically to grasp that which will benefit it – and it is this inability about which utopians of all ages have complained and complain to this day. Being unacceptable to the statistically average brain, utopias compel their supporters to knock ideals of virtue and happiness into such a statistically average brain by force.

In this respect it is the utopias' own fault that they come to be realised as caricatures of themselves. The force which accompanied socialist and communist attempts to introduce socialist and communist ideals into eastern Europe made nonsense of their meaning. History has played an ugly game with utopias: in the course of some sixty years, the hitherto greatest utopia of all has been turned into a social order whose immobility and intellectual sterility is reminiscent of the nightmares of ancient utopias. The pure socialist utopia, meanwhile, continues to float freely in space like a cloud, as Rosa Luxemburg used to say. The way it has been put into practice corresponds to human nature – it is unequal, selfish, materialistic, acquisitive, and it gives scope to majority folly. And the remnants of utopian terminology still to be found in the vocabulary of politicians' public speeches are no more than a propagandist swindle.

It has to be asked why a system which long ago divorced itself from its utopian foundations does not acknowledge this rupture and admit that it exists for quite another purpose: that its utopian springs have long ago dried up, being replaced by purely pragmatic motives which have to do with the acquisition and maintenance of power. This could be done with little or no risk, since the system relies on the stability of human nature. Its retention of the old utopian terminology can only be explained in terms of a sentimental respect for the faith of its ancestors, this being common to all ideologies, but in particular as a practical political device: by using the old utopian teminology, it tells the people that the existing order is the legitimate heir of the old ideals, indeed their only possible realisation.

Everything that George Orwell invented several decades ago in a feverish moment of inspiration has more or less come to pass. The process which was meant to make man freer, to enhance his rights and his dignity, has ended in a status quo which in a complicated way serves completely different ends. Since Orwell wrote his famous novel, many people have wondered, like his hero Winston Smith, *why* a system should survive which has become alienated from its original aims and thus shows all the signs of absurdity, having to cover up this fundamental contradiction with all manner of lies.

Now, thirty-six years after *1984* – surely one of the most exciting books in world literature – came to be written, the answer to Smith's puzzle is fairly simple. Millions of people in our part of Eurasia, who observe life around them with basically non-ideological eyes, can see a number of phenomena which add up to provide the answer. These people have known for a long time that real socialism does not constitute an advance towards communism, nor does it attempt to create equality and a classless society, or any such utopian visions. They know that it is, by and large, just another system, its stability based on human nature, they know that the basic motivation of all social activity comes from a desire to satisfy material needs, to acquire things, a desire for conventional material values such as influence, money, houses, cars, and everything else that can be owned by a citizen of a real socialist state. And, as in any other system, possession is made sweeter by the way it differentiates people one from the other. In real life this basis of the system is not as well concealed as in Orwell's fiction. In Eastern Europe people can sometimes see how the privileged caste lives and glimpse their mansions at least from a distance, and so they do not have to seek any mysterious explanation for the functioning of the political system.

Things were not quite as transparent where Orwell was concerned. Perhaps he thought that the answer to his *why* was hidden in some fated historical law. I have to confess that I, too, felt unwilling for a long time to accept the primitive explanation, one that has to do with the stomach rather than with the mysterious life of ideas. I refused to accept that it could all be so simple. Unfortunately, the great historical mystery ceased to be a mystery a long time ago; and in the end natural material existence always triumphs over unnatural ideas.

It would be wrong, however, to blame the utopias for this powerlessness. They do not as a rule contain any instructions on how to make use of the ideal of equality for the establishment of a new class system, nor how to establish a social order which would so quickly turn away from its original purpose.

Even so, we know enough to have taken the measure of utopias, being fully justified in distrusting them and blaming them for many a historic disaster. I began to feel hostility towards them from the moment I realised how treacherous they were. I thus concurred with Karl Popper, who said that they are dangerous, malignant and self-destroying, and that mankind would be better off tackling concrete evils rather than attempting to pursue abstract good (1).

I was backed in my hostility towards utopias by our Czechoslovak historical experience. The Czech people have usually had to pay a heavy price for their defeated utopias. I believe that it was this realisation which prompted even T.G. Masaryk – despite his admiration for the Hussites – to advocate honest, everyday labour, and it was this that made him suspicious of all abstract schemes intended to provide an answer to all our ills. However, at a time of social upheaval he was thought by many to be old-fashioned. Czech poets, for instance, turned their backs on him, enthralled as they were by the holy concept of revolution – yet another form of utopia, as Melvin J. Lasky so convincingly shows in his book, *Utopia and Revolution* (2). And it was over this very concept of revolution, beloved of the poets, that the people of Czechoslovakia experienced their greatest disappointment. To this day Czech spiritual life suffers from the confrontation of utopian abstraction and the liquidation of concrete evils – as evidenced by discussions among the dissidents regarding Ludvík Vaculík's *feuilleton* on bravery.

With all they have gone through, the Czechs and Slovaks find it difficult to look favourably on abstract schemes for the pursuit of worthy aims. One such scheme has degenerated into expressions of fanaticism, violence and ideological falsehood. A few years ago I came to the conclusion that it was all over. And yet …

And yet – let us try to imagine a world without utopias. Let us erase everything utopian from our entire cultural heritage, all the dreams and strivings for a better ordering of society, for the realisation of the age-old ideas of equality, fraternity, liberty, love and the dignity of human existence. Do this, and history is robbed of one dimension, the dimension of dreams, of transcendence, of journeys beyond the frontiers of our everyday experience.

Even were we to consign utopias to the realm of the fairy-tale, the history of human thought would be sadly impoverished. Utopias are not mere fairy-tales, they encompass all our unrealistic desires, and if we abandon them now, the spiritual heritage of mankind will turn to dust. Mankind will cease to be mankind, becoming like ants, which may be more efficiently organised, but unlike human beings will never send their ant-hills soaring like the Tower of Babylon.

If Plato's desire for order, beauty and harmony in society is to disappear from history, the same must happen to Christ's equally utopian faith in the brotherhood and love of man, and man's liberation from his material and instinctive determination. In short, we lack precise criteria on which to base an anti-utopian censorship.

It is certain that without the ancient fanatical faiths in God's kingdom on earth millions of people would not have died in the various struggles to put these utopian dreams into practice. There would have been far fewer victims of the injustice perpetrated on their fellow-men by the zealous prophets of the future. Columbus would have stayed at home; Robespierre would have enjoyed a longer life had he stuck to his legal practice. Undoubtedly, millions of people in Russia would have led more peaceful lives had it not been for Lenin and Stalin. But then most probably a village lad named Yuri Gagarin would not have been the first man in space. And who knows if just this will not one day be important, when man decides to abandon his ruined planet.

History without utopias would doubtless be less tragic. Yet at the same time it would be deprived of the tragedy of human existence, as described for us Europeans by Greek myths and Christian legends. And what would man be then?

Although I have had more than enough opportunity to rage at failed and moribund utopias, now, years later, I have made my peace with them. Not that I believe in their power to save mankind, and as a cure for that belief I would recommend everyone to read their Orwell. Nevertheless, I have made my peace with utopias, realising that without them our world would be that much worse. While they give birth to ideas far removed from everyday life and human nature, utopias at the same time confirm our tragic humanity, the unnaturalness of our human fate, the fantastic activity of the super-animal brain which makes man unique among his fellow-creatures. A world without utopias would be a world without social hope, a world of resignation to the status quo and the devalued slogans of everyday political life.

As we approach the end of our century, we have fewer utopias to choose from. And people view them with more suspicion based on bitter experience. Many utopias are dead. In industrial societies, however, they have managed to realise the utopia of relative prosperity and even outstrip the utopia of technical progress. In some happy

countries these two utopias have come about without slaughter, by
dint of unusual tolerance. It would be enough if these utopias were
sufficiently strong to spread to our entire planet, doing away with the
hunger and poverty of the Third World. I am of the opinion that even
the pollution which accompanies industrial prosperity is better than the
chaos and brutality which plagues those societies in which people are
unable to satisfy their basic needs.

Today the world is in such a state that it needs new utopias. None of
the serious problems facing mankind can be solved by mere
pragmatism. If we are just to maintain the present level of development
and civilisation, we shall have to gain acceptance of projects which go
beyond the everyday and which may in many respects look like
utopias, because their realisation will require the overcoming of social
selfishness on the part of classes, groups and individuals.

We can already witness the great vitality of the utopia which is
trying to preserve for mankind unpolluted air, water, forests and seas,
everything that is still left of Nature, which has been sacrificed to the
realisation of another utopia, that of prosperity, and that is the true
unnatural demand which is really worthy of man.

We are also concerned with the utopia of peace and disarmament.
This is less successful because it corresponds to the instinctive desire to
preserve life and contains a comprehensible idea which suggests how
well off mankind could be if it were to put the immense material
wealth which at present goes into the manufacture of weapons to some
sensible use. This particular utopia speaks to all human nature, coming
into conflict only with man's natural aggressiveness and stupidity.

I shudder to think of what would remain of the world I live in, were
it not for utopias. We would be left with hopeless submission to an
order which is only too natural, because it can, as yet, modestly feed
the people, give them employment and a secure daily round. It is
unable to provide for the unnatural demands of man, for the utopian
ideas of its beginnings such as justice, freedom and tolerance, and to
carry them further. This order no longer understands such demands,
considering them unnatural and utopian; a remarkable case of
amnesia.

Had I not come to terms with utopias, but maintained my old
hostility, I could not rejoice at their rebirth. I did rejoice when they
reappeared in an extremely modest guise in 1968 – when they did not
proclaim anything more than respect for the human face; i.e. respect
for man. Perhaps that is why, when it was defeated, this utopia did not
leave behind that old depressing stench. Not being given the slightest
chance of realisation, this utopia could not be caricatured. It therefore
lives on, moving from place to place. It is a very modest utopia indeed,
aiming only at the well-tried benefits of freedom, tolerance of different
views and everything that flows from this. In this case there is no

question of not coming to terms with this utopia – to live without it would be to live without human dignity.

This chapter is dedicated to Dr Vilém Prečan, who lives in Hanover and whose friendship has realised for me the utopia of a unified Europe.

References

1. Popper, Karl, 'Utopia and violence', *Hibbert Journal* (1948), reprinted in Popper, *Conjectures and Refutations*, Routledge, London 1963.
2. Lasky, Melvin J., *Utopia and Revolution*, Chicago 1976.

15

The Necessity of Utopia

Mark Holloway

The earliest written utopias in post-classical times were usually thought of as comprehensively structured artefacts, complete in all their parts, and of rigid and unchanging character. In this they were largely a reflection of ideas of the time which saw society in general as an ordered mechanism run like clockwork, or like the solar system itself. The conception of human society as a developing organism, subject to constant changes which alter its character as it moves through time, has only been accepted as valid in comparatively recent years. No very convincing attempt was normally made to show how the static kind of utopia had come into being. It was there, *sui generis*, flourishing, fully-formed, and without disruptive or rebellious citizens strong enough in numbers or dissatisfaction to endanger its continued existence. And whether its purpose was to awaken the reader to the possibilities of change or to contain implied criticism of the society in which author and reader lived, utopia itself was usually remote geographically or in time.

A few centuries later, as man in the most prosperous and inventive societies developed socially and technologically, utopia, or at least some of its most prominent features, actually came within sight and seemed possibly attainable, if not at once, then in the very near future. The world had by this time – eighty to a hundred years ago – begun to seem much smaller. The Industrial Revolution had speeded up communication, most of the world had been explored and charted, the internal combustion engine had started on its adventurous and ever-accelerating journeys on and above the earth, and the improvement in weapons, particularly in small arms, was such that the path of the advancing white man could be cleared with unprecedented efficiency. It was a time of much confidence and optimism on both sides of the Atlantic, and utopian writers began to see the possibility of achieving utopia in what Wordsworth called 'the very world which is the world of all of us.'

It was at this point that written utopias came in from the cold: it is probably true to say that utopia only became a necessity when it was recognised as a means to an end rather than an end in itself. Instead of a vision or mirage hovering on the horizon it became a carrot dangling tantalisingly only a foot or two in front of the human donkey. Oscar Wilde in 1891, and H.G. Wells a decade or so later, agreed on the necessity of utopia. They also agreed that it was not an end in itself. A map of the world that did not include it was not worth looking at, thought Wilde, in spite of the fact that it was only a staging-post to further utopias. 'When Humanity lands there, it looks out, and seeing a better country, sets sail. Progress is the realisation of Utopias.' The aphorism contains an approximate geographical truth as well as a metaphorical one. When the planet seemed huge and was largely unexplored, the most fanciful utopia might still have been discovered actually to exist somewhere on earth. But before the world had run out of unexplored places and noble savages, there had been a wholesale transatlantic emigration by the poor and oppressed peoples of Europe. In the nineteenth century especially, America was Wilde's 'better country' of the time, to which seekers after utopia were hastening. By 1917, however, some, like John Reed, the American journalist, were hastening in the opposite direction, and the staging-post for utopia for the next two or three decades for many people was Soviet Russia. Nevertheless, by the time of the Second World War, it had become almost impossible for an honest man to find utopia anywhere on a map of the world; and in literature, by this time, dystopia had been sighted and described.

Utopia had not entirely disappeared, however. It had slipped out of the atlas on to the drawing-board or into the government white paper. Le Corbusier was building his Unité d'Habitation at Marseilles while Aneurin Bevan was introducing the National Health Service in Britain. Utopia, instead of shifting from country to country round the globe, actually or metaphorically, had become fragmented, like much else in life, and pieces of it were to be found here and there fulfilling partial needs and aspirations and indicating lines of advancement which reformers had drawn up and governments had passed. It was largely a matter of planning, and in some cases it was becoming difficult to separate utopian dream from contemporary reality. In a world increasingly able to translate dream into fact or at least into factitiousness, in which dream and reality are confused, a sharply defined and inclusive utopia is difficult to describe and will probably be out of date before it is completed.

In the period since World War II there has been a technological revolution out of all proportion in its far-reaching effects to the period of time in which it has taken place. The widespread development of radio, television and telephone communications, including the use of satellites; the placing in orbit of other satellites for other purposes; the visits to the moon, the probes into the solar system, and the construction of space laboratories; the development of optical and radio telescopes and of the electron microscope; the discovery of the structure of DNA; the development of a huge range of drugs; the conquest of smallpox, and the prevention and partial elimination of other diseases; the introduction of life support systems and the advances in replacement surgery; the vast expansion of the electronics industry following the invention of semi-conductors, transistors, and more recently the silicon chip; the universal use of computers, copying machines and microfilm; the immense expansion of air travel; the plastics revolution – nearly all this, and much more, has occurred in the lifetime of anyone who is now about thirty-five, and the rate of technological development does not seem to be slowing down.

The social and moral results of this multifaceted technological progress have been as revolutionary as the scientific inventions themselves. The Welfare State – so long as it lasts – guarantees freedom from dire poverty, treats ill health, provides education for the young and makes life much easier for the old and the disabled. In the first two decades after the war, the 1950s and 1960s, the young had never prospered so well. They lacked for little compared with any previous generation, and were able to disregard completely the traditional caution and circumspect behaviour of their parents and elders who had grown up in a harsher economic and social environment. They took off, in the 1960s, into a world increasingly geared to satisfy their material desires. Of the freedom they found, they made more, taking over, at ever younger ages, the entrepreneurial activities which had been started for their entertainment. They made a huge impact on popular culture, notably in music, dress, and leisure activities. The first generation that grew up from puberty on the Pill was able to liberate itself completely in sexual behaviour, and that freedom spread until it embraced widespread toleration of behaviour such as cohabitation without marriage, male and female homosexuality, experimentation with drug-taking, squatting, and student strikes and sit-ins. Enough older people, embracing the good in the new freedom, supported the young to create the so-called Permissive Society, in which the paradoxical situation arose that it became normal not to expect normality. Each individual must be allowed to 'do his own thing'. For anyone who believes in freedom, this was obviously a good thing in principle, and in a sense it was an element of utopia, actually achieved.

But where so much had been attainable by so many, more was wanted, and wanted immediately. To want for something – not the necessities, for these were almost guaranteed by the state, but the cars, motor bikes, radios, television sets, hi-fi equipment and other

glittering toys and gadgets stacked so enticingly in shop windows –
seemed almost indecent, a form of cultural starvation. Desire for
material goods should be followed instantly, or at any rate as soon as
practically possible, by possession. In shops with open display counters,
this appetite led to million-pound annual losses through theft. In
finance, it led to an ever-increasing number of people being mortgaged
for years, if not life; in business, to a vast proliferation of expense
accounts. And in case any of these activities should cause stress or the
least amount of discomfort, instant palliatives were available. The
mood-changing pills of Huxley's *Brave New World* have been with us
for two or three decades and are likely to stay: uppers and downers,
sweeteners and sharpeners, mind-bogglers and sense-confusers are
swallowed daily in their millions. For even further comfort and
reassurance, no one need ever be exposed to the devastating effects of
silence, which might engender feelings of loneliness or isolation. All
can have muzak wherever they go, even in lifts where for half a minute
or so they would otherwise be deprived of it; and in any case – music
or muzak, noise or voices, can be carried around in the hand or pocket.
Nor need one suffer from unpleasant weather: one's car defeats the
climate just as, with the right clothing and other equipment, one can
overcome the inconveniences and dangers of any climate in the world.
Guided tours of Everest are almost within the scope of travel agents. If
you want to visit the moon, you will have to wait a few years. If your
heart wears out, get a new one. If you don't want children, stop them.
If you want a sexual orgy in fact or by proxy, just buy these
video-cassettes and have it at home, alone or in as much company as
you please. You can have practically anything at home, at second
hand, via the little screen. Soon there will be instant access to all the
knowledge in the world – except, no doubt, the secret obscenities
perpetrated by governments.

But here we come up against another paradoxical situation: the
more immediately and efficiently we can communicate, world-wide,
the less do we need the actual physical presences of our bodies
anywhere but at home. 'As to living', wrote the author of *Axel*, ten
years before Wilde published his remarks about utopia, 'our servants
will do that for us.' Our electronic servants have proved him right:
technologically, utopia is here to stay and proliferate in all directions.
Hand in hand, though, as always, walks the devil: one finger on one
button can annihilate a city half way across the world; a huge
percentage of the gross national product of many countries is poured
directly, in ever greater quantities, into the armaments industry, the
most colossal waste bin ever known in the history of man. Dwindling
resources are consumed in ever greater amounts by an artificially
stimulated public that is constantly exhorted by advertisers and
manufacturers to spend more and more year by year whether it wants

to or not. How is it possible for anyone to believe that this process can or should continue? Yet it is fervently advocated by governments, popularised by the media, and so far, up to a point, absorbed and approved by the majority of citizens. That majority of citizens, meanwhile, is being slowly but surely subjected to an insidious process of alienation. Our nerve-endings are extended through the roof and pick up signals from the whole world, but the more information we receive in this way, the more our senses risk being dulled and blunted. As the camera zooms in on the pool of blood still dripping from the kerb where a victim was assassinated only a few minutes ago, we note that the newsreader maintains a bright, informative voice – the same intonation and expression that he or she has been trained to use for all items of news. We drink our tea or eat our supper apparently unaffected. If any good comes of such impartiality, it is accompanied by a great risk that our senses and judgments may become so accustomed to the extremes of human behaviour that abnormality will appear to be normal. The frontiers of what is permissible, or bearable, are continually being pushed back. Why should anyone be surprised at the increase in violence and pornography, in rape and juvenile crime? The important question in this matter is whether there is, or should be, a limit to this continual pressure, this continual extension or abuse of freedom? As in the case of the stockpiling of armaments, it seems to me that if the process is not stopped voluntarily it is likely to be stopped disastrously, in chaos and bloodshed.

Prophets of doom warn of a dark age complete with poisoned earth and atmosphere and hugely widespread famine and disease among such humans as may survive. The possibility reminds us of the ancient teleological problem: what is the destiny of man? The only honest answer is, we do not know. But one is tempted by a side question: whether a mechanism or force, working towards an end, no matter what that end may be, is directing our development? Are we wholly, or in large part, the product of our genes, and are these genes the ruthless and indestructible core around which experimental temporary forms of life (of which we, mankind, may be one) assemble and evolve? Do these genes need us simply for the evolution of ever more complex life-forms in a process that we do not understand? If this is the case, have they already been programmed, as it were, to carry us forward into an atomic war in which mutations of *Homo sapiens* will occur, capable of superseding our species and living more successfully than we have done?

In this, as in many other matters, it might be salutary to keep a small corner of one's mind open to such a possibility, although, generally speaking, it is difficult to think of life being so crudely determined when we see around us in every living form such subtleties and varieties and manifold gradations of the sensitive living substance constantly adapting and modifying themselves to fit into their environments. If we do not have free will and are controlled by our genes, I believe nevertheless that we should continue to act, as we have done for many years, *as though* we had free will. We have the mind for it, and we might well ask: for what other reason does consciousness exist? Even if consciousness has come to us as a capricious experiment on the part of some far-removed force we do not understand, and if we and it are destined for extermination, possibly self-inflicted, in what better way can we make the most of our situation while we exist than by *pretending* to free will, whether we have it or not? Without it, it seems to me, no development is possible. We need to believe we have it; no other course will suit the sort of animal we are, or give us equal satisfaction.

Belief in free will is one thing: belief in the perfectibility of man is quite another thing, and utopian plans had better *not* depend upon the latter. Perfection could never be achieved without the omniscience that could foresee those sudden enlargements of knowledge or technique which occur from time to time, and have seemed in our more recent history to occur with increasing frequency. When they do occur – one has only to think of Copernicus and Galileo or Darwin and Freud or Ford and Edison – they at once reveal the imperfections or incompleteness of previous thought or technique.

Another fact which makes the achievement of perfection unlikely is that within the species of man the inequalities of development are such that from our present vantage point it is difficult to believe that we shall ever react with the same unanimity as is the normal behaviour of most other species. Two nations have sent men into space while there are still societies of men on earth living as most of mankind lived in the Stone Age. Between these extremes representatives may be found of almost every type of society that has ever existed. All of them are passionately or doggedly devoted to their own religious or political faiths and the daily routine imposed upon them by their social organisations and their economic and geophysical environments. To plan for perfection in such circumstances is therefore a futile exercise, likely to lead to disillusionment and pessimism. It is no accident that dystopias have emerged recently as products of frustrated attempts at perfection. However, just as we should, in my view, proceed *as if* we had free will, so also, I think, we should proceed *as if* man could continually improve his situation in the world.

If we do not proceed on this assumption, recent history suggests that we are likely to be overtaken by events. We cannot afford to advance technologically, as we have been doing, without a corresponding advance in morality. A century ago this unequal development resulted in an ever-widening gap between the rich and powerful and the poor; now it not only accelerates the speed with which that gap increases, but also threatens the whole planet with death. It is evident, therefore, in what way we need to improve our situation in the world. We need a radical re-formation of ethical behaviour. This had better begin with the realisation that in certain highly important aspects man is one and indivisible as the planet also is, although both we and our dwelling-place are composed of myriads of small units for most ordinary purposes. The Earth, and mankind, may both be regarded as bodies containing millions of cells, as a single animal does. If these cells do not act for the benefit of the whole, the animal is sick. Man may never have enjoyed superb health, but he has never before been in such imminent danger of committing suicide. Mankind is sick, and is infecting his environment.

It should also be noted that the physical varieties and differences within our species are relatively few and relatively unimportant compared with the non-physical differences: multi-racial societies have already shown for a good many years that they can live, in certain circumstances, in peaceful co-existence. By contrast, some of the fiercest wars have been fought between white men who, if examined individually simply as physical specimens, we would find it difficult or imposible to sort into national, religious or political categories. Man is divided and plunged into conflict, or is united into national or supranational groups with policies and ways of life that have more in common than they have in disagreement, almost entirely by attitudes of mind. If our species is to survive, we must see to it that our disagreements do not remain lethal or potentially lethal. Disagreement itself is as vital to our survival and well-being as is the abolition of war.

As I have tried to show, utopias of yesterday are the realities of today. It is this characteristic which makes them a necessary study for anyone who is concerned that the future should be an improvement on the present. Utopian speculation occurs all the time, not only among specifically utopian thinkers, but also in the planning and statistical departments of governments, especially purely speculative and research departments concerned with the future – the so-called Think Tanks – and among those consultants who have set themselves up as pundits in the pseudo-scientific study of futurology. Prophecy seems to me to be very much the same hit-and-miss affair that it has always been, even when based on extrapolations of present trends. Examples of prophetic fallibility are numerous. Who, for instance, in 1953 – one generation ago – could have predicted that this country would now be self-sufficient in oil? And who then, only eight years after the annihilation of Hiroshima and Nagasaki, would have predicted that by now the Japanese would have a virtual monopoly in certain sections of the electronics industry, or would be exporting millions of cars to Europe? Who could have said a few years before it happened, that

Cuba would become a communist state, or that the USA would be finally humiliated in Vietnam in such a manner as to shake that nation's morale to its foundations? Nevertheless, in spite of inevitable mistakes and omissions in forecasting the future, it seems to me an excellent thing that governments should now have departments specifically devoted to thinking about the future. The more people who think about it, the more likely is it that some of us may actually live to see it. The media are fond of referring to a third world war, which they assume will be nuclear, as 'the unthinkable'. But it has been very carefully and calculatedly thought about by Mr Hermann Kahn and his associates for many years – in what I would call a strongly dystopian manner. Such possibilities *must* be thought about, but ought never to be taken for granted, or thought inevitable.

If we are to survive as a species, it may be taken for granted that there will always be an unknown territory ahead of us. The secrets of this planet, of the solar system, of this galaxy, of outer space, and of man himself may be delivered to us more frequently and in greater numbers as our technology improves, but I take it as axiomatic and necessary that the supply of these secrets is literally endless, or at any rate co-terminous with the existence of man. We cannot forsee a time when mankind will not be striving to find or make the right key with which to open the door to the next roomful of knowledge in order that he may absorb it and try to shape it to his own ends by whatever means. Nor is it likely that he will ever again be allowed time, as he was in his infancy, to assimilate the treasures in one such roomful of knowledge before another and another door is unlocked or forced partly open. The Golden Age, if any ever existed, was the unweaned babyhood of man, when he lay in the lap of Nature, identified himself closely with her, and with Mother Earth, and could not yet toddle out of his very limited immediate environment to see and describe and make comparisons and ask himself questions and so awaken his intellect. As a metaphor, the Christian myth about the tree and the fruit of knowledge is a correct diagnosis: once he has tasted it, the taster is forever addicted, for ever exiled from paradise, from that happiness which can be equated with absolute innocence and lack of self-consciousness, an unblameable irresponsibility and dependence.

The doors of discovery open and open, and we strive to digest on the moral level the food provided by brain and hand and tool. It is always rather more, and more varied, food than can be comfortably assimilated. I am inclined to believe that this arrangement, although often distressing, and even dreadful in its possible consequences with regard to our future, is, in some cosmic manner, fitting. We have been made to realise that we are our own worst enemies. The richest nations have been made to realise that they are living not only in luxury compared with the rest of mankind but also in ever increasing danger; and almost all mankind is filled with anxiety, either about physical starvation and disease and war and oppression or about moral starvation and illness of will. Anxiety may not provide the best climate for wisdom to grow up in, but it is better than the stale air of complacency. Where there is anxiety there will be no lack of suggestions for reducing or ending it. Where there is complacency, action is not envisaged.

If there is one thing we learn from history it is that a perfect society has never existed, even when able and intelligent men have deliberately set out to create one. Nevertheless, the degree of success achieved in small-scale societies, such as those which existed in America in the nineteenth century, was impressive. In most cases, these societies were successful in so far as they were united by common beliefs which in themselves were usually limiting and restrictive and demanded the surrender of individual freedom to an extent which most people nowadays would not tolerate. But any judgment of such societies should recognise that they had considerable success within the context of the greater society by which they were surrounded.

Where there has been an attempt to convert a whole country into utopia, as in France at the time of the Revolution, and in Russia after the arrival of Lenin from exile, the vision was soon eclipsed by the black shadows of ensuing reality. The existence of any society with idealistic beliefs requires very strong motivation and devotion on the part of all the individuals of which it is composed. This can easily lead to dogmatism and tyranny, and if at the same time the majority is persuaded or a powerful minority insists that the end justifies any means, including killing and torture, then the society immediately betrays the ideal and the purpose for which it was founded. There is another difficulty: any truly revolutionary idea which involves a complete reorganisation of society from top to bottom, even when accepted in one country or state, is immediately seen as a threat by neighbours who do not accept it, and it must be said in defence of the French and Russian revolutions, that the idealists were bitterly opposed by foreign governments who were afraid of the liberalising ideas of the revolutionists, who soon found that they were forced to defend themselves against invading armies. This tragic situation has been repeated on a smaller scale many times elsewhere. The old is prepared to defend itself with all the viciousness it can muster against whatever it supposes is a threat from the new.

This being a fact of life, it seems important to draw the conclusion that successful change will have to be slow, and by consent of the majority. This is unlikely to be obtained except piecemeal over a considerable length of time. It also seems likely that it will require a mature parliamentary and democratic experience and a responsive but not volatile electorate. Where these conditions do not exist, change is likely to be sudden, impermanent, and often costly in lives.

For these and other reasons, any idea of utopia being created at a stroke, either in one country or on a global scale, must be thought of as fantasy. Utopia will come about, if at all, solely by persuasion, and by education drawn from experience and example. In other words, it will evolve by a process of adaptation. The part we shall have to play in this process is that of keeping the growing tips of all viable experience from hurt and destruction, of constantly being aware from moment to moment of what endangers life on this planet and doing all we can to eliminate or prevent it. We must nurse and nurture the roots that already unite mankind, and try to extend them until they are seen to be far more essential to our well-being than outworn and divisive creeds. It follows therefore that any truly utopian society must be founded on respect for the sanctity of life, and must demand as a prerequisite for its existence the abolition and outlawing of war.

If the world were consulted, a huge majority of its inhabitants would agree on what makes life desirable. That agreement should be used as a basis for emphasising the *unity* of mankind. This is already demonstrated effectively and unchallenged in such organisations as the Red Cross, the World Health Organisation, the lifeboat and air-sea rescue organisations, the international communications networks, and many other bodies of an international kind. Such basically human organisations, founded upon compassion without regard to race or creed, can be and should be extended and increased in strength and numbers. Somehow the United Nations must be made truly effective. Above all, if we and other countries feel we are threatened by the USSR or any other system of society of which we disapprove, we had better, and very quickly, demonstrate in practice and unmistakably that our own way of life is better. To my mind this means abolishing the profit-motive, which is a disgusting basis for any kind of decent life, and showing by example rather than by lip service that we will have no truck with oppressive regimes, or with cruelty and intolerance of any kind. If we can do this and at the same time put positive faith and effort into trying to create a world government – at first solely to police the world and stop aggression, we shall have made a good contribution towards creating the conditions favourable to the growth of a utopian society.

16

Utopian Thought: a Framework for Social, Economic and Physical Planning

Peter Hall

The question that must logically be addressed here is: can planning be effectively undertaken without a utopian element? Planning as an activity, by definition, seeks to achieve a goal different from the outcome that would be likely without planning. It assumes that this goal is desirable to the group of people for whom the planning is undertaken. Insofar as the achievement of this goal lies in the future, and must therefore involve a degree of uncertainty, one might say that all planning must by definition involve an element of utopianism.

Most reasonable people would probably think this logic strained. In the first place, planning is commonly defined to include almost any kind of purposive activity, by however small or private a group. A motor or computer manufacturer 'plans' to produce a new model, the details of which are shrouded in complete secrecy from his competitors and thereby from the public; the desired new model may represent some kind of utopia for him, but it is doubtful whether it represents most people's idea of the word. Just occasionally we might allow it, as with Ford's vision of making the car available to everyone or Sinclair's similar vision for the computer. But even then we would have reservations, as when Sinclair tells his interviewer that computers 'do no harm – but I don't believe they are going to save the world' (10, p. 55). Utopias, we might feel, should have a more obsessive quality than that.

Particularly, perhaps, they should result from a disinterested vision: a view of a future state, economic or social or physical, which offers no immediate or obvious prospect of material reward for its inventor. Here of course we face a problem: Marxist analysis would hold that no action could be disinterested in that sense, and indeed some of Marx's earliest battles were fought with the utopian socialists on just that basis. One must take a philosophical stand here: mine is that Marxist analysis offers a profound and satisfactory explanation of a large part of the behaviour of people in history, but that the ideas of individual thinkers do also play a role, as Marx's life itself illustrates. Utopias demonstrably have their place, and only a determined attempt at logic chopping could ascribe all of them to the operation of class interests. That is a common-sense view, and I would hold that common sense is often the best guide.

Physical planning utopias

The role of utopias in physical planning has varied quite sharply from one time period to another. The greatest period of visionary idealism, in which physical designs for ideal cities were propounded, dates from approximately 1880 to 1940. This short span of only sixty years includes Soria's *La Ciudad Lineal*, Fritsch's *Die Stadt der Zukunft*, Howard's *Garden Cities of Tomorrow*, Garnier's *Cité industrielle*, Le Corbusier's *La Ville radieuse* and Wright's *Broadacre City* as well as many other less well-known examples (9). They have several features in common. All were physical realisations of a desired ideal state. None was built in precisely the form that was suggested, and several were never built at all. The concept that was best realised in practice – Howard's Garden City, with two actual examples started within a quarter of a century of publication of his book – was interestingly designed by an amateur, and was the only one to contain detailed financial calculations about how it should be achieved (6). The plans of the professional architect-planners – Garnier, Le Corbusier, Wright – were the most unsuccessful in practical terms, though their subsequent indirect influence was considerable.

All these exercises consist of an idealised physical form which embodies a certain vision of the economy or society that will be contained in it. In a few this vision is restricted to an engineer's vision of efficiency, as in Soria's Linear City which was to extend without limit along its rapid transit system, and might eventually connect Cadiz to St Petersburg. But in most, the planner has a vision of a different kind of society. With Le Corbusier, it is 'machine-age civilisation': a benevolent technocracy will release mankind from the over-congested early twentieth-century city. With Wright, it is a return to the simpler rural society of his Wisconsin boyhood. With Howard, it is a combination of the virtues of town and country: easy access to employment and social contacts, but fresh air and unspoilt nature. And beyond that, Howard saw the creation of a literally new socio-economic order through the ownership of land by the local community and its appropriation of rent for public works, coupled with individual or co-operative house construction for owner-occupiers.

Given the vision, it is pertinent to ask how it was to be achieved.

Wright seemed to think it could be done directly by appealing to normal American commercial instinct: people would return to the countryside, as indeed some were returning in the Great Depression of the 1930s, but would be liberated by cheap electricity and universal car ownership. Howard appealed to idealistic capitalists willing to lend their money at modest rates of interest, but also believed that once the idea had gained momentum ordinary commercial processes would suffice; he specifically counselled against government action, saying to his lieutenant Frederic Osborn that 'you will be older than Methuselah before they start' (8, p. 8). In interesting contrast, Le Corbusier looked to the centralising force of the French state, and dreamed of a new *Roi Soleil* who alone could realise his vision; significantly, during World War II he appealed directly to the Pétain government (4, p. 248).

Directly or indirectly these different visions have had their influence. The British government, before Osborn reached the age of Methuselah, did begin to build new towns (and, by the time Osborn died at 90, had started 28). A generation of architects paid their tribute to Le Corbusier, both before and after his death in 1965, by building high rise blocks modelled on his *Unité d'habitation* in Marseille (though usually lacking its communal facilities). Wright's Broadacre City did come to pass in American suburbia after World War II, though without the agrarian base that he had seen as central to it. A traveller across Europe or North America today can see the landscape of Howard, the landscape of Le Corbusier, the landscape of Wright. It is interesting that the extent of these landscapes does hinge a good deal on the kind of agency that built them – and thus on the prevailing socio-economic system. Corbusian landscapes are typical of centralised regimes where the state provides for its citizens, whether on the outskirts of Paris or the outskirts of Warsaw. Wrightian landscapes in contrast are typical of free enterprise, owner-occupier societies like the United States, Canada or Australia. Howardian landscapes are more typical of mixed economies with social democratic governments, like Britain in the 1940s and 1960s or Sweden at almost any time since World War II (though Sweden also has Corbusian features).

The point is that visions of utopia do matter. It is difficult to believe that cities would look like they do now without the visionaries. That is partly because the successful visionaries were good at understanding what was happening in the world ahead of ordinary mortals and harnessing these trends. Howard seems intuitively to have realised that decentralisation was starting to occur away from the congested cities of Victorian England; he simply channelled it. Le Corbusier grasped, as early as the 1920s, that technological change was going to affect the way we built buildings and the way we moved around cities;

he similarly incorporated these facts into his grand design. Wright understood, even by the early 1930s, that the car was going to open up the American countryside to low-density urbanisation; he even appreciated, half a century ahead of his time, the impact of new electric-based technologies on patterns of work.

Equally, there are plenty of examples of utopian visions that have passed into limbo, to be discovered there by scholars: megastructures thousands of feet high, gigantic linear cities strung along motorways, human ant-heaps or latter-day cave dwellings. (All these have actually appeared as serious suggestions within the last twenty years – most of them in that time of great visions, the 1960s.) They were not taken up because, though interesting and even fascinating to fellow-professionals, they did not connect with the broad movement of technological, economic or social change.

Utopia plus social realism, then, seems to be a necessary condition for successful planning. We can equally say that utopias come unstuck. The Corbusian vision looks pretty ragged in the Everton Piggeries. The Howard vision, equally, looks frayed in some of the less successful, harder-to-let new town estates. In both these cases there are plenty of excuses and justifications, and some of them at least sound convincing. Corbusian planning was applied to clients, if that is the word, who had no tradition of high-rise living and had lived a hand-to-mouth existence in the two-up, two-down slum terraces off Scotland Road. Given that and an exceptionally high child density (Corbusier had worked in inter-war France, a society distinguished by an exceptionally low birth rate), the result was predictable. The name new town is invoked for all kinds of development that are its antithesis, such as the notorious overspill development at Kirkby on the outskirts of Merseyside. But the fact is that if a society tries to rebuild and to rehouse as fast and as furiously as Britain did in the 1960s, first there are going to be some good designs and some not so good (cf. 3); and secondly the sheer pace will ensure social dislocation and hence social malaise.

Populist utopias

The question should be, not why some planned utopian visions went wrong, but whether society can build satisfactorily without them. In almost all western societies, a high and rising proportion of new housing is provided by market methods in settlements that – though 'planned' in the sense that some public authority approved a plan – certainly do not represent an ideal form. In Anglo-Saxon countries this generally takes the form of suburban extensions on previously undeveloped land at the urban periphery. In Britain in the 1930s and to some extent more recently, and to a more limited degree in the United

States, some experts have condemned this process for being wasteful of land and for producing long, costly and tiring journeys to work. Most of this criticism however proves to be fairly marginal or without substance. Travel surveys almost everywhere show that most commuter journeys are short – even in such supposed apotheoses of urban sprawl as Los Angeles. If land is wasted through irregular suburban growth or through land awaiting development, the process is usually no more than temporary.

When the criticism is examined more closely, however, an interesting point emerges. Very little criticism comes from the supposed victims, which is logical because if they were so dissatisfied it might be supposed that they would do something about it. Rather, it came and comes from a vocal minority of architects, geographer land-use planners, and writers yearning for a lost past. All are united in their concern to preserve a countryside and a way of life that they see as threatened. For them, suburbia is a hermaphrodite world, not town, not country, and therefore to be condemned. Pressed more closely, they may admit the charms of a few select planned suburbs – Bedford Park, Hampstead – but they rail against the extension of the same principle to the masses. This applies equally to the classic period of English suburbia, the 1920s and 1930s, and to that of American suburbia, the 1950s and 1960s (5).

Yet this too was a utopia of a sort – a populist utopia, realised by and for people who had never read the strictures of the critics. Now that time has begun to soften it, even they may discover its charms. Older nineteenth-century suburbs are 'gentrified' by just those people who would not, as yet, consider living in their twentieth-century equivalents; but their turn, too, will come. Both the suburbs of the 1870s and those of the 1930s were, as one Victorian writer put it, a railway state (7); their form derived from the commuter station and the related shopping parade. The American suburbs of the 1960s and the English suburbs of the 1980s are in contrast car-based; they relate to motorway interchanges, to local distributor roads and to big shopping centres. But each has a very characteristic form which is the product of the then prevailing technology; to condemn them as 'sprawling' or 'formless' is to miss the point.

Socio-economic utopias

Planners' utopias need not have a physical expression; equally, they may exist in the abstract socio-economic realm. The French economic development plans of the post-World War II era, and the British plans that were modelled on them in the 1960s, both had as their aim the rapid creation of a different kind of economy and society: modern, technologically advanced, investing generously in new infrastructure, generating almost effortless economic growth. Marxist analysis sees this as the attempt of the capitalist state to satisfy the productive requirements of the capitalist economy (1); equally however the French plans can be interpreted as the attempt of a tightly-knit bureaucratic class to impose its own values on a resistant French public. In either event the aim was unrealised; eventually the plans met with resistance and finally with lack of success. The British plans from the beginning were cursed by over-optimistic forecasting, which represented a form of wish-fulfilment on the part of the academics and bureaucrats who produced them, and which took little account of historical realities (2). It was small wonder, perhaps, that the ill-fated British National Plan of 1965 should have collapsed in the midst of economic crisis after barely a year. There is a possible parallel here with the failure of physical planning utopias, such as those of the Soviet 'urbanists' and 'deurbanists' of the 1920s; both took all too little regard of social or economic reality, and were finally overruled by Stalin's edict of 1931 which sharply returned the Soviet Union to a more conventional form of planning (11, pp. 96-8).

Conclusion

From this we can draw a general conclusion: utopias in planning, as in any other activity, can have a real effect if and only if they are underpinned by a strong sense of the art of the possible. That means that their authors must have a powerful appreciation of the constraints presented by the existing socio-economic framework, but may then feel free to let their fancies rove. The story of planning is littered with the ruins of utopias that ignored this golden rule. The successes without exception heeded it.

References

1. Castells, M., *City, Class and Power*, Macmillan, London 1977.
2. Chapman, G., 'Economic forecasting in Britain 1961-1975: a critique of assumptions', *Futures* 8, 1976, pp. 254-60.
3. Esher, L., *A Broken Wave: the rebuilding of England 1940-1980*, Allen Lane, London 1981.
4. Fishman, R., *Urban Utopias in the Twentieth Century: Ebenezer Howard, Frank Lloyd Wright and Le Corbusier*, Basic Books, New York 1977.
5. Hall, P., 'The urban culture and the suburban culture', in Eells, R. & Walton, C. (eds) *Man in the City of the Future*, Macmillan, New York 1967.
6. Howard, E., *Garden Cities of Tomorrow*, Faber and Faber, London 1946.
7. Kenward, J., *The Suburban Child*, Cambridge University Press 1955.
8. Osborn, F.J., *New Towns after the War*, J.M. Dent, London 1942.
9. Reiner, T.A., *The Place of the Ideal Community in Urban Planning*, University

of Pennsylvania Press, 1966.

10. Sinclair, C., Interview in *Practical Computing*, July 1982, pp. 54-64.

11. Starr, S.F., 'L'urbanisme utopique pendant la revolution culturelle Sovietique', in *Annales: Economies, Sociétés, Civilisations* 32, 1977, pp. 87-105.

17

The Grasshopper: Posthumous Reflections on Utopia

Bernard Suits

The medieval fantasy 'The Land of Cockaygne', in which Cockaygne's inhabitants are provided with such striking amenities as cooked larks that fly into one's mouth and pigs that run about squealing 'Eat me', is viewed by many recent writers on utopia with, at best, amused condescension. For some writers, it would seem, Cockaygne is too utopian to qualify as a genuine utopia, on the ground that its author has given no indication whatever as to how such avian and porcine altruism can be brought about. One might well wonder whether practical objections of this kind can properly be directed against *utopias*, of all things. Still, among utopian investigators there is disagreement on precisely this issue, an issue I do not propose to resolve nor, indeed, to pursue. Instead, I suggest that Cockaygne, whether it is or is not a proper utopia, can be viewed fruitfully, and not altogether whimsically, as an early version of a society enjoying well advanced automation. What we have in Cockaygne is medieval high tech, adumbrating, as it does, such modern amenities as garage doors that open themselves and voice-activated bugging devices – that is, states of affairs that come about automatically when needed. All Cockaygne lacks is the silicon chip. But we have the chip, and so while Cockaygne may have been a charming joke to its contemporary audience, it need not be merely that for us. In this chapter I will outline a utopia which is, in part, an updating of The Land of Cockaygne.

I first advanced my utopian theory in a book called *The Grasshopper: Games, Life and Utopia* (University of Toronto Press, 1978). I propose here to add a postscript to that book. The grasshopper of Aesop's fable of the grasshopper and the ant is the book's protagonist and the spokesman – sorry, spokesinsect – for my position. In the book the Grasshopper does two things. He advances a definition of games, and he argues that the ideal of human existence – that is, Utopia – must consist fundamentally, if not exclusively, in the playing of games. His definition of game-playing is as follows: to play a game is to attempt to achieve a specific state of affairs, using only means permitted by rules, where the rules prohibit use of more efficient in favour of less efficient means, and where the rules are accepted just because they make possible such activity. Or, for short: playing a game is the voluntary attempt to overcome unnecessary obstacles.

The Grasshopper believes that Utopia must consist in playing games because unless people play games in Utopia there will be nothing whatever to do, and everyone will die – or go mad – of boredom. Why does the Grasshopper believe that that would be so? Because the Utopia towards which all of us are – and always have been – striving is that state of affairs where there is no need for what the Grasshopper calls instrumental actions – that is, actions whose values lie not in themselves but solely in their further purposes: things like dieting, or root-canal surgery, or studying German verbs, or working for a living. The aim of all such input of human busyness – frenzied, stressful, painful, or just plain tiresome – is to achieve a payoff of periods which are free of frenzy, stress, pain, and tedium. We put up with frenzy, stress, pain and tedium only because we expect them to lead to things which are valuable in themselves. Well, the Grasshopper reasons, if that is what human beings are essentially engaged in doing with their lives, the ideal which inspires all of this busyness must be a condition totally free of instrumental necessities.

And so the Grasshopper outlines a picture of the indicated Utopia – a state of existence where all activities are valued solely for themselves, where no striving of any kind is required, where, thanks to the total implementation of computerised automation, anything anyone could ever desire is immediately available without effort – from healthy gums to healthy psyches. The Grasshopper then asks what the Utopians would do to pass the time, and at first it appears that they would have nothing whatever to do. To begin with, it is obvious that all the activities of the workaday world would vanish. There would simply be no tasks which had to be performed by human beings, from running trams to running governments. Nor, the Grasshopper argues, would there be love, friendship, art, morality, science, or philosophy. For all of these depend, in one way or another, upon instrumental necessities. Space does not permit me to go into the Grasshopper's detailed arguments in support of this surprising conclusion. For that I must refer you to the book. But for now, let me quote a passage which sums up the Grasshopper's argument that Utopian existence must consist in playing games.

We appear to be left with game playing as the only remaining candidate for Utopian occupation ... What we have seen thus far is that there does not appear to be anything to *do* in Utopia, precisely because in Utopia all instrumental activities have been eliminated. There is nothing to strive for precisely because everything has already been achieved. What we need, therefore, is some activity in which what is instrumentally *necessary* is inseparably combined with what is intrinsically *desirable*, and where the activity is not itself an instrument for some further purpose. Games meet this requirement perfectly. For in games we must have obstacles which we can strive to overcome *just so that* we can possess the activity as a whole, namely, playing the game.

The Grasshopper then adds one more refinement to his picture of Utopia. All kinds of activities, he agrees, can be valued for themselves, even those normally regarded as instrumental – e.g. fixing the kitchen sink, if that happens to be what turns you on. And so all the occupations of the workaday world ought to be included in Utopia, at least as options, since there are likely to be Utopians who would rather be building houses or running large corporations or fixing the kitchen sink than doing anything else. Does this destroy the Grasshopper's game-playing Utopia? Not at all, says the Grasshopper, for all such activities, if they were to exist in Utopia, would be games. Since everything any Utopian might need – from sinks to symphonies – is made immediately available to him by the computers, any effort a Utopian put into the production of those commodities would be quite unnecessary. And so Utopians who *worked* at producing such things would be engaged in the voluntary attempt to overcome unnecessary obstacles; i.e. they would be playing games. By way of illustration of this point, the Grasshopper considers two cases, that of John Striver, a Utopian house builder, and that of William Seeker, a Utopian scientist. Since better houses can be produced more efficiently by the computers than the houses Striver can build, his carpentry has no more significance than does the building of model airplanes. And since any problem Seeker chooses to address has already been solved, and the solution is immediately retrievable from the memory banks of the computers, Seeker's scientific investigations have no more significance than do the efforts of crossword puzzle devotees. And indeed their attitudes to their respective tasks are identical. 'Don't tell me the answer!' the crossword addict commands 'The whole idea is to do it by myself.' I ask the reader to keep Striver and Seeker in mind for future reference.

One more thing needs to be known about the Grasshopper. He is subject to a recurring dream in which it is revealed to him that everyone alive is really engaged in playing some elaborate game without realising that that is what he is doing. Then, still in the dream, the Grasshopper goes about persuading everyone that that is indeed the case, and when each is persuaded he immediately ceases to exist. Appalled as he is by the results of his teaching, the Grasshopper cannot stop, but quickly moves on to the next creature with his news, until he has preached the truth throughout the universe, and has converted everyone to oblivion.

With the meaning of this dream unresolved, the Grasshopper dies. But toward the end of the book he is miraculously resurrected, and he and his interlocutor, an insect named Skepticus, discover an interpretation of the dream. It begins with the Grasshopper telling Skepticus of a vision that has recently come to him (the Grasshopper, like Socrates, is subject to visions when convenient).

> This vision of mine [the Grasshopper says to Skepticus] was a vision of paradise lost. I saw time passing in Utopia, and I saw the Strivers and Seekers coming to the conclusion that if their lives were merely games, then those lives were scarcely worth living. Thus motivated, they began to delude themselves into believing that man-made houses were more valuable than computer-produced houses, and that long-solved scientific problems needed re-solving. They then began to persuade others of the truth of these opinions and even went so far as to represent the computers as the enemies of mankind. Finally they enacted legislation prohibiting their use. Then more time passed, and it seemed to everyone that the carpentry game and the science game were not games at all, but vitally necessary tasks which had to be performed in order for mankind to survive. Thus, although all of the apparently productive activities of man were games, they were not believed to be games. Games were once again relegated to the role of mere pastimes useful for bridging the gaps between our serious endeavours. And if it had been possible to convince these people that they were in fact playing games, they would have felt that their whole lives had been as nothing – a mere stage play or empty dream.
>
> *Skepticus.* Yes, Grasshopper, they would believe themselves to be nothing at all, and one can imagine them, out of chagrin and mortification, simply vanishing on the spot, as though they had never been.
>
> *Grasshopper.* Quite so, Skepticus. As you are quick to see, my vision has solved the final mystery of my dream. The message of the dream now seems perfectly clear. The dream was saying to me, 'Come now, Grasshopper, you know very well that most people will not want to spend their lives in playing games. Life for most people will not be worth living if they cannot believe that they are doing *something* useful, whether it is providing for their families or formulating a theory of relativity.'
>
> *S.* Yes, it seems a perfectly straightforward case of an anxiety dream. You were acting out in a disguised way certain hidden fears you had about your thesis concerning the idea of existence.
>
> *G.* No doubt. But tell me, Skepticus, were my repressed fears about the fate of mankind, or were they about the cogency of my thesis? Clearly they could not have been about both. For if my fears about the fate of mankind are justified, then I need not fear that my thesis is faulty, since it is that thesis which justifies those fears. And if my

thesis is faulty, then I need not fear for mankind, since that fear stems from the cogency of my thesis.

S. Then tell me which you feared, Grasshopper. You alone are in a position to know.

G. I wish there were time, Skepticus, but again I feel the chill of death. Goodbye.

S. Not goodbye, Grasshopper, *au revoir*.

The book ends on this note. Now I would like to resurrect the Grasshopper a second time so that the two can continue their colloquy from the point at which it was interrupted by the Grasshopper's death:

S. I see you're back.

G. Yes, resurrected again.

S. Jolly good. Then let me put to you the same question that your death prevented you from answering.

G. By all means.

S. Which do you believe, then, Grasshopper, that your thesis is faulty, or that the fate of mankind is in jeopardy?

G. Since I believe that my thesis about Utopia is substantially correct, Skepticus, it must be the possible fate of mankind that occasioned the anxieties manifested in my dream.

S. You mean that if Utopia contains very many people like Striver and Seeker, then Utopia will turn out to be not a paradise, but a kind of hell.

G. Just so, Skepticus.

S. A strange Utopia, Grasshopper! Indeed, so strange that one might wonder whether it might not be better for mankind to remain in their 'non-utopian' condition instead of seeking the 'utopia' your investigations have disclosed. And I place quotation marks around the words 'utopian' and 'non-utopian' since these expressions appear to have traded meanings with one another. Paradoxically, Utopia is really what we have been calling our non-utopian existence, for in that existence there is, quite simply, more *scope for action* than there is in the Utopian world you describe.

G. Well, to be sure, Skepticus, in making the transition from this life to Utopian life there is a trade-off: scope for action, as you call it, is exchanged for intrinsicality, that is, for actions which are valuable solely in themselves.

S. No doubt, Grasshopper, but as we have seen, the intrinsically valuable things left to do in Utopia are exceedingly limited in range, and thus not all that appealing to all that many people. Scarcely anyone, I should think, would be eager to trade off the richness of this life, despite its shortcomings, for a life confined to checkers, tiddly-winks, and noughts and crosses. So perhaps we ought to give up the quest for Utopia, for the best Utopia there can be already exists in our own back yards.

G. I think, Skepticus, that you have misunderstood a rather important aspect of what I have been saying about Utopia. Your argument that it might be better for us to accept a non-Utopia over a Utopian existence rests upon a false premise, namely, that we have a choice in the matter. The Utopia I envisage is not a state of affairs which is ideally *desirable*; it is simply a state of affairs which is logically *inevitable*. For it seems perfectly clear to me that all our efforts in our present non-Utopian condition are directed towards removing the necessity for precisely those efforts. Labour and the introduction of labour-saving devices are one and the same thing. We work so that we won't have to work; nothing else makes any sense to me.

(Skepticus ponders this for a bit, and then speaks.)

S. Grasshopper, I have a suggestion. I believe that you have mis-identified Utopia.

G. Indeed.

S. Yes. John Striver and William Seeker were disillusioned – were they not? – only when they discovered that their striving and seeking were futile and empty. The things striven for had already been achieved, and the things sought had already been found. So what they were doing was not really necessary for *producing* anything. They weren't engaged in *really* instrumental – that is to say, useful – activities at all. But in constructing or in visualising Utopia we can easily change all that. In the Utopia I am suggesting, everybody will work, or seek knowledge, or whatever it might be, but they will *really* be doing those things. There are no computers at all. Everyone really works, but things are so arranged that everyone derives intrinsic value from the thing he works at. This is not a novel idea, of course, but is perhaps as much the ideal of our present non-Utopian existence as is the work-free society that you regard as the only Utopia. For what it actually amounts to is no more than the familiar wish to be happy in one's work. And examples of this kind of thing come readily to mind. One hears professors of philosophy, for example, speak of their good fortune in actually drawing salaries for doing what they would be doing even if they were not paid for it.

G. Or so they claim.

S. Yes, well, and for some of them, certainly, it is an honest claim.

G. It's the same with prostitutes, I suppose.

S. I beg your pardon?

G. Some prostitutes, one may surmise, also are paid for doing what they would be doing anyway. Not enough of them, I understand, though I am not myself expert in such matters. In any case, I see what you mean. You are imagining a condition where a real service is performed, but where performing the service is intrinsically valuable to the performer. And so we have that melding, as it were, of intrinsic and instrumental values that I had earlier argued was achievable only by playing games. All professionals are at the same time amateurs, for they love their professions, whether they are philosophers or erophiles.

S. Precisely, Grasshopper.

G. We might call the principle which inspires your alternative Utopia the Happy Hooker Principle.

S. Well, that, perhaps, or maybe the Felicitous Philosopher Principle would be better.

G. Happy Hooker Principle has a nice ring to it, though, don't you think? But whatever we choose to call it, there are difficulties, are there not?

S. Difficulties?

G. Why, yes. The Happy Hooker Principle might work very well when applied to prostitutes and philosophers, but what about physicians and lawyers?

S. I'm afraid I don't follow you.

G. Well, you will be required, will you not, to build all kinds of evils into your Utopia, or else professions like medicine and the law will cease to exist. You will have to make sure that your Utopia contains a suitable amount of sickness and crime, so that physicians and lawyers will really have something to do.

S. Come now, Grasshopper, I have learned enough philosophy from my conversations with you not to be put off by irrelevancies such as that. Just as your work-free Utopia involves a trade-off, as we noted earlier, between intrinsicality on the one hand and scope for action on the other hand, so my Utopia involves a trade-off between enjoyable professions and the evils that go along with those professions.

G. You mean that for the sake of your Utopia, you will accept the continued existence of crime and disease?

S. Certainly. Faint hearts will never win Utopia.

G. Well, I must say you display a striking ability to rise above other people's misfortunes.

S. Your sarcasm, Grasshopper, is quite uncalled for. And besides, in accepting such evils for the sake of Utopia we will be more fair about it than is the case in our non-Utopian existence.

G. How is that?

S. Physicians will have to take their turn as patients, and lawyers will have to take their turn as clients. And there can, of course, be reciprocal exchanges which cut across professions as well.

G. You mean that F. Lee Baily will get a heart disease in order to give Christian Barnard something to do, and in exchange for this service

Barnard will commit a serious crime in order to give Baily something to do?

S. Yes, that's the idea. A good plan, too, since it is not the unfortunate victims of an imperfect society who must serve as the necessary raw material, so to speak, for their more fortunate professional neighbours, but the professionals themselves. And since in the Utopia I propose everyone will be a professional, there will be a complete reciprocity of give and take in this way throughout all society.

G. Yes, I see, Skepticus. There does, however, seem to be a possible difficulty.

S. A difficulty?

G. Yes. These Utopians in their roles as victims would be inclined, I should think, to make it as easy on themselves as they could. After people had got the hang of the thing, there might be a falling off in their zeal in the roles of patient or client. F. Lee Baily would show up in Barnard's counsulting room with only a mild skin disease, and Barnard would require the services of Baily merely for some routine conveyancing of real estate. Or either might just pretend to have a medical or legal problem which they didn't in fact have. If such a sorry state of affairs came to pass, one can imagine Barnard throwing up his hands in disgust and, in desperation, performing surgery on himself, in which case he would no doubt be a man after his own heart, but he would be a very dissatisfied Utopian. My point is that the activities of Utopians would have a tendency to become very much like *games*. 'I think I'll play doctor with Lee,' says Barnard, or 'It's time to play lawyer with Chris,' says Baily.

S. Well, Grasshopper, we would simply have to insist that the citizens of Utopia come up with real and serious illnesses and commit real and serious crimes. After all, it's my Utopia, and I can have them do anything I want them to do.

G. I agree, Skepticus, you cetainly can. I will not quarrel with you over that. For, in any case, it is not the possibility of *pretended* maladies and *pretended* crimes that would turn your Utopia into a life of game playing. Even if, as you say, everyone came up with real and serious medical and legal problems, such a state of afairs would still be game playing. For all are engaged in bringing about the existence of obstacles just so that such obstacles can be overcome. Tennis is not a game, after all, by virtue of the players *pretending* they have a net. The net is real. Your society is, in fact, nothing but a series – indeed, a network – of interlocking games. It is just that the stakes in these games are very high. What you have described, therefore, is not only a condition of game playing, but of very heavy game playing indeed. Notice that my objection to your alternative Utopia is not directed to the medical and criminal horrors it entails – that would be a quite different kind of objection. Rather, it is that you were proposing a *non*-game Utopia as an alternative to my Utopia of game playing, but it has turned out, upon examination, to be a game Utopia after all. All that bears out, Skepticus, what has been my conviction from the beginning. A game Utopia is a logical inevitability.

S. Very well, Grasshopper, I see I shall have to acknowledge that my Utopia is indeed a life of games. And so I shall accept, at least for the sake of the present argument, that a game Utopia is *logically* inevitable. But, Grasshopper, even if that is so, it does not mean that a game Utopia is also *historically* inevitable. It's just like the case of the monkeys.

G. I beg your pardon?

S. The monkeys and the typewriters. If you put a bunch of monkeys in a room full of typewriters, it is logically – or at least statistically – inevitable that they will, given enough time, produce the complete works of Shakespeare. But such an otherwise inevitable (not to say tiresome) state of affairs can easily be prevented. You simply have to keep monkeys away from typewriters. Similarly, in order to retain the richness of our non-Utopian existence, all we need do is delay the arrival of the relatively empty Utopia you envisage, and, with sufficient effort and ingenuity, delay it indefinitely.

G. Indeed, let us consider that possibility, Skepticus. How would we implement your plan? That is, what would the recommended delaying tactics be like?

S. Well, Grasshopper, I'm not sure about the tactical details, but I'm quite clear as to what the overall strategy would be. In general, it would be the elimination – or a least a massive withholding – of labour-saving devices. For it is the elimination of work which threatens to bring your Utopia ever closer.

G. Yes, I agree completely that that is the indicated strategy. We would have to take care that enough impediments or barriers to our productive goals remained so that there would still be something to do. Thus, if an automobile were invented that ran, not on petrol or electricity, but on, say, will-power, we would see to it that such a machine was never put into production. And similarly with thousands of other such innovations that would be bound to come up – innovations which we naively look upon as 'improvements', but which we now see are not improvements at all, but a thousand nails being driven into the coffin of any meaningful existence we can hope to have. For the total elimination of problems from our lives would also quite literally be to drain those lives of anything significant to do.

S. Precisely so, Grasshopper.

G. What you are recommending, in other words, is that in order to stave off my Utopia we must all become ludic Luddites.

S. Ludic Luddites?

G. Precisely.

S. Would you mind running that past me one more time?

G. Certainly. The Luddites, you will no doubt recall, went about the English Midlands in the early nineteenth century smashing up machinery that was causing technological unemployment.

S. Ah, yes, the Luddites, to be sure. But what kind of Luddites did you say *we* must become?

G. Ludic ones, Skepticus, from the Latin *ludus*. It means *game*. Just as the historical Luddites were anti-technology in order to escape the dreariness and despair of British bread-lines, you are proposing that we become latter-day Luddites in order to escape the dreariness and despair of Utopian game rooms.

S. Just so, Grasshopper. Ludic Luddite. It has a nice ring to it, I must say. Not quite the punch of Happy Hooker, but an arresting alliteration after all. And in contrast to felicitous philosophers and happy hookers we are, with ludic Luddites, progressing quite rapidly in our investigations.

G. Well, at least we are progressing quite rapidly through the alphabet. And in order to end what bids fair to becoming a somewhat tiresome word game, Skepticus, let us go at once to the end of the alphabet, for there awaiting us is an alliteration that expresses the very heart of your objection to my theory of Utopia. Since you see my Utopia as a place whose residents are deprived of any genuine reasons for significant endeavour, I suggest that you might want to express their condition as one of zero zeal.

S. The Zero Zeal Effect! I like that. But tell me, Grasshopper, why are you waxing so inventive in support of my anti-Utopian thesis?

G. Because I believe that it deserves all the support it can get, Skepticus. Indeed, I have one more consideration to advance in defence of your position. The point you wish to make can be made clearly, I think, by considering the following analogy. Imagine a group of people whose life consisted exclusively in playing (North American) football. All they ever did was plan plays, try to make yardage on the ground or in the air, defend their goal line against attacks by opposing teams, and so on. And now suppose that they invent labour-saving devices as humans always try to do; they introduce kicking machines, then armour for blockers, and jet-propelled shoes for running backs and receivers. Things go on in this way for some time, with victories coming with ever increasing ease and frequency. Finally they realise that they can solve all of their problems, so to speak, wholesale. They adopt the tactic of slaughtering any opposing team that appears on the playing field, and so are finally free to make touchdowns or field goals at will, whenever they want to. But of course that is not to play football at all. Their Utopia has finally arrived and has instantly self-destructed.

S. Bravo, Grasshopper, bravo. The message is clear, is it not? They should never have introduced greater efficiency into their lives, for the logical consequence of such a strategy is to empty their lives of any significance whatever. And that is precisely why we ought to prevent Utopia from arriving. All of life is like the football game, and we are in danger of destroying it by our misguided, indeed tragic, efforts to improve it.

G. In other words, Skepticus, what you are saying is that we ought not to remove all the obstacles from our paths, for the price of such improvement is that here will be nothing left for us to do.

S. Precisely, Grasshoper.

G. Thus, even though we could – at least in principle – make all the tasks of life quite unnecessary, we ought voluntarily to refrain from taking such measures.

S. Certainly, Grasshopper, that is clearly the conclusion we have reached. Why do you keep labouring the point? What are you getting at?

G. Just this. It strikes me that a completely accurate way to describe the state of affairs which you regard as an indefinite postponement of Utopia is as follows. Everyone is engaged in the voluntary attempt to overcome unnecessary obstacles. In other words, the attempt to postpone Utopia indefinitely is to make a game of life. A life dedicated to the postponement of Utopia finds such a fitting analogy in the football example just because such a life has itself become a game. Your efforts, therefore, to delay the game-playing Utopia I envisage are not a delay of that Utopia at all, but the construction of it right now.

S. (a thoughtful pause) You baited the trap, and I took the bait.

G. Not I, Skepticus, but the argument, which has a will of its own.

S. Yes, and, evidently, a fate of its own. Twist and turn as we will, a life of game playing appears to be our final destiny.

G. Quite right, Skepticus. There is, alas, no Divine Improvidence which shapes our ends.

S. Then the only thing to do, perhaps, while recognising that a game-playing Utopia is inevitable, is to give thanks that it will not arrive in our life-time, relax, and hope for the best.

G. Yes, Skepticus, we could do that, and thus turn life into a game by a mere act of will.

S. How do you make that out?

G. Well, instead of going to all the trouble of inventing interlocking games like the Baily-Barnard games, or all the trouble of aborting scientific and technological improvements, we accomplish the same thing simply by rejoicing in the fact that those improvements have not yet been made. We make life into a game by adopting a game-like attitude towards all of the problems life presents. For we regard those problems just as we would the obstacles that are intentionally erected in the games we play.

S. Well, Grasshopper, you have convinced me that the future of mankind is irremediably bleak.

G. Not quite, Skepticus. I think the future may be bleak for some but not for others.

S. What do you mean?

G. Be patient for a moment and I'll tell you – just as soon as I finish this vision. (In due course the Grasshopper speaks.) In the vision I see myself and a multitude of other Grasshoppers all engaged in playing the most elaborate, subtle, and challenging games. For a game-playing Utopia need not confine itself to checkers and tiddly-winks, as you suggested earlier. Rather, we ought to be devising really magnificent games now, so that when eternal summer finally arrives, we will have all kinds of absorbing things to do. And I mean *really* magnificent games; games so subtle, complex, and challenging that their inventors will be seen as the ludic Einsteins of the future. And the Utopians will look back on names like Queensbury, Naismith, the Parker Brothers, even Rubik, with the same indulgent condescension with which today's physicists look back on those ancient investigators who proclaimed air, earth, fire, and water to be the basic elements of nature. The ants all exhort us to store up food for winter, but the more serious problem is to store up games for summer. But to return to my vision. All of us Grasshoppers are playing all these wonderful games, when there comes a knock at the door of Utopia. It is an ant, and I see that it is the same ant who turned me from his door in the autumn of my life. 'Please, Grasshopper,' he begs, 'give me something to do.' 'Why, Ant,' I reply, 'What on earth do you mean? How can an Ant be in need of something to do? Get about your business of storing up food for winter, splitting firewood and so on.' But the ant replies mournfully, 'I can't do that. The technology that our ant industry has produced is now so advanced that we can obtain food for winter, and all the other necessities of life as well, merely by activating our computers. So there is nothing at all left for us to do. But you Grasshoppers seem to find plenty to do. My goodness, look at all that activity in there.' Now, the temptation to turn the pitiful creature from my door is very great. But I don't do that. Instead, I invite him, and all the members of his race inside. There, those who are able to learn and enjoy our games survive as happy Utopians, and their metamorphosis from ants into grasshoppers is a beautiful sight to behold. But those who cannot change must go back outside, where the whole race of ants – cold, bored, perplexed, and futile – dies out forever.

Postscript

Verbatim reports of discussion are neither fashionable nor economically feasible, and summaries that try to give some part of every argument are difficult to write without distortion. Here we make no attempt to recapture the content and flavour of the many hours of debate that led to the composition of this book; instead we concentrate on one theme, the utility of utopian thought, using comments made formally and informally during the symposium, and in later correspondence.

The scale of reactions to utopia ranges from total acceptance to total rejection. Total acceptance amounts to regarding a whole utopia as a fixed blueprint for rebuilding society. Total rejection may come either from practical people, who see such speculation as the product of a lunatic fringe of unrealistic dreamers, or from intellectuals who stress the dangers of concentrated power and the threat to freedom. Aware, no doubt, that it is not yet clear whether Orwell's *Nineteen Eighty-Four* and other anti-utopian writings make an unanswerable case against utopia for all time and in all its forms or merely give a useful warning that utopia could be turned upside down if taken too literally, few contributors supported either extreme. Their chief concern was to examine ways of using utopia that might help to solve social problems and at the same time avoid the dread results described by Šimečka. Several standpoints were clarified during the discussion; these will be mentioned in ascending order of the extent of their reliance upon utopia.

On the micro scale of small communities there were few reservations. These may, in spite of the dangers, constitute a safe social laboratory for providing knowledge of social groups and for testing new ideas, regardless of whether communities last or fall apart after a short time. They are useful provided that the success of a community is not taken as proof that the same results would follow if the organisation were reproduced on a large scale.

There was also general agreement with those who have long argued that utopia can be used as a standard for judging existing society; a mirror which highlights imperfections and, by giving a glimpse of a possible better future, gives direction and acts as a spur for action. Used in this way utopia potentially provides a useful tool for piecemeal social engineering; its function being to encourage thought and action rather than to offer solutions. Used well it could become an efficient means of keeping pace with technological developments that have been the prime movers in recent history. There was also some support for the hypothesis that utopia has been most useful in social engineering when broken down into its strands, in planning and education for instance, where new professions have selected specific proposals for testing in practice on a narrow front. However, when discussion did focus on architectural and planning utopias it developed into an attack on the professions – the mistakes of the past few decades being much easier to grasp than the undoubted benefits.

The next standpoint viewed utopia as an inevitable part of ideal planning. Once the planning horizon is placed several decades ahead, the planner is forced into the unknown; existing trends become unreliable and questions arise as to the desired nature of future society, for to some extent we are capable of engineering a future and not just reacting to events. Any attempt to plan on a comprehensive basis thus involves utopian speculation, and the more there is discussion of possible futures the more likely it is that better solutions will be found and that a wider consensus will emerge. From this standpoint the problem is to use utopia intelligently; but there is an implicit assumption that progress towards an ideal, or an approximation to an ideal, leads to an acceptable end. Logically this is open to doubt as the approximation may be lacking in some essential feature, the absence of which could bring about dystopia.

The final standpoint rejected the idea of piecemeal planning and *evolutionary* ideal planning. Both these options were seen as too slow to meet the alarming problems of poverty, the arms race, pollution and population growth. A swift change in our perceptions of world society is urgently needed, and only utopia can provide the stimulus and the solutions. The advocates of the necessity of utopia were, however, not calling for the blind acceptance of a particular form of utopia. Their demand was for radical rethinking, for using utopia as a method of clarifying problems and issues, for determining goals, for forming policies, and for testing alternatives. The difficulties are of course immense and the dangers obvious. Nevertheless after the set-backs earlier in this century we are in a better position to forsee and avoid errors. We are aware of dystopia, theoretical knowledge has improved, and we are alive to the need for establishing constraints to safeguard basic human rights. Furthermore, improvements in planning techniques would enable continuous monitoring to take place. The age of innocence has passed. On the other hand, some contributors felt that a swift transformation of society could be accepted only as a last ditch exercise; otherwise the risks would still be too great. This group was certain that it is not feasible to model a new form of society in sufficient detail and with sufficient reliability to predict the likely consequences.

The relation between utopia and the perfect moral commonwealth was touched upon rather than debated. According to some theories only one is needed to achieve the goal of perfection; in practice both may be necessary for improvement. Only if we accept Robert Owen's contention that environment determines behaviour is it sensible to consider utopian planning without complementary modifications in the consciousness of the people involved. In an age when participation is becoming part of the planning process it may be that the struggle towards a perfect moral commonwealth should proceed in advance of utopian design.

Index